Myth and History
in the Book of Revelation

Myth and History
in the Book of Revelation

JOHN M. COURT

John Knox Press
ATLANTA

ISBN 0-8042-0346-6

Library of Congress Number 79-16586

This book is published simultaneously by John Knox Press in the United States of America and by SPCK in Great Britain in 1979.

John Knox Press
Atlanta, Georgia

Printed in Great Britain

Contents

Acknowledgements

Thanks are due to the following for permission to quote from copyright sources:

T. & T. Clark Ltd: *Revelation* (International Critical Commentary Series) by R. H. Charles.

Wm. B. Eerdmans Publishing Co: *Theological Dictionary of the New Testament* edited by G. Kittel and translated by G. W. Bromiley.

Hodder & Stoughton Ltd: *The Letters to the Seven Churches of Asia* by Sir W. M. Ramsay.

SCM Press Ltd: *The Rediscovery of Apocalyptic* by Klaus Koch, translated by M. Kohl.

Note on References and Abbreviations

Biblical references are made in accordance with the Revised Standard Version from which the majority of quotations are taken. References to Classical texts and other extra-biblical sources are abbreviated according to the appropriate standard reference works. References to theological journals and standard works of reference follow accepted practice when abbreviated.

Author's Preface

A preface might be the last opportunity to prepare the reader for what is to come. This is doubly necessary when the reader is invited not only to scan these pages but to open the chapters of the Book of Revelation, and to look again at their mysteries. One could have some sympathy with William Wordsworth when he referred to such mysteries as

> Characters of the great Apocalypse,
> The types and symbols of Eternity,
> Of first, and last, and midst, and without end.

Within the perspective of modern biblical scholarship one would have less sympathy with George Eliot's creation, the mother of 'Felix Holt', who 'regarding all her troubles about Felix in the light of a fulfilment of her own prophecies, treated the sad history with a preference for edification above accuracy, and for mystery above relevance, worthy of a commentator on the Apocalypse'.

The attitude of approach to the work can be everything. For that reason one must begin with a survey of the real options still available for the interpretation of the Book of Revelation. It is possible that a judicious combination of such methods of exegesis may yield new fruit. This study concentrates on the possibilities of combining a detailed understanding of the Book's historical background with a critical appreciation of the traditional mythology which the author employs. In the Apocalypse, where number symbolism is of importance, the selection of seven main themes to demonstrate the interrelationship of history and mythology could well provide a significant sample.

The letters to the seven churches of Asia Minor; the often neglected, but highly significant, sequence of plagues; the 'interlude' of the two witnesses; the portent of the woman clothed with the sun; the figure of the beast with seven heads; the image of Babylon the harlot; the vision of New Jerusalem – each theme, with its own difference of emphasis, substantiates and justifies the concept of this relationship. Some general conclusions are offered about the significance of the relationship, and some suggestions are made about the broader contexts of the book, the connections between the Apocalypse and apocalyptic, between the Apocalypse and the New Testament, and between the Apocalypse and its function in the early Christian world. I have ventured in the hope that such a treatment may combine accuracy with relevance, without sacrificing edification and an appropriate sense of mystery.

This work originated in a protracted programme of research for which the University of Durham awarded the degree of Ph.D in 1973. A substantial revision was necessary to produce the manuscript of this book which was completed in the summer of 1977. Had circumstances been different, I should have liked to incorporate references to many more of the recent works in this field.

No preface is adequate to express my debt of gratitude. First of all to Professor C. K. Barrett, of Durham University, I owe my enthusiasm for biblical studies; without his expert guidance, patient interest and firm encouragement this work would never have reached its conclusion. To the Revd Dr W. A. Whitehouse, first Professor of Theology at the University of Kent, I am indebted for opportunities within a full teaching and administrative programme to complete my writing. To Landesbischof E. Lohse and Professor H. Conzelmann I am grateful for their special help and interest during my time at the University of Göttingen. I would thank these and all others who can recognize their contributions to these pages; while I hope that I have not misrepresented them, obviously the responsibility is mine not theirs. Only my wife knows the full extent of my debt to her; to have lived with me and a work on the Apocalypse is more than anybody should be expected to endure.

Keynes College
University of Kent
Canterbury

John M. Court
26 January 1979
St Polycarp of Smyrna

1

The Interpretation of the Book of Revelation

It is important at the beginning of this work to offer some indication of the range of possibilities still open to the interpreter of the Book of Revelation. Some methods of interpretation have a remarkably long history of active use; others have moved in and out of fashion in a way that is not unrelated to the history and internal politics of the Christian Church; others are comparatively modern, being based on the scientific techniques of nineteenth- and twentieth-century criticism.

In presenting a catalogue of possibilities, it is necessary to stress that such methods are not by any means mutually exclusive options. The history of criticism sometimes tends to give this impression, as do the individual proponents of one particular theory, when they advocate it at the expense of another. But the remarkable feature of any survey of recent commentaries as, for example, the one offered by André Feuillet, is that the comments made, to indicate the characteristics of this or that work, highlight first one aspect and then another of the total story about the Book of Revelation. One writer is interested primarily in its contemporary relevance, another in its literary unity, another in its eschatological themes, another in its historical allusions. But more than one of these emphases could be combined in a more comprehensive study of the Book. That such methods of study are by no means incompatible can be demonstrated easily from R. H. Charles's work; in the Introduction to his Commentary he devotes a section to 'The Methods of Interpretation Adopted in this Commentary' in which there is 'an enumeration of the methods, which have stood the test of experience and been found necessary for the interpretation of the Apocalypse'; and in his survey 'History of the Interpretation of the Apocalypse', his headings do justice to the combination of methods used by individual interpreters in the assessment of the book at various periods.

What is offered here is not by any means a history of interpretation, but rather an introductory survey of methods that have been

1

used and can still be used. Each method is considered in the light of a few examples of its application, which can serve to illustrate the advantages and disadvantages. The order in which the methods are considered is approximately chronological, namely that of the first major appearance of each method, so far as this can be determined from extant material. The systems of exegesis may be tabulated as follows:

1   Chiliastic

2   'Alexandrian' – spiritual or allegorical

3   Recapitulation theory

4   Historical applications – *weltgeschichtlich* or *kirchengeschichtlich*

5   Eschatological – *endgeschichtlich*

6   Contemporary-Historical – *zeitgeschichtlich*

7   Literary analysis

8   Comparative studies – *religionsgeschichtlich* and *traditionsgeschichtlich*.

1   Chiliastic

The earliest commentaries on the Book of Revelation are thought to belong to that category labelled 'millenarian' because of the preoccupation with the literal concept of a reign of Christ on earth, with the righteous from the 'first resurrection', for a period of one thousand years before the Final Judgement. The textual basis for this chiliastic interpretation is found in Rev. 20.1–6. And the literalism which characterizes the interpretation of this passage is the dominant attitude in the reading of the book as a whole.

A connection with Asia Minor may well prove to be significant for this method of interpretation. Montanism was born in Phrygia, and characteristically was concerned with the imminence of the Millennium and the actual descent to earth of the Heavenly Jerusalem. Sir William Calder[1] argued that Montanism originated in the region of Philadelphia as a direct result of the influence of the Book of Revelation and, in particular, of the letter to Philadelphia in Rev. 3. The fact that such could be the immediate response to the book, the prototype of all commentaries, is not of course an infallible guide to the actual meaning of the book. A single idea could have widely different values in the background to the author's thought, in his own use of it, and in the response of his readers.

Feuillet draws attention to the importance of sectarian movements from Montanism to the present day, in keeping alive this chiliastic interpretation.[2] R. H. Charles, referring to the rejection of the literal interpretation of Rev. 20, tells how 'a realistic eschatology was crushed out of existence in the Church for full 800 years ... revived by Joachim of Floris [sic] ... again abandoned for some centuries and declared heretical by the Augsburg and Helvetic Confessions'.[3]

It is clear that, apart from its use for the highly chiliastic views of some sects, the millenarian category of interpretation does not by itself provide an adequate definition for the exegesis of the Apocalypse as a whole. Reduced to more suitable proportions, it could do duty as a designation for a basically literal as opposed to a purely symbolic understanding of one aspect of the final consummation depicted in Revelation. But it may even be inaccurate to recognize the Millennial kingdom as a separate item in the Seer's order of events; R. H. Charles's painstaking reconstruction of the end of the book[4] has the virtue of logic, but the Seer may not have been so logical in employing traditional features within a total collage of the Consummation.

2 'Alexandrian' – spiritual or allegorical

I am inclined to label the spiritual or allegorical tradition in the interpretation of Revelation as 'Alexandrian' because its roots seem to be firmly embedded in the school of exegesis associated with the Christian Church at Alexandria. Origen stood within this exegetical tradition and exercised a formative influence upon it, but it was not by any means a Christian innovation. In his exegesis of Scripture, Origen separates out three levels of meaning – the literal, the moral and the spiritual.[5] This formal structure is on analogy with human psychology, corresponding to the body, the soul and the spirit in man; it is supported by Scriptural texts, such as the Septuagint reading of Prov. 22.20 – 'Describe these things in a threefold way.'

Origen held to the principle of verbal inspiration of Scripture; the Scriptures were written by inspiration of the Holy Spirit and have a deeper meaning than that which appears upon the surface of the record. Because these two convictions were held closely together, what Origen regarded as the unattractiveness, or the factual error, in the literal meaning of some parts of Scripture did not invalidate his conclusions about Biblical inspiration. On the contrary, spiritual truth can be preserved in material falsehood; literal unattractiveness, absurdity or error can be positive signs of a hidden meaning which is of primary or sole importance. The search for the spiritual meaning of Scripture involves extensive use of allegory and typology, employing it much more widely than just to explain awkward passages. Figurative interpretations are required at every point in Scripture.

The ever-present problem which faces any allegorical interpretation is that of establishing any effective control over the interpretation, such that one meaning can be said to be justified over against another. The difficulty is sharpened in the view of the modern scholar with his concern, which was by no means necessary to the ancient mind, that the exegesis should be related to the original situation and intention of the Biblical writer. As C. K. Barrett expressed it, the effect of the allegorical method is 'to emphasise the authority of the work interpreted and at the same time to rob it of any serious historical meaning'.[6]

One of the few methods of control over such exegesis which were attempted by some commentators was the use of an historical frame of reference. This was employed spasmodically by Origen, when he developed the figurative meaning of some texts in historical terms. A more satisfactory example can be cited from an earlier period, when the exegesis of the Old Testament at Qumran (Midrash Pesher) employed a certain amount of fairly crude allegory, but usually combined this with an 'historical' kind of interpretation. As Millar Burrows describes it,

> the interpretation put upon the Scripture is primarily historical, not in the sense that it corresponds to modern conceptions of historical criticism and interpretation, but in the sense that everything is supposed to refer directly to the history of the group itself. Not only are events of the writers' own times interpreted in the light of Scripture; it is even more characteristic that the Scriptures themselves are interpreted in the light of recent events.[7]

The Qumran sect saw the Scriptures as fulfilled in themselves and the events which befell them.

Not so much in the form of exegesis as in the conviction underlying it that their present time is the eschatological time in which the prophecies of Scripture are fulfilled, the Qumran community and the New Testament Church came close together.[8] The allegorical method was used to apply the passage being quoted to the desired historical setting. The use of allegory itself is a fairly clear indication that the commentator began with certain convictions about the historical situation and then imposed these on the text. Individual paragraphs of text are interpreted separately; the continuity is provided not by the original context, but by the new historical context.

Another attempt at the control of allegorical exegesis, by the method of maintaining a consistent line of thought as the basis of the interpretation, is illustrated by the work of Tyconius the fourth-century Donatist.

> The greatness of Tyconius' achievement lay in his typological interpretation of scripture within a fixed pattern of thought: the struggle of the City of God, the members of the Body of which Christ is the Head, with the City of the devil, the infernal antitype of the Body of Christ.[9]

3   Recapitulation Theory

It is usually said that the originators of the Recapitulation theory were Victorinus of Pettau and the Donatist Tyconius; certainly these two give the first clear expression of the idea. Victorinus' work is the earliest extant commentary on the Apocalypse,[10] while Tyconius' views have to be reconstructed from quotations. In brief, the Recapitulation theory holds that the Apocalypse is not a strictly consecutive account of a sequence of events, but a description which repeats the same facts in different forms, such as the seven seals, trumpets and bowls.

But we should also notice what is at least a connection in terminology between this theory and the comments of Irenaeus about the interpretation of the beast's number, 666. Irenaeus was inclined not to commit himself irrevocably to a single theory about the name of the beast, but he interpreted the number as the totality of all apostasy:

> And the number is six hundred and sixty-six, that is six times a hundred, six times ten, and six units. [He gives this] as a recapitulation of the whole of that apostasy which has taken place during

six thousand years. .... And there is therefore in this beast, when he comes, a recapitulation made of all sorts of iniquity and of every deceit, in order that all apostate power, flowing into and being shut up in him, may be sent into the furnace of fire. ... The digit six being adhered to throughout, indicates the recapitulation of that apostasy, taken in its full extent, which occurred at the beginning, during the intermediate periods, and which will take place at the end (Iren. *haer*. 5.28.2; 29.2; 30.1).

Irenaeus used the term *recapitulatio* (*anakephalaiōsis*) widely, in more than one specialized context. It may be that we should acknowledge him as the real originator of this recapitulatory tradition in the exegesis of the Apocalypse, just as we acknowledge him as the expounder of a 'physical' theory of the atonement on the basis of Eph. 1.10.

Victorinus, the bishop of Pettau, was a martyr in the persecution of Diocletian. According to his commentary, there is a chronological progression in the Apocalypse as far as the sixth seal, when the stage of the *novissima persecutio* is reached; thereafter the punishment of the unbeliever is described, firstly in the seven trumpets and then repeated in the seven bowls. For Tyconius, the Apocalypse described the war of Christ with the devil; the seven heads and ten horns of the beast symbolized the totality of powers hostile to Christ, the *civitas diaboli* under the leadership of the *rex novissimus*.

It is clear from the outset that not all writers will apply the Recapitulation theory in the same way. Much depends on whether this method of interpretation is associated primarily with an exegesis which recognizes some chronological sequence within the book, as in Victorinus' commentary. Such a sequence may relate to historical events or to future expectation; what is important is that within the Apocalypse the sequence comes to a halt, and the action is 'replayed'. A distinct type of recapitulation occurs in Tyconius' work, and there would seem to be some relationship between this and the language of Irenaeus. In what is basically a spiritual interpretation, the system of recapitulation emphasizes the totality of the forces involved.

The theory of Recapitulation presumably arose to give a more satisfactory account of the apparent repetitions, both of ideas and of forms, within the Book of Revelation. At times it has assumed the status of a dogma in exegesis; once accepted, all the details of the book from the seven letters to the New Jerusalem are brought into relationship with it. The textual justification of the theory rests primarily on the parallelism between the three sequences of plagues. Even here, the theory seems to do violence to the epithet 'last' of the plagues in Rev. 15.1. But only a full reappraisal of the three sequences can provide an adequate basis on which to judge the value of this theory.[11]

4 Historical applications – 'world-historical' or 'church-historical'

The *weltgeschichtlich* and *kirchengeschichtlich* methods of interpretation were favoured especially by medieval commentators. The type of calculation, applying the apocalyptic data to the course of contemporary events, has remained strangely attractive in spite of the recurrent anguish and disappointment it causes. In the context of thought concerning the Millennium, there was a renewal of speculation about the world's end in the eleventh century, particularly in France, the period of 1000 years of the Christian Church being calculated either from the Birth or the Ascension of Christ.

The name of Joachim of Flora (*c*. 1132–1202) is associated with a much more detailed evaluation of the Apocalypse as a description of the seven periods in the history of the Church.[12] These represent six times of suffering for the Church, followed by a Sabbath (the Millennium), and then the eighth period which is the final consummation and eternal rest. The first four periods are times of strife for various orders in the Church against their opponents: first, the *apostoli* against the *Judaei* (chs. 2–3); second, the *martyres* against the *Romani*, from Nero to Diocletian (chs. 4–7); third, the *doctores ecclesiae* against the *Ariani*, the Arian *reges Constantinopolitani, Vandali, Gothi, Longobardi* (chs. 8–11); and fourth, the *virgines* against the *Saraceni*, the Muslims as the enemies of Monasticism (chs. 12–14). The fifth period is the time of conflict between the Church in general and Babylon, the degenerate Holy Roman Empire;[13] this period is depicted by Joachim in terms of contemporary events. It is followed by the sixth period, that of Antichrist, in which Babylon comes to judgement; thereafter the Church is renewed for the Millennium by a return to the poverty and simplicity of apostolic times, under the influence of the new order of monks devoted to the contemplative life.

The main force of Joachim's interpretation lies in the prophetic statement of an eschatological message for his own times; the relationship between the individual conflicts of the first five periods is established by means of a theory of recapitulation, each conflict being taken up into the total conflict of the Church. A more systematic and strictly chronological statement of the *weltgeschichtlich* method is provided by Nicholas of Lyra (*c.* 1270–1340); he retained the scheme of seven ages, and expounded the Book of Revelation as a continuous history of the Church from its foundation to the end of time.

The majority of modern scholarly exegesis no longer sustains such an application in detail of the imagery of the Apocalypse to the history of the world or the Church or to events of the commentator's own day. But there are occasional attempts to read from Revelation's sequences of seven a schematic guide to the broad stages of world history, attempts which have inherited the inspiration of Joachim of Flora.

It is at least a more reasonable argument to suppose that something is applicable to more than one concrete situation because it is in a sense 'timeless', rather than to imagine that a work composed in the first century A.D. must of necessity contain a 'blueprint' for events in the distant future, whether of later persecutions, the Middle Ages or the Reformation. The major objection to so many expositions of world history through the pages of the Apocalypse is the arbitrary manner in which the age precipitating the final crisis is identified with the age of the interpreter. Even if it is true, and not a gross simplification, that writers in the apocalyptic tradition were concerned principally with the timing of the End and did no more than revise previous predictions, which events had proved incorrect, is this any justification for the commentator who, instead of writing a commentary, puts on the Seer's mantle and brings his work up to date?

5   *Eschatological – endgeschichtlich*

The eschatological method of interpretation cannot be distinguished sharply from the first category, the chiliastic. As R. H. Charles rightly pointed out, 'strictly speaking, Chiliasm forms a subdivision of Eschatology'.[14] But whereas the earliest interpreters tended to concentrate on the Millennium, which was still regarded as a prophecy for the future, liable to imminent earthly fulfilment, the thorough-going eschatological interpretation of the whole book first arose in the sixteenth century as a reaction against the proliferation of 'world-historical' interpretations.

It was the Jesuits who reacted most strongly to the bombardment of anti-Catholic exegesis from the Protestant Reformers who used the Apocalypse as ammunition for their attacks on the Papacy and the Church of Rome. These Jesuits proposed a strictly eschatological interpretation: the Apocalypse is concerned with the end of the world and the signs which herald it; the calamities, wars and persecutions which it predicts apply almost exclusively to this last age of history. Therefore it is no longer necessary to force John's imagery to make it apply to past or present realities; there is every reason to believe that John's oracles will be fulfilled literally – *haec verba intelligenda sunt ut sonant.*

The pioneer, and a notable exponent, of this method-of exegesis was the Spanish Jesuit Ribeira (*Commentarius in sacram beati Joannis Apocalypsim*, Salamanca 1591). According to Ribeira, only the first five seals refer to the early history of the Church, from the preaching of the Apostles up to the time of Trajan. From the sixth seal to the end of the book, everything relates to the last age, and therefore the figures for $3\frac{1}{2}$ years (42 months or 1260 days) can be understood literally. Basically, the Apocalypse is in two parts: up to ch. 11 there is a description of the calamities prior to the reign of Antichrist; between chs. 12 and 20 the reign of Antichrist and the accompanying persecutions are predicted.

In contrast, the modern application of the eschatological method by Lohmeyer[15] is much more comprehensive and, indeed, absolute. Everything in Revelation, from ch. 4 to ch. 21, is strictly eschatological. Historical identifications are therefore not appropriate; indeed, Lohmeyer believed that John was working with what is essentially an atemporal or *zeitlos* concept of salvation, in which past, present and future are in certain senses interchangeable.

Paul Minear in his investigations of ontology in the Apocalypse regards John's data as historical, ontological and eschatological in character:

he is speaking of present, existent realities in such a way as to discourage a disjunction between the present demands for endurance and the future reward of life in the kingdom. On

Patmos and in the seven cities of Asia the eschatological reality and the historical reality had become fused.... We may separate the two dimensions – the visible and the invisible, the historical and the eschatological – but John assumes their compresence.[16]

On the subject of the cities in Rev. 11.8 Minear comments:

the prophet describes not only a coalescence of heavenly and earthly forces; he sees also in a single situation the coalescence of many times and places. ... He saw each story as fully historical, and yet as fully eschatological. ... He perceived each separate place-time in terms of its content, i.e. that corporate historical action which 'filled it'. He discerned behind this action a 'trans-historical model' which linked each story to the others. This is a comprehensive rather than a disjunctive mode of seeing and thinking. It apprehends events in terms of their inner structure as responses to God's action.[17]

Such conclusions, although based originally in whole or in part on the eschatological method, seem to me to go far beyond the strict confines of the exegetical technique. Because the commentator is freed by his own arguments from historical controls which will limit his exegesis, his final results may closely resemble the spiritual interpretation of a modern 'Neo-Alexandrian'. Nor is the eschatological theme itself always sufficiently well defined (and restricted by an historical investigation of the type of thinking characteristic of the period) that it can act as a control on the exegesis.

On the supposition that Oscar Cullmann's presentation of Christian eschatology and *Heilsgeschichte* reflects at least one tradition of eschatological thinking within the Early Church, it may be most instructive to examine the work of Mathias Rissi, as he applies Cullmann's thesis directly to the Book of Revelation.[18] According to Rissi, the intention of the Apocalypse

is not simply to devise a general theology of history, but to lay out, quite concretely, a prophetic interpretation of that history which lies between those two divine interventions which are so very decisive for all human history, between the historically datable first appearance of Jesus Christ and his return.

John expresses an 'expectation of the near End' from 'certainty that the last time has broken in with the historical coming of Jesus Christ'; Rissi explains the repeated 'anticipation' of the eschatological events by a version of the Recapitulation theory. 'The tension of the End time', which is the time of Christ's lordship, the time of Antichrist and the time of the Church,

> is resolved by the Parousia of Christ, the final revelation and the accomplishment of salvation. ... John describes the End under various aspects and shows thereby that he is not satisfied with the mere laying out of a rigid scheme of eschatological events and that he is aware of the inadequacy of our conceptions. But he accommodates all elements in a total compass and presents the materialization of salvation as a consequence of events whose unfolding lies grounded in the nature of salvation history.

In this way the 'final creative act of consummated history is bound to the redemptive act of Jesus, who is enthroned with God in Paradise as mankind's atoning Lamb'.

6   Contemporary-Historical – *zeitgeschichtlich*

R. H. Charles observed: 'Quite sixty years pass before we find any references to [the Book of Revelation] and over a hundred before any writer deals at length with its expectations.' Thus, since the real historical horizon of the book was lost, and its historical allusions had become unintelligible for the most part, the use of the 'Contemporary-Historical' method of exegesis, 'unless in isolated passages, had become practically impossible'.[19] The possibilities of this exegetical method only came to light and were given serious consideration in the sixteenth and seventeenth centuries, as part of the same reaction against the fantasies of 'world-historical' exegesis which had also created the eschatological method.

The first steps were taken by Hentenius, a professor at Louvain, who summarized his understanding of the Apocalypse in the preface to an edition of Arethas' commentary in 1547. He divided the prophetic section of Revelation into two parts: chs. 6–11 dealing with *synagogae abrogatio*, and chs. 12–19 concerning *excidium gentilismi*. This very influential analysis was combined rather quaintly with an identification of ch. 13 with Mohammed and Islam's persecution of the Church. The date of the Apocalypse was given as in the time of Nero. Very similar ideas are taken up, but without the reference to Islam, in the important commentary of Alcázar (*Vestigatio arcani sensus in Apocalypsi* Antwerp 1614 and 1619).

In more recent exegesis, the emphasis on references to events contemporary with the author has been maintained in a number of works, and for a variety of reasons, not least the rationalist desire to exclude from consideration supernatural and prophetic elements. An obvious example is provided by the work of Ernest Renan, *L'Antéchrist* (Paris 1871, E. T. London 1890). He offers historical identifications for numerous details in the Book of Revelation: e.g. 6.6 refers to the famine prices of A.D. 68; 8.7 to the disastrous storms of 67, 68 and 69; 8.8 to the volcanic island of Thera; 8.10 to the fall of a meteorite which was associated with the pollution of drinking water; 8.12 to a series of eclipses or the dreadful storm of 10 January 69; 9.2 to the volcano (Solfatara) of Puteoli; the two witnesses in ch. 11 must be prominent members of the Jerusalem church.

Another important and an unfairly neglected example is offered by the work of Sir William Ramsay of Aberdeen. As a young man he was influenced deeply by the speculation of the Tübingen school; but 'the story of his researches' as a practical archaeologist, painstakingly relating the evidence of inscriptions and other discoveries to the issues of New Testament interpretation, 'is also the story of his gradual conversion to the view' of the accuracy and reliability of the New Testament writings.[20] J. G. C. Anderson described him as 'the foremost authority of his day on the topography, antiquities, and history of Asia Minor in ancient times'.[21] As W. Ward Gasque says in his study of Ramsay, 'even in his later, more apologetic writings he is expressing judgements formed during his early work in Asia Minor as a scientific archaeologist and classical historian'.[22] With these interests it is natural that Ramsay's attentions in the Book of Revelation should have been directed to *The Letters to the Seven Churches of Asia and their place in the plan of the Apocalypse*. In the preface to that work he wrote: 'The Apocalypse reads the history and the fate of the Churches in the natural features, the relations of earth and sea, winds and mountains, which affected the cities; this study distinguishes some of those influences.'[23]

Two works by French Roman Catholics offer notable examples from more recent scholarship of the *zeitgeschichtlich* method of interpretation. P. Touilleux's *L'Apocalypse et les cultes de Domitien et de Cybèle* was published in Paris in 1935 in reaction against Allo's use of the Recapitulation method.[24] According to Touilleux, John adopted the 'fiction' characteristic of Jewish apocalypses, that of describing events of the past or present as if they were future prophecies. The Apocalypse was actually written under Domitian, but gives the impression of being a revelation received about A.D. 68 in the reign of Vespasian.

The work of S. Giet, *L'Apocalypse et l'histoire*, published in Paris in 1957, originated in a comparison between material in the Apocalypse and Josephus' account of the Jewish War. Giet argues for a date of composition of the greater part of the Book of Revelation about 74/5 in the reign of Vespasian. Detailed correspondences are discovered between Rev. 8.13–11.19 and Josephus' account of the three phases in the Jewish War with Rome.

Interpretations in terms of the contemporary historical situation, although justified as being in accord with the tradition of apocalyptic writing, are always most vulnerable because of the limited nature of historical data to corroborate the identifications. And where there are such data, the commentator's eye lights automatically on any 'parallelism', even though it may be only chance coincidence. The modern reader has access to only a minute proportion, and not necessarily the most useful proportion, of the information available to the earliest reader, who naturally did not think of documenting what were to him obvious identifications. We can only proceed with extreme caution, assessing our historical allusions in the light of the book's total context. And so, for example, we recognize that, attractive though many of Giet's identifications appear, his assessment is based on a strictly limited portion of the book; the difficulty with his dating lies in the absence of evidence to support a context of actual persecution, despite all the indications he offers of a powerful impetus given to the Imperial cult by Vespasian.

7   *Literary Analysis*

The technique of literary criticism, applied systematically to the text of the Book of Revelation, is really a development of nineteenth-century scholarship. But it was anticipated, to a limited extent, by Grotius in his application of the 'contemporary-historical' method of exegesis.[25] Since he wished to assign different parts of the text to

different historical settings, and since he observed that there was
more than one tradition as to the place and date of composition,
Grotius conjectured that the Book was made up of several visions
which had been written down at different times, either on Patmos in
the time of Claudius or at Ephesus under Vespasian.

The application of literary criticism in the nineteenth and early
twentieth centuries produced a variety of theories which can be
classified under three headings, as R. H. Charles suggested: firstly,
redactions, where the present text has been amended by one or
more editors; secondly, independent documentary sources fused
together or merely juxtaposed; thirdly, fragments of material from
other sources, Jewish or pagan, interpolated by the author into his
work in such a way that the unity is disrupted by elements which are
not assimilated completely.

Subsequent developments in literary analysis can be illustrated by
two examples: the two-volume commentary by R. H. Charles – the
result of no less than twenty-five years' work – which appeared in
the I.C.C. series in 1920; and the hypothesis suggested by M. E.
Boismard in his article ' "L'Apocalypse" ou "Les Apocalypses" de
Saint Jean',[26] and set out in the introduction to the Book of Revelation in the Jerusalem Bible.

R. H. Charles analysed several different sources utilized by the
author in his work; he also believed that the text had suffered
considerably after the author's death at the hands of a faithful
disciple who was incompetent and rather stupid as an editor.
Charles recognized the inadequacy of literary-critical methods
without a study of the distinctive form of Greek employed by John;
he therefore provided in his introduction, and in the sections on
diction and idiom within the commentary itself, an extensive exposition of Revelation's linguistic peculiarities and characteristics. He
was particularly concerned to point to deviations from Classical
Attic Greek, and tried to demonstrate that what appear as
irregularities are in fact consistent features of John's style. Largely
on the basis of this analysis, Charles distinguished the parts of the
text which were composed by John from those which represent
independent sources and from interpolations and editorial glosses
in the text. G. Mussies comments on Charles's analysis that,
although it is extensive, it 'is not complete, especially not if
measured by the new demands resulting from the developments in
linguistics of the last fifty years. For a solution of the problems . . . it

is absolutely necessary that the linguistic description be as complete as possible.' Mussies's own work[27] aims 'to extend Charles' description to subjects not yet discussed or not sufficiently treated of, and to compare the result thus obtained with the morphological system of non-literary Koine-Greek, so as to discover the facts that are peculiar to the Apocalypse'.

R. H. Charles identified and dated various sources used by John, and drew attention to numerous interpolations, glosses and corruptions in the text which may be due to editorial activity. But his hypothesis about the incompetent editor has the most significant effect on the order of the text after 20.3, where Charles offers the following reconstruction of the logical order originally intended by the author: 20.1–3; 21.9–22.2; 22.14–15, 17; 20.4–6; 20.7–10; 20.11–15; 21.1–5b; 22.3–5; 21.5c, 6b–8; 22.6–7, 18a, 16, 13, 12, 10; 22.8–9, 20–21. Charles believes that the author died leaving his work in its final form only as far as 20.3, while the rest of the work existed as a number of documents waiting for their final editing.

According to the theory of M.-E. Boismard, the 'strictly prophetic part of Revelation, chs. 4–22, is made up of two different apocalypses written by the same author at different times and later fused into one by some author'.[28] This theory recognizes both the unity of style in the work and the problems of frequent doublets in the narrative. The analysis is made by examining internal affinities within the material, by separating the doublets and by remedying the incoherences, and is set out in the Jerusalem Bible introduction, as follows:

	TEXT I	TEXT II
Prologue: The small book		10.1–2a, 3–4, 8–11
Satan attacks the Church	12.1–6, 13–17	12.7–12
The Beast attacks the Church		13
Proclamation and preludes of the Great Day of wrath	4–9; 10.1–2b, 5–7; 11.14–18	14–16
The Great Day of wrath: Babylon's wickedness described	17.1–9, 15–18	17.10, 12–14
Babylon's fall	18.1–3	(cf. 14.8)
The elect preserved		18.4–8
Lament for Babylon	18.9–13, 15–19, 21, 24	18.14, 22–23
Canticles of triumph	19.1–10	18.20 (cf. 16.5–7)
The messianic kingdom	20.1–6	
The eschatological war	20.7–10	19.11–21
The Judgement	20.13–15	20.11–12
The Jerusalem to be	21.9–22.2; 22.6–15	21.1–4; 22.3–5; 21.5–8
Appendix: The two witnesses		11.1–13, 19

The analysis concludes with a brief reference to chs. 1–3: 'The letters to the seven churches ... which were certainly intended to be read as an introduction to the two prophecies, must originally also have existed as separate text.'

Obviously there is great value in a description of the language of Revelation such as that produced by Charles and carried further by Mussies. But the application of literary criticism to source analysis, in the most comprehensive sense, can be a misleadingly destructive method when conducted in isolation; these examples, considered in the light of the most recent scholarship, appear as rather primitive attempts, devised in a vacuum, to cater for all those seemingly problematic inconsistencies in style and content. In contrast, the mathematical techniques of modern computer analysis indicate the substantial unity of the book; of the passages which do not appear to belong to the same population as the remainder, only in the case of ch. 12 can the variation not be explained simply in terms of special features required by the subject-matter.[29]

8   Comparative studies – *religionsgeschichtlich* and *traditionsgeschichtlich*

The final category of methods of interpretation represents another substantial contribution made by scholars of the nineteenth and twentieth centuries, associated with the rise of comparative studies in religion. It is recognized that the symbols and imagery employed in Revelation are not necessarily the special creation of the author, but the majority of them may well be borrowed from tradition. Although the traditions of the Old Testament and Inter-Testamental Judaism, as well as early Christian traditions, clearly have contributed much to the author's thinking, it is desirable to define more exactly the circumstances in which this happened, and also to look further afield and consider the possibilities of other contributions from traditions beyond Judaism. Several scholars did significant work as pioneers in elucidating the debt of Revelation to these other religious traditions.

Particular attention has centred on the imagery of Rev. 12, especially that of the woman with child, pursued by the dragon. Many different solutions have been advanced for the problem of the mythological ancestry of this image. The Greek myth of Leto, pregnant by Zeus, and pursued by Python the serpent son of Earth, was advocated by A. Dieterich. H. Gunkel favoured the Babylonian mythology about Marduk the child of Damkina, the earth mother, and his conquest of Tiamat. A. Jeremias preferred the Mandaean version of the Babylonian myth in terms of Manda d'Hayye who fought against the monster of the waters of chaos before the creation of the world.[30]

Bousset found parallels in Egyptian mythology in the story of Isis, Horus and Set, and thought that the total picture represented a combination of Iranian and Egyptian ideas. H. Lietzmann thought in more general terms of a widely current legend of a heavenly Saviour figure, such as could be seen depicted in Virgil's Fourth Eclogue.[31] The classic commentary by Wilhelm Bousset, first published in 1896, is an important exposition of this method, applied to the Apocalypse as a whole. Another notable example is the work of Franz Boll (*Aus der Offenbarung Johannis: Hellenistische Studien zum Weltbild der Apokalypse*, Leipzig–Berlin 1914).

For Boll the important background to the Book of Revelation was constituted by the ideas of astral mythology, which derived from the 'science' of the Babylonians, but had been developed in the Graeco-Roman world. He concluded from the comparisons he made that the visions of Revelation were not the genuine results of spiritual experience, but were merely a literary elaboration of pagan data.

This method of interpretation affords a clear recognition of the 'traditional' character of the book, and emphasizes the importance of understanding it in relation to earlier traditions and the contemporary world of ideas. It is vital that it should be considered in an accurate perspective, so that it can, in its own right, contribute to the reconstruction of Christian origins and the assessment of those factors which were most influential in the development of Christian self-expression.

Of course the sheer variety of parallels drawn to the imagery of Revelation raises its own kind of problems. It is necessary to establish a history in miniature of the development of a particular set of ideas, so that Revelation's own position in this history can be described with some probability. At the same time it needs to be recognized that superficial parallels are not a complete guide to a real historical relationship and dependence; within our imperfect knowledge of the situation, there is always the possibility of movements of syncretism which establish artificial connections beyond the bounds of the original sources, as well as the case of complete coincidence where similar ideas are produced spontaneously in different places as a result of a general stimulus. In all our reconstructions the note of uncertainty must remain.

Much of the symbolism of Revelation is allusive, and therefore open to several possible identifications within traditions near and far. In such circumstances the best 'rule of thumb' seems to be to choose the traditional context that is nearest, temporally and geographically. It must be possible not only to suggest a relationship but also to indicate how that relationship can function. Inevitably this creates a preference for the early Christian and Jewish traditions, and frequently it will appear that this preference is vindicated in detailed exegesis of the surrounding text. But to say this is not to exclude at the outset many interesting possibilities raised even by the more eccentric exponents of the *traditionsgeschichtlich* method.

W. G. Kümmel, in his *Introduction to the New Testament* concludes: [32]

'To be sure, today we are one in principle in respect to the correct method of exposition of the Apocalypse, at least where such exposition proceeds from scientific presuppositions: The Apocalypse can only be understood in accordance with the intentions of the author and with our historical distance from his time, if we first of all ask about the traditional meaning of the images and conceptions [*traditionsgeschichtliche Methode*], then seek to determine which expectations the author proclaims in respect to the imminent end [*endgeschichtliche Methode*], and finally observe to what extent, by means of reference to the history of the immediate past or present, the time of the end is regarded as already realized in the present [*zeitgeschichtliche Methode*].'

I certainly would agree that these three elements are essential to the interpretation, without necessarily following Kümmel's exact order of priorities, or failing to recognize some valuable insights contained within some of the other principal methods.

My own inclination is to begin with an investigation of the historical situation as reflected in the Apocalypse, because this can illuminate the possibilities of dependence upon other traditions, as well as indicating how the author may be using eschatological concepts within a broadly defined structure of *Heilsgeschichte*, and satisfying the requirements of frequent historical allusions. But this is, in a measure, to anticipate my conclusions. The special purpose of this study is to investigate the relationship between these three major elements revealed in interpretation – history, traditional mythology and eschatology. In the sense in which the eschatological element is taken for granted in a study of the Book of Revelation, in so far as it belongs to the apocalyptic genre, this study will concentrate on the interrelationship of the two factors – the historical background and the use of traditional mythological ideas – which have influenced the presentation of the book.

This study must begin from a fresh critical appraisal of the data of the Apocalypse. But one cannot hope to cover every aspect of the Book in a specialized study, unless one is prepared to take more than twenty-five years in writing a multi-volume commentary. Therefore a sample of the material will be used, a sample which it is hoped can be regarded as broadly representative of the whole.

2

The Letters to the Seven Churches

Within extant apocalyptic literature a unique feature of the Book of Revelation is its collection of seven letters addressed to the churches of Asia Minor. E. J. Goodspeed called it 'this extraordinary façade',[1] a portal made up of seven individual letters introduced by a general covering letter. Because it is a unique feature of the Christian Apocalypse it will be especially important to examine this section in detail both for historical clues and for its relationship to earlier tradition. But the underlying question about these letters, whether they are individual letters originally circulated separately and now collected together, or whether we have an artificial construction devised to suit the author's particular purpose, also needs to be answered. This answer should be of significance for the historical side of the inquiry, although care must be taken to keep that significance in perspective. These letters do not have to be individual pieces of writing, each for their own destination, in order that they may be thought to tell us something of the situation in the churches of Asia, as the author of Revelation saw it.

Sir William Ramsay decided, from his investigation of the background to letter-writing, that the form of the letter had become established as the most characteristic expression of the Christian mind, and it was therefore almost obligatory upon any Christian writer. This was the explanation he offered both for the epistolary framework of the Book of Revelation, and for the inclusion of the seven letters in the Book.[2] The epistolary introduction and conclusion are out of keeping with the Jewish apocalyptic form which lies between, but are used because the writer, in spite of the style he had chosen for his work, was unable to lose the strong pastoral instinct of a successor to Paul. 'Just as the Roman Consul read in the sky the signs of the will of heaven on behalf of the State, so St John saw in the heavens the vision of trial and triumph on behalf of the Churches entrusted to his care.' He must record his vision in the appropriate apocalyptic form; but, equally, he must enclose it in a letter to the churches. For similar reasons the author feels himself obliged to use the letter form within his work, and so again he abandons the apocalyptic form briefly and expresses his thoughts within seven letters, although he makes some attempt to maintain the symbolism prescribed by the traditional principles of apocalyptic. He has recognized the inadequacy of the Jewish literary form; it 'breaks in his hands, and he throws away the shattered fragments', according to Ramsay's view of this disaffection. The author is presumed to have come to this realization during composition; the seven letters were therefore the last part of this work to be conceived, although they were carefully fitted in near the beginning.

This means that the letters to the seven churches are, strictly speaking, 'literary epistles', further removed from the type of the 'true letter' than any other New Testament composition. They are deliberate imitations of the accepted literary form which seems to have become almost obligatory for any Christian writing.

For Goodspeed the view of the seven letters as literary epistles, written in deliberate imitation of an accepted literary form, had a special significance which he expressed in his theory about the influence of the Pauline epistles.

> The letters of Paul had individually no effect upon other Christian writings. It was only after they were gathered into a collection and, as we should say, published that their literary influence began. The distinction between the letters scattered among the churches to which Paul wrote them and the same letters gathered into a collection and published, must be sharply drawn.

The striking picture of Paul presented by the Book of Acts led to such a revival of interest in the man that his letters were collected together, and Ephesians was written by these editors as an introduction to their collection, so that the Pauline epistles might become 'one great encyclical to all the churches'. The form of Revelation with its seven letters, which are really one letter containing messages to all seven churches, reflects this recently formed Pauline corpus.

The Book of Revelation

> begins with a collection of letters, represented as dictated by Jesus, and individually addressed to seven churches of the province of Asia, a missionary field which beyond any other Paul had made his own. ... It is evidently the effect of a whole collection of his (Paul's) letters to churches, which has so impressed the

prophet John and his public that it shapes into letter-collection form the whole first division of his apocalypse.

This collection is not a true one, made up of actual letters that had previously been written, because the collection is obviously written as a whole. There is only one letter salutation which stands at the beginning of the introductory or covering letter in the first chapter; each letter, therefore, apart from certain local details, is intended for all seven. For Goodspeed it was unthinkable that anyone should write in this way without having seen an actual collection of Christian letters. But once the author had seen the incidental values of this 'corpus' method, he would necessarily use this technique rather than write all the letters to all the churches.

This theory is a neat reversal of the comparison made in the Muratorian Canon which states that 'the blessed Apostle Paul himself, following the rule of his predecessor John, writes only by name to seven churches'.[3] As a theory it possesses a certain attractiveness, but it remains a hypothesis because there is so very little evidence to examine which would prove or refute it.

Could there be seven actual letters once circulated to the churches addressed, but now collected in this symbolic arrangement to suit some purpose of the author? This view was more popular among commentators in the past than it is today. Spitta, for example, thought that chapters 2 and 3 contained real letters that had been sent with the body of the work to each of the communities.[4] R. H. Charles argued that the letters should be dated earlier than the rest of the book, and had been sent to the churches towards the end of the reign of Vespasian. They had been edited subsequently by the author and incorporated in his Apocalypse, which dated from the time of Domitian.[5] Goguel also argued that the letters were written ten to fifteen years earlier than the remainder of the work, because their different emphasis, with the minimum of references to persecution, pointed to a different situation of composition.[6] A diametrically opposite conclusion, however, was drawn from the same data by Dibelius, in suggesting the possibility that 'these writings were first conceived when Domitian was dead and the worst danger was over'.[7]

Many commentators have endeavoured to show that the letters are inseparable from the rest of the work; attention has been drawn to the many connecting links in words and ideas. This does not, of course, preclude an independent existence of the letters at some stage, so long as common authorship of the letters and the Apocalypse is maintained. A more serious objection to the idea of real and separate letters can be drawn from 'the sevenfold design of the letters and from the careful symmetry of their arrangement'.[8] A somewhat extreme analysis of this design was offered by Austin Farrer[9] on the basic pattern of the half-week; there are four sequences of sevens, each divided into a greater and a lesser half-week $(4 + 3 = 7)$, in the Book of Revelation taken as a whole. Farrer wrote about the letter sequence: 'the messages fall into two cycles, the last three going back over the ground traversed by the first four'. He draws attention to the repetition of themes, and also to the use of 'texts' for the messages, selected from the vision of Christ in ch. 1. The symmetry of the composition, the balance between the letters and the interplay of themes among themselves and with the preceding vision, all these can be seen even without so mathematical an exposition as Farrer offered. The role of the writer of the Apocalypse has been enhanced considerably by these observations, but even this does not preclude the possibility that there are still actual letters to be found, written by the same author, but buried deeply in his subsequently imposed editorial pattern.

Even this possibility can be excluded for practical purposes, when these letters are extracted and examined. Features of the process of composition of this collection of letters are: a common plan followed in each letter; the opening formula with its instructions to the scribe; the identification and the credentials of the speaker in the 'text' with which each letter opens, taken from the Seer's vision of the Son of Man; the 'promise' with which each letter closes, expressed in apocalyptic imagery which is taken up elsewhere in the book; the formula which introduces the appraisal of the situation and the statement of merit or demerit; the verdict itself, calculating the failures of the churches and giving a direct command to each church to cope with its situation; and the exhortation to use the ears one has, and hear what the Spirit says – not to this one particular church currently being addressed – but to 'the churches'. This last formula of exhortation occurs in two positions, but even this variation seems systematic and not random; the formula precedes the promise to the conqueror in the first three letters, and follows it in the other four. When allowance is made for all these features of pattern imposed in the letter collection, what remains of the individual letters, discounting any further patterns in content as well as form, is so small a unit that it is most unlikely to resemble an original letter transmitted independently, or to offer any basis on which an original could be reconstructed, unless there had been some kind of 'postcard correspondence' in the Early Church.

It was said that a decision whether the seven letters are independent letters or an artificial construction might be of significance in an historical investigation. If there had been traces of an actual correspondence, this would itself furnish a major historical clue. But an artificial collection can also offer evidence which may point to an historical interpretation, and we must investigate those features of the seven letters which have been held to demonstrate this.

Ramsay regarded the author of Revelation as seriously fettered by the fanciful and unreal form of Apocalyptic. But when he began to write the letters, 'he comes into direct contact with real life, and thinks no longer of correctness in the use of symbols and in keeping up the elaborate and rather awkward allegory. He writes naturally, directly, unfettered by symbolical consistency.'[10] Ramsay argues that the 'direct contact with real life' is shown in the way the characteristics of each church are described in terms of its natural scenery and geographical environment. The interpretation of the first of the seven letters offers a striking illustration of the method of Ramsay's argument. The characteristic which belongs distinctively to the city of Ephesus is change – the variations in the natural conditions and the site of the city.

'The scenery and the site have varied from century to century. Where there was water there is now land: what was a populated city in one period ceased to be so in another, and has again become the centre of life for the valley: ... The city followed the sea, and changed from place to place to maintain its importance as the only harbour of the valley.'

This is reflected in the letter:

'A threat of removing the Church from its place would be inevitably understood by the Ephesians as a denunciation of another change in the site of the city, and must have been so intended by the writer. Ephesus and its Church should be taken up, and moved away to a new spot, where it might begin afresh on a new career with a better spirit. But it would be still Ephesus, as it had always hitherto been amid all changes.'[11]

C. J. Hemer has undertaken a reappraisal of Sir William Ramsay's work in which many of his conclusions are vindicated and some new suggestions offered. He goes further than Ramsay in relating the symbol of 'the tree of life' in 'the Paradise of God' particularly to the church in Ephesus. The tree is associated on coinage with Artemis of Ephesus and a primitive tree-shrine occupies the site of the later temples (identified by D. G. Hogarth);[12] this tree represented a connecting link with the sacred tree of Ortygia where it was believed the goddess was born.[13] The continuity of shrines and temples on the one site provided a fixed focal point of religious interest contrasted with the changeable nature of the site of Ephesus itself. This fixed point 'was a place of salvation for the suppliant' of Artemis, 'surrounded by an asylum a bow-shot or more in radius, enclosed by a boundary wall'. This sacred enclosure is alluded to by the word *paradeisos*,[14] a development from the original idea of a royal park. Mark Antony enlarged the bounds of the asylum, including within it part of the city itself, with disastrous consequences because there the criminal had refuge from the law. Augustus, Tiberius, and the proconsul under Claudius, all had to intervene to control the abuse of the right of asylum. M. P. Charlesworth says that Domitian 'apparently extended the boundaries of the temple of Ephesian Artemis'.[15] Apollonius of Tyana was highly critical about the evil consequences of asylum in a holy place.[16] To the church at Ephesus especially 'the promise of a city-sanctuary pervaded by the glory of God would be meaningful';[17] if the 'tree of life' also alludes to the cross of Christ,[18] then such a promise provides a complete contrast with the threat of the movement of church and city back under the dominance of the Artemision.

A similar kind of argument based on the local circumstances of another church, the church of Laodicea, is put forward by two other supporters of Sir William Ramsay's approach, M. J. S. Rudwick and E. M. B. Green, in an article on 'The Laodicean Lukewarmness'.[19] They offer an explanation of the terms 'hot', 'cold', and 'lukewarm' used in the letter, terms which Ramsay rather curiously neglected in his historical/geographical exposition.[20] Apparently, the site of Laodicea was originally chosen because of its control over an important road junction.[21] The site lacked a natural water supply and so had to derive its water from hot mineral springs near by, along a special siphon type of aqueduct; the water would have cooled in the pipes, but still be warm when it reached the city. Accordingly

> Laodicea would have been notorious as a city which, for all its prosperity, could provide neither the refreshment of cold water for the weary, as, for example, its neighbour Colossae could, nor the healing properties of hot water for the sick, as its neighbour Hierapolis could. Its lukewarm water was ... only fit to be 'spewed out of the mouth'.[22] The church in Laodicea would have been intended to see in itself a similar uselessness. It was providing neither refreshment for the spiritually weary, nor healing for the spiritually sick. It was totally ineffective and thus distasteful to its Lord.

The author who makes such deliberate and specialized reference to local conditions may write from a close pastoral understanding of the situation of his churches, and in his writing have the fortunate gift – or inspiration – of selecting some feature from the church's environment which admirably symbolizes the characteristic attitude of belief or practice he wishes to praise or condemn. By these highly significant allusions he depicts the spiritual condition of the churches. Alternatively the detailed characterization of the churches may be the work of a writer who

> surveys them from the point of view of one who believes that natural scenery and geographical surroundings exercise a strong influence on the character and destiny of a people. ... In the relations of sea and land, river and mountains ... he reads the tale of the forces that insensibly mould the minds of men.[23]

The second alternative clearly represents Ramsay's understanding of the situation. Not only is it expressed in the terms he used, but also the scheme of his book shows that considerable stress was laid on describing each church's environment before expounding the appropriate letter.

We might question the way Ramsay saw the methods of an author in a first-century situation. Would it not be more characteristic of a nineteenth-century sociologist than of a first-century Christian pastor to be concerned to emphasize the connection between the forces of the natural environment and the spiritual condition of the local community of the Church? Expressed in its most extreme form, this belief in the determining influence of the environment would leave little opportunity or justification for a pastor's praise or blame. In a situation where, granted the weakness of human nature, conformity was almost inevitable, the function of a writer in letters such as these would amount to stating the reality of the situation for those who had failed to recognize it. The characteristic expression of the promise to the one who overcomes cannot have been made with much hopefulness or conviction; whereas, apart from Ramsay's view of the author's situation, we might be disposed to recognize not only a realistic approach to practical problems in the churches, but also a confidence and optimism that is in tune with the mood of encouragement found elsewhere in the Book of Revelation. Certainly it is on the basis of this latter assessment that so much use has been made of Rev. 2 and 3 by countless churches other than the original Asian seven, for the purpose of practical devotion.

In assessing the general validity of this method of interpretation by contemporary references, as employed by Ramsay and his successors, it is necessary to weigh carefully the details of the argument. For what Ramsay believed to be reality, in the historical and geographical references to individual churches, other commentators have seen as part of a symbolic structure. Where Ramsay separated out the material of the letters as belonging to a special category, others have drawn attention to the close relationship of this material to that of the rest of the Book.[24] This would mean either that the historical method of interpretation is not to be reserved for the letters but is applicable to the whole Book, or that it is not an appropriate method for the Book as a whole.

But a thorough assessment of all the detailed allusions that have been suggested, together with historical and geographical reconstructions to provide a suitable background for their consideration, would be a completely impracticable project within the limits of this chapter. Since Hemer makes the significant point that evidence for an interpretation of the letters by local reference is essentially cumulative, I have endeavoured to represent, on the pages now following, a visual impression of this cumulative argument, indicating the range of detail which has been assessed.

The numbers on the biblical text as printed refer to the

appropriate historical and geographical data in the notes alongside. For purposes of comparison I have indicated references to the Old Testament and later Jewish writings by a variation in the type: **bold** represents what scholars usually regard as a direct quotation; ***bold italic*** represents a suggested allusion.

EPHESUS

The words of him who holds the seven stars in his right hand, who walks among the seven **golden lampstands**. (1) I know your works, your toil and your patient endurance, and how you cannot bear evil men but have tested those who call themselves apostles but are not, (2) and found them to be false; I know you are enduring patiently and bearing up for my name's sake, and you have not grown weary. But I have this against you, that **you have abandoned the love you had at first**. (3) Remember then from what you have fallen, (3) repent and do the works you did at first. If not, I will come to you and remove (3) your lampstand from its place, unless you repent. Yet this you have, you **hate** the works of the Nicolaitans, (4) which I also **hate**. He who has an ear, let him hear what the Spirit says to the churches. To him who conquers **I will grant to eat of the tree of life**, (5) which is **in the paradise of God**. (6)

EPHESUS[25]

Priority of Ephesus attributed to its status, either as official capital of Roman Asia, or as commercial centre of region; or explained on geographical grounds as the natural starting-point for a traveller.

1   Allusion to status as leading city (one as centre for all seven) cf. reference to Sardis, ancient capital of Lydia.

2   False apostles – local opposition?

3   Idea of movement alludes to change in site of city during history: Ionian city moved by Croesus (c. 550 B.C.), moved again by Lysimachus (c. 287 B.C.). Silting-up caused by the river Cayster was a threat to the harbour and eventually made necessary the moving of city and harbour and the dredging of the channel.

4   Nicolaitans – local opposition?

5   Tree-shrine of Artemis on the site of later temples. Tree as symbol of Artemis.

6   Artemision offered asylum within its sacred enclosure.

SMYRNA

The words of **the first and** the last, who died and came to life. (1) I know your tribulation and your poverty (but you are rich) and the slander of those who say that they are Jews and are not, but are a **synagogue of** Satan. (2) Do not fear what you are about to suffer. Behold, the devil is about to throw some of you into prison, (3) that **you may be tested**, and for **ten days** (4) you will have tribulation. Be faithful (5) unto death, and I will give you the crown of life. (6) He who has an ear, let him hear what the Spirit says to the churches. He who conquers shall not be hurt by the second death.

SMYRNA[26]

'The symbolism of weeping, burial and resurrection attached to myrrh (=**smurna**) may have been reflected in the portrayal of a city of suffering.' (Hemer)

1 Destruction of Old Smyrna by Alyattes of Lydia *c.* 600 B.C. Inhabited as a village until new city was founded *c.* 290 B.C. around Mt. Pagos. Aristides speaks of a city risen from oblivion since Alexander, uses image of phoenix.

2 Relations of church with local Jews? Special antagonism of the Jews of Smyrna illustrated later by conduct at martyrdom of Polycarp; cf. *CIG* 3148.30.

3 Imprisonment not a penalty, but a temporary measure, a period of suffering pending trial or execution.

4 Possible reference to Niobe tradition in Homer's Iliad 24.602–17 where tenth day terminates period of mourning. Niobe tradition has local relevance: Hittite carving (Tas Suret), or natural rock feature on Mt. Sipylus, identified as Niobe.

5 Proverbial faithfulness of Smyrna to her allies. (cf. Cicero *Phil.* 11.25; Livy 35.42.2).

6 Crown as reference to physical appearance of city on Mt. Pagos authenticated by ancient writers (Aristides and Apollonius of

Tyana) and by use as emblem of city. May also be related to agonistic imagery of martyrdom in arena (cf. Ignatius to Polycarp and Martyrdom of Polycarp).

Perhaps also local custom conferring crowns on the dead, or honouring visits of officials.

PERGAMUM

The words of him who has the sharp two-edged sword. (1) I know where you dwell, where Satan's throne (2) is; you hold fast my name and you did not deny my faith even in the days of Antipas my **witness**, (3) my **faithful** one, who was killed among you, where Satan dwells. But I have a few things against you: you have some there who hold the teaching of **Balaam**, (4) who taught Balak to put a stumbling block before **the sons of Israel**, that they might **eat** food **sacrificed** to idols and **practise immorality**. So you also have some who hold the teaching of the Nicolaitans. (4) Repent then. If not, I will come to you soon and war against them with the **sword of** my **mouth**. (1) He who has an ear, let him hear what the Spirit says to the churches. To him who conquers I will **give** some **of the hidden** manna, (5) and I will give him a white stone, (6) with a **new name** written (7) on the stone which no one knows except him who receives it.

PERGAMUM

Ruler-worship was developed under the Attalid dynasty and carried over when the kingdom was reconstituted as the province of Asia. Questioned how long Pergamum retained status of capital and seat of proconsul; likely rivalry with Ephesus and Smyrna.

1   Ctr. with proconsular *ius gladii* (historical or present) or authority of spoken word (e.g. judge's sentence, as in the trial of Antipas).

2   Earliest and greatest centre of Ruler-worship (Imperial cult – 29 B.C.). Possibly also refers to 'armchair' appearance of city-hill to traveller from Smyrna.

Satan – allusion possible to other great shrines of Pergamum: throne altar of Zeus Soter, and worship of Asklepios Soter, both symbolized by the serpent (Biblical = Satan).

3   Celebrated local case, otherwise unknown?

4   Nicolaitans =? Balaam – local opposition?

5   Manna – food of Messianic banquet (associated with the original manna, as preserved Ex 16.32–4), ctr. with food offerings in

Imperial cult or other religious feasts. 'Manna' in pagan Greek and Latin (Galen of Pergamum and Pliny *H.N.*) indicated crumb of frankincense, pinch of incense used to prove loyalty to Emperor.

6 White marble used for inscribed stones at Pergamum, ctr. coarse dark brown granite of Acropolis buildings. White ctr. black voting pebble which condemns a man on trial.

7 Later analogy of Aristides' vision of Asklepios during *incubatio* at Pergamum, commemorated by a token he was given, associated with new name 'Theodorus' he received, suggests an interpretation if this was local practice at the Asklepieion.

THYATIRA

The words of the Son of God, who has **eyes like** a flame of **fire**, (1) **and whose feet** are like burnished **bronze**. (2) I know your works, your love and faith and service and patient endurance, and that your latter works exceed the first. But I have this against you, that you tolerate **the woman Jezebel**, (3) who calls herself a prophetess and is teaching and beguiling my servants to **practise immorality** and to **eat** food **sacrificed** to idols. I gave her time to repent, but she refuses to repent of her immorality. Behold, I will throw her on a *couch*, (4) and those who commit adultery with her I will throw into great tribulation, unless they repent of her doings; and I will **strike** her *children* **dead**. And all the churches shall know that I am he who searches **mind and heart**, (5) and I will **give to each** of you **as** your **works deserve**. But to the rest of you in Thyatira, who do not hold this teaching, who have not learned what some call the deep things of Satan, (6) to you I say, I do not lay upon you any other burden; only hold fast what you have, until I come. He who conquers and who keeps my works until the end, I will **give** him power over the **nations**, and **he shall rule them with a rod of iron**, (7) **as when earthen pots (8) are broken in pieces**, *even* as *I myself have received* power *from my Father;* and I will give him the morning *star*. (9) He who has an ear, let him hear what the Spirit says to the churches.

THYATIRA[28]

Exceptional prominence of trade-guilds as basis of city's organization, associated in origin with military function of city, as supplying auxiliary services of garrison.

1   Attributes perhaps reflect those of city's god Tyrimnus, assimilated to Helios and Apollo, and later explicitly linked with Imperial cult (Caracalla).

2   Unique word (chalkolibanō) – trade term for metal work in Thyatira – used for alloy of copper or bronze with metallic zinc (produced by distillation).

3   Teacher from local opposition? Or refers to syncretism of Sambathe Sibyl (cf. Schürer).

4 RSV sickbed. Greek ambiguous, of couch for dining or illness. Allusion to religious activities of trade guilds, feasts especially. Status of women in guild feasts not clear.

5 As this is addressed to all the churches, this is a point at which local allusion is less likely.

6 Allusion to, or caricature of, slogan of local 'Gnostic' group.

7 Allusion to military power of city, perhaps represented by Tyrimnus with his battle-axe.

8 Guild of potters – *CIG* 3485=*IGRR* 4.1205.

9 Emblem of authority, with Messianic connotations, Ctr. with claims of Emperor (if Imperial cult was active threat here, perhaps in persecution by trade-boycott). cf. Domitian in A.D. 95 (Statius *Silv.* 4.1.1–4).

SARDIS

The words of him who has the **seven spirits** of God and the seven stars. (1) I know your works; you have the name of being alive, and you are dead. (2) Be vigilant (3) (RSV Awake), and **strengthen** what remains (4) and is on the point of death, for I have not found your works completed (5) (RSV perfect) in the sight of my God. Remember then what you received and heard; keep that and repent. If you will not be vigilant (RSV awake), I will come like a **thief**, (3) and you will not know at what hour I will come upon you. Yet you have still a few names in Sardis, people who have not soiled their garments; (6) and they shall walk with me in **white**, (7) for they are worthy. He who conquers shall be clad thus in white garments, and I will not **blot** his name **out of the book of life**; (8) I will confess his name before my Father and before his angels. He who has an ear, let him hear what the Spirit says to the churches.

SARDIS[29]

Sardis was proverbial in ancient literature, both for its wealth and its history.

1   Reference appropriate, cf. Ephesus, because of status of Sardis as ancient capital of Lydia.

2   *a.* City in decay, or, at least no longer seat of power.
    b. Local religious preoccupation with themes of death and life.
    c. Allusion to differing views on fate of Croesus – apotheosis or self-deception.
    d. Situation of temple of Artemis with Acropolis of ancient Lydian capital to East, and Necropolis hill to West. Royal Lydian Necropolis near by at Bin Tepe.
    e. Citadel imposing from a distance, but material of hill liable to crumble and be eroded.

3   City captured, in spite of its strength, through lack of vigilant defence (in 546 by Cyrus, and again in 214 by Antiochus III). 'Coming like a thief' describes method of assault at a weak point by a few men.

4   By nature of site, Sardis suffered most severely in the earthquake of A.D. 17 perhaps losing much of S.W. of citadel.

5 'Unfinished' un-fluted columns of Cybele temple?

6 Immorality censured by Apollonius of Tyana. Inscriptions refer to chastisement with disease of those morally unclean when performing vows.

7 *a*. Ancient centre of woollen industry.
  b. White toga worn at Roman triumph and at festivals – such pomp had departed from Sardis, but remained for faithful Christians.

8 Ctr. with citizen register, or membership of synagogue. (Jewish curse of the Minim: 'May they be blotted out') Later archaeological evidence indicates large body of Jews in Sardis (3C. Synagogue building), confirms earlier evidence (e.g. Josephus) for Jewish community here.

PHILADELPHIA

The words of the holy one, the true one, who has **the key of David**, who **opens** (1) **and no** one **shall shut**, who **shuts and no** one **opens**. I know your works. Behold, I have set before you an **open** door, (1) which no one is able to shut; I know that you have but *little power*, and yet you have kept my word and have not denied my name. Behold, I will make those of the synagogue of Satan (2) who say that they are Jews and are not, but lie – behold, I will make them **come and bow down before your feet**, and learn that **I have loved you**. Because you have kept my word of patient endurance, I will keep you from the hour of trial (3) which is coming on the whole world, to try those who *dwell upon the earth*. I am coming soon; hold fast what you have, so that no one may seize your crown. (4) He who conquers, I will make him a *pillar* (5) in the temple of my God; never shall he go out of it, (3) and I will write on him the name of my God, and **the name of the city** (6) of my God, the New (RSV new) Jerusalem (7) which comes down from my God out of heaven, and my own **new name**. He who has an ear, let him hear what the Spirit says to the churches.

PHILADELPHIA[30]

1   City as 'open door' towards Phrygia, controlling the route from Smyrna and Lydia. Afforded missionary opportunity for church (cf. 1 Cor. 16.9;2 Cor. 2.12; Ignatius Phld. 9.1.) Philadelphia originally founded as 'missionary' centre for Greek ideas?

2   Reference to Jewish community? (cf. Smyrna). Ignatius offers evidence of proselytizing – Phld. 6.1, 8.2. The reference to 'shutting' may then also allude to Jewish power of excommunication.[31]

3   Church facing prospect of disaster. Image of city living under constant threat of earthquake in volcanic region. Slow recovery from major earthquake of A.D. 17. Many inhabitants lived outside city in surrounding country to avoid greatest danger.

4   Games and memorials to athletic prowess prominent in Philadelphia, which had reputation as 'Little Athens' because of its festivals and temples.

5 Pillar as image of stability (ctr. earthquakes). Possible allusion to a local use of inscribed pillars.
   ? ctr. *stēlai* (Ignatius Phld. 6.1).

6 City took Imperial names in gratitude for aid:
   Neocaesarea (Tiberius)
   Flavia Philadelphia (Vespasian – Domitian)
   Honours seemed hollow after Domitian's edict against vines (A.D. 92) which affected Philadelphia's major product.

7 Does the unusually square and symmetrical town-plan of modern Alasehir represent a practical working-out of New Jerusalem prophecy? Cf. important belief in descent of New Jerusalem for Montanism, which Calder saw as originating in district of Philadelphia.

LAODICEA

The words of the **Amen**, the faithful and true witness, the **beginning** of God's **creation**. (1) I know your works: you are neither cold nor hot. Would that you were cold or hot! So, because you are lukewarm, (2) and neither cold nor hot, I will spew you out of my mouth. For you say, I am rich, **I have prospered**, and I need nothing; (3) not knowing that you are wretched, pitiable, poor, blind, and naked. Therefore I counsel you to buy from me gold (4) *refined* by fire, that you may be rich, and **white garments** (5) to clothe you and to keep the shame of your nakedness from being seen, and salve (6) to anoint your eyes, that you may see. Those whom I love, **I reprove** and **chasten**; so be zealous and repent. Behold, I stand **at the door** (7) and knock; if any one hears my **voice** and **opens** the door, I will come in to him and eat with him, (8) and he with me. He who conquers, I will grant him to sit with me on my throne, (9) as I myself conquered and sat down with my Father on his throne. He who has an ear, let him hear what the Spirit says to the churches.

LAODICEA[32]

City stood on the crossroads, controlling trade routes.

1   Cf. terminology of Colossian heresy suggested by Col. 1.15ff. Parallel situation at neighbouring Laodicea.

2   Local water supply by aqueduct required as city grew, since river water was petrifying and unpalatable. Aqueduct fed from spring 5 miles away at Denizli. Water as drunk tended to be lukewarm, ctr. cold water of Colossae and hot healing springs of Hierapolis.

3   Ostentatious independence of city in reconstruction after earthquake of A.D. 60 (cf. Tacitus *Ann*. 14.27.1). Public buildings paid for by individuals.

4   Trading city was centre of banking.

5   Ctr. local speciality of clothing made from raven-black wool of local sheep (colour attributed by Vitruvius to water which sheep drank).

6   Local medical school produced influential specialists in oph-
thalmology (e.g. Demosthenes Philalethes). 'Phrygian powder'
– eyesalve made from alum available locally.

7   Perhaps alludes to monumental triple gate (Ephesian Gate) of
city donated in rebuilding, with dedication to Domitian. The
whole city, not just the Acropolis, was contained within a ring-
wall with three gates. 'Closed door' symbol on Phrygian tombs.

8   Ctr. enforced hospitality exacted by Roman officials from
Laodicea as affluent *conventus* capital.

9   Allusion to Zenonid dynasty, resulted from Roman offer of
throne to Polemon after resistance to Labienus Parthicus in 40
B.C.

It can only be stressed that the strength of this argument is cumulative. While individual features of the interpretation are open to dispute, and, if considered in isolation, might not command total respect, the fact that they all combine to present an intelligible picture of the cities and churches of the period, using such references to past events and present characteristics as are attested elsewhere, makes a convincing argument that is practically conclusive. The range of allusions suggested covers almost all the special features of the seven letters. Another significant point is that, as is indicated by the juxtaposition of Old Testament references, and possible allusions, with the topical details in the summary, the author seems to be using Old Testament and other traditional themes and adapting them to have a specific application in the current situation of the churches. So we have a combination of traditional ideas with references to the contemporary situation, a combination which we shall observe at many other points in the Book and which appears to be important for the Book as a whole.

3

The Plague Sequences

The three plague sequences, the seven seals, the seven trumpets and the seven bowls, have an important role to play in any interpretation of the structure of the Book of Revelation. Upon the critical appraisal of their function within the Book depends a judgement about the chronological order and historical nature of the events described. Is the divine process, which John sees to be at work, moving forward through these sequences of events, taken consecutively; or do these sequences reiterate, in a scheme of recapitulation, a single set of circumstances? A characteristic of much of the interpretation of these passages, as for example those theories about the seven seals reviewed by R. H. Charles in his commentary,[1] is the apparent arbitrariness with which one exegetical method is chosen for one element in the picture, and another for the next element. I shall endeavour to set out an interpretation which offers greater coherence both in method and in general theme, and also provides adequate consideration of the details.

As D. S. Russell observed, there is a significant continuity between the ideas about the Day of the Lord presented by the Old Testament prophets, and the apocalyptic picture of the signs of the End, with its sequence of judgements and woes associated with hope in the final triumph of God:

> the Apocalyptists took up the prophetic teaching concerning the future hope as expressed in the Day of the Lord, enlarging and enriching it out of the store of their own religious insight and experience.... They were trying, in effect, to say what they believed the prophets would have said in the changed circumstances of their day.[2]

The two aspects of the prophetic picture of the Day of the Lord, the dreadful day of judgement, and the heralding of the golden age of God's kingly rule, are held together as essentially complementary. In practical terms, the 'transformation' envisaged could well change the situation from one extreme to the other, from apparent prosperity to the irrevocable judgement of God's wrath, and from imminent disaster to an age of blessedness. Nor did the transformation necessarily accord with popular expectation, a point which the prophet Amos stressed. The judgement of God could be seen to operate on a national basis (against Israel's enemies) or on a religious and ethical basis (according to which Israel as God's people or as individuals were equally, if not more, liable to judgement). The future hope expressed by the prophets was associated with the 'end' of an historical era; later the temporal dimensions were changed as the Apocalyptists envisaged the end of the world.

The Day of Yahweh 'has been expanded into a phenomenon of cosmic significance',[3] depicted in the colours of traditional mythology. A variety of traditions contribute to the total picture and in so far as the expectation is systematized, elements from different traditions are to some extent blended together. Within the cosmic dimension, Yahweh's enemies are not always identified specifically with historical nations; the prophetic oracle may have originated in concrete circumstances or may have been given an historical application subsequently, but the material transcends these limitations. As world powers, the enemies are characterized in mythological terms and given labels such as Gog and Magog, names better known for the mythological aura which surrounds them than for any remote historical reality they may represent. Subsequently, in apocalyptic writing, these mythological world powers can be identified again with historical realities.

An important contribution to the imagery describing the Day of Yahweh is made by the Israelite's nomadic and agricultural experience, which John Gray describes as under the 'influence' of 'the deserts south and east of Palestine'.[4]

From this quarter came the locusts, before which 'the land is as the garden of Eden and behind them a desolate wilderness' (Joel 2.3). From there the sirocco blew as a blast from a fiery furnace, the ordeal of fire of which Amos speaks, which dried up even the subterranean waters (Amos 7.4). The whirlwind or dust storm also came from the great empty quarter (Amos 1.14). The 'darkness' or obscuration associated with both sirocco and dust storm, owing to the fact that the atmosphere is heavily charged with fine particles of dust, is also connected with the desert. Such a darkness obscures the heavenly bodies, and both sun and moon appear 'blood-red'. A prolonged visitation of the sirocco, called in Palestine the Hamsin (lit. 'fifty'), with drought and famine, causes plague. All these are common manifestations of the presence of Yahweh in the Hebrew prophets.... They are not rare, supernatural phenomena, but are all too common in the experience of dwellers in Palestine in all ages, and to ancient Israel (e.g. Amos) they signified the dreaded presence of Yahweh their desert God.

When, as a result of outside influences and internal disillusionment working upon the fundamental concept of God's activity in history, Judaism evolved a cosmic eschatology within and beyond the nationalistic future hope, and the phrase 'the latter end of the days' was applied to the end of history itself, and not merely to the end of an historical era, many features of the description of the Day of Yahweh were developed to achieve a new significance and emphasis as 'signs of the end'. The 'wise men' (whether Apocalyptists or scribes) claimed the ability to discern when the end was approaching, on the basis of the series of omens preceding it.[5] The current world-view, best described as a modification of pessimistic dualism, envisaged two ages – the present age dominated by evil powers, and the age to come which is the golden age – and believed that the turning-point between these ages was imminent. By this criterion the culmination of evil could indicate the proximity of the end.

> It is this culmination of sin and wickedness which brings this world to an end, the last tribulation, so familiar to both the apocalyptists and the rabbis, and called by the latter 'the travail of the Messiah (or Messianic age)'...: tumult and war, pestilence and famine, bad seasons and dearth, apostasy from God and His Law, the disruption of all moral order, and disorder even in the laws of nature.[6]

Apocalyptic tradition since the Book of Daniel had declared: 'There shall be a time of trouble, such as never has been since there was a nation till that time' (Dan. 12.1). Subsequent writers developed the details of this expectation in a number of signs marking the nearness of the End.[7]

These 'signs of the end' can be grouped by subject-matter into three broad categories:

1 Ominous happenings of every kind – 'signs in sun and moon and stars' – portents in the heavens and on earth; failure in the powers of nature, resulting in bad seasons and poor crops; famines, earthquakes, destruction by fire.[8]

2 Rebellion and warfare; all men at enmity with each other; persecution. Nation rises against nation; men provoke one another to fight; friends attack each other as if they were enemies; utter lack of any human sympathy, so that even the closest bonds of the family are broken.[9]

3 These first two categories presage the last desperate resistance to God by Satan, his army and the evil world powers, when God comes to wind up the present world order. Son of Man or Messianic figure coming from heaven as judge and as agent of deliverance from oppression.[10]

A special terminology is developed to refer to these 'signs of the end' in later Jewish and Christian writings. One term, 'the travail pains of the Messiah', has been mentioned in its singular, Rabbinic, form. The idea of *hai ōdines* goes back in the Old Testament to the imagery of Hos. 13.13 (cf. Isa. 26. 16–19; Mic. 4. 9–10). Later developments of the idea, within an eschatological context appropriate to the birth or appearance of a Messianic figure, include 1QH 3. 7–10, where it is understood to be applied to the Qumran community itself; Mark 13.8, where *archē ōdinōn* is associated with earthquakes and famines; and Rev. 12. 1–6. Another term is *thlipsis*, which is used by the Septuagint (and Theodotion) to translate the Hebrew *tsārāh* at Dan. 12.1 and elsewhere. Daniel's general prophecy of 'a time of trouble' is reiterated in subsequent writers who concentrate on expounding its features in detail (cf. Ass. Mos. 8.1; Mark 13.19). Another word, *telos*, is self-explanatory when used in this connection, being applied to the climax of these expectations, the End itself. A sharp distinction is not always maintained when these three terms are applied to parts of the total range of subject-matter associated with these expectations. John 16.21 suggests that, even in literal usage, *thlipsis* can be employed where *ōdin* might be more exact. Nevertheless it would appear that these three terms – *ōdines*, *thlipsis* and *telos* – correspond in a general way to the three categories of subject-matter already analysed.

References to the 'Little Apocalypse' of Mark 13 have appeared already in this brief review. Many scholars have seen a threefold structure of expectations, similar to our classification, within the material of Mark 13 and its parallels. As T. Colani wrote in 1864, 'Our discourse presents not only this division, but it uses precisely these three technical words.... We have here a very complete summary of the apocalyptic views spread among the Jewish Christians of the first century.' The threefold division within the 'Little Apocalypse' to which Colani refers seems to have been recognized first in the analysis offered by H. J. Holtzmann which

> was adopted by almost all subsequent exegetes: it narrates (1) *archai ōdinōn*, the beginnings of the woes, represented first according to their 'world historical' character, 13.5–9, and next according to their significance for the development of the kingdom of God (the time of the mission), vv. 9–13; (2) *hē thlipsis*, the tribulation, including the destruction of Jerusalem, vv. 14–23; (3) *hē parousia*, the coming of Christ, vv. 24–27

depicted as *to telos* 'the end'.[11]

While hesitating to add yet one more variant to the multiplicity of modified analyses and sub-divisions of Mark 13 which has resulted from more than a century of development of the 'Little Apocalypse' source theory, I feel that there is a more satisfactory, if less admirably balanced, way of understanding the material of this chapter in terms of the proposed classification of 'signs of the end'. I would retain the significance of the technical terms as 'signposts' within the Marcan chapter, but take a different view of the order in which the three elements are expounded from that to be found in Holtzmann's analysis. It is important to recognize that Holtzmann's original work was conditioned by a threefold understanding of the parousia, which even he did not retain throughout his working life.

The first section in this chapter is by far the largest, comprising 13.5–23. In its present form this is a carefully structured account of the *thlipsis*, the last words of the section reverting to the opening theme of false prophecy. Verses 19–23 make a fitting conclusion for what has gone before, and 13.19 gives the section its title, using the words of Dan. 12.1 to prophesy days of unprecedented tribulation. In the context of Mark's Gospel these traditional ideas are applied by the evangelist to current circumstances in his readers' experience, pointing to their real significance as 'signs of the end'. This represents only the first of three stages, and 13.7–8 serve to make this clear. The 'wars and rumours of wars' are part of the first stage, the *thlipsis*; the third stage, the end, is not yet. Before the end are two stages: there is firstly the international strife which is part of the present tribulation; even when numerous earthquakes and outbreaks of famine occur, these only represent the beginning (archē) of stage two (the woes): the first anticipations of the full range of cosmic signs disrupting the natural order of heaven and earth. Mark 13.8[12] thus points ahead to the second section of this 'apocalypse', represented by 13.24f.; these are the cosmic woes, the supernatural portents which herald the appearance of the Messiah, the 'birth-pangs' which precede his coming to the world. The third section (Mark 13.26f.) then represents the final stage, the *telos*, when the Son of Man comes 'with great power and glory'. As the judgement takes place 'he will send out the angels, and gather his elect from the four winds'.

When we come to examine the plague sequences of Revelation against this general background of thought, there is a major question which warrants some preliminary consideration. Since these ideas have evolved into three separate sequences of seven 'plagues' it is necessary to ask what special significance is attached to each sequence; why, indeed, there should be three of them; and how they are related to one another and to the construction of the book as a whole.

According to one method of interpretation, which we have already examined, the appropriate response is that these three sequences are simply repetitions of one another. The Recapitulation theory asserts that the seven bowls reflect exactly the same events as the seven seals; the substance is the same and only the form has been changed. Clearly in the accounts of the three sequences of plagues there are differences and similarities. The problem for the Recapitulation theory was to show how events which appeared to be different were different only in the way they were described. For the chronological theory the converse is a problem: how can the interpreter make a clear distinction between sequences which have superficial similarities?

A valuable starting-point for a consideration of the seven seals (Rev. 6.1–7.1; 8.1) is R. H. Charles's presentation of the case for the dependence of this section on the material of the 'Little Apocalypse' in the Synoptic Gospels. He sets out the parallels as follows:[13]

MATT. 24 (vv. 6, 7, 9a, 29)	MARK 13 (vv. 7–9a, 24–25)
1 Wars	*1* Wars
2 International strife	*2* International strife
3 Famines	*3* Earthquakes
4 Earthquakes	*4* Famines
5 Persecutions	*5* Persecutions
6 Eclipses of the sun and moon; falling of the stars; shaking of the powers of heaven.	*6* (as in Matthew)

LUKE 21 (vv. 9–12a, 25–26)	REV. 6. 2–17, 7.1
1 Wars	Seal *1* War
2 International strife	*2* International strife
3 Earthquakes	*3* Famine
4 Famines	*4* Pestilence (Death and Hades)
5 Pestilence	*5* Persecutions
6 Persecutions	*6* Earthquakes, eclipse of the sun, ensanguining of the moon, falling of the stars, men calling on the rocks to fall on them, shaking of the powers of heaven, four destroying winds (cf. Luke 21.25).
7 Signs in the sun, moon and stars; men fainting for fear of the things coming on the world; shaking of the powers of heaven.	

As Charles declared, 'Even a cursory comparison of these lists shows that they practically present the same material.' If we follow the traditional and widely accepted relative dating of Revelation and the Synoptic Gospels, then any dependence must be by the author of Revelation on the Gospel tradition. The dependence cannot be narrowed down to the use of a single Gospel: the fourth seal is only paralleled in Luke (21.11), whereas the substance of Rev. 6. 12–13 is described in similar language in Matt. 24.29 and Mark 13.24f., but only alluded to in Luke 21.25 as 'signs in sun and moon and stars'. R. H. Charles prefers the conclusion that John was dependent upon the 'Little Apocalypse', as a document underlying the present Gospels, rather than that he made use of two Gospels, or used oral tradition.

The relationship between the seven seals and the apocalyptic material of the Synoptic Gospels is set out in terms of parallels of substance and parallels of order (although there is some flexibility here and Charles's arguments for amendments explicable in terms of literary policy are not overwhelming); there are practically no parallels of wording, either as literary allusions or as direct quotations, but only unavoidable parallels in the usage of obvious words. In these circumstances the matter is stated much more happily in terms of a somewhat fluid tradition of apocalyptic ideas, moulded according to a fairly precise pattern of expectation. To this tradition Mark, perhaps Matthew (if his variations are significant), Luke (if his divergence from Mark 13 results from his use of fresh material as well as his creative reinterpretation of Marcan tradition in accordance with eschatological presuppositions),[14] and certainly the author of Revelation are indebted.

This relationship can be tabulated afresh, as in the accompanying chart. I believe that this gives a fairer picture of the total situation: it indicates the significant parallels in order which are important for the total pattern; it indicates the parallels in subject-matter found in the apocalyptic chapters of the Gospels; and it indicates the further parallels in supporting detail, subordinate to the overall pattern, which show that the author of Revelation is working out this pattern in several particulars in the light of material from the apocalyptic tradition of the Gospels. If we consider the material in this way, we shall avoid the worst excesses of the literary analysis and permit other relationships to be examined which are obscured by Charles's presentation. Two examples of the latter may be mentioned:[15] firstly, according to Charles, 'While the predictions in Rev. 6.15–17 are wanting in the first two (gospels), their equivalent is found in Luke 21.25'; presumably the Lucan reference should also include 21.26, but in any case a further helpful parallel is provided by Luke 23.30. Secondly, of the four winds of Rev. 7.1 Charles says: 'this feature may have its parallel in Luke 21.25, where the nations are said to be distressed, in perplexity at the roaring of the sea and the waves'; this may offer some similarity in idea, or it may not, but more to the point would be the reference, in the next stage of the traditional pattern (Mark 13.27; Matt. 24.31; no // in Luke), to 'the four winds', which is one of the infrequent verbal parallels.

SEVEN SEALS IN REVELATION	APOCALYPTIC TRADITIONS OF THE SYNOPTIC GOSPELS
1 6.1–2 White horse	Wars and rumours/wars and tumults
Bow	(Matt. 24.6; Mark 13.7; Luke 21.9) (A)
Crown, victor, cf. 19.11,	Matt. 24.5; Mark 13.6; Luke 21.8 'many will come in my name'
2 6.3–4 Red horse	Nation against nation (Matt. 24.7; Mark 13.8; Luke 21.10) (B)
Sword	Matt. 10.34
3 6.5–6 Black horse Scales	Famines – *limoi* Matt. 24.7 (C); Mark 13.8 (D); Luke 21.11 (D or E)
4 6.7–8 Bilious-yellow horse *thanatos*/Hades	Pestilence – *loimoi* Luke 21.11 (E or D) variant reading Matt. 24.7; Mark 13.8
5 6.9–11 Souls beneath the altar (Persecution, martyrdom)	Persecution/Christian witness Matt. 24.9–14 and 10.17–22 (E) Mark 13.9–13 (E) Luke 21.12–19 and 12.11–12 (G)
'How long?'	Mark 13.20 (shortening of days) // Matt. 24.22 cf. Luke 18.7–8
6 6.12–17 A great earthquake	Great earthquakes Luke 21.11 (C) cf. Matt. 24.7 (D), Mark 13.8 (C)
sun, moon, stars	Mark 13.24f. // Matt. 24.29 (Luke 21.25, 21.11b?)
like fig tree	Fig tree (Matt. 24.32f.; Mark 13.28f.; Luke 21.29ff.)
fear of what is coming 'saying (RSV calling) to the mountains ... Fall on us'	Luke 21.26 'to say to the mountains: Fall on us' (Luke 23.30) cf. Hos. 10.8
7.1 Restraining 'the four winds'	Gathering elect 'from the four winds' at coming of Son of Man Mark 13.27; Matt. 24.31.

Interlude – Sealing (7.2–17)

7 8.1 Silence in heaven for half an hour
8.2ff. Trumpets.

NOTE
Capital letters used as symbols in right-hand column are indication of the order of events in the Gospel accounts.

According to this scheme, the author of Revelation has utilized here a substantial proportion of the main body of apocalyptic tradition within the Synoptic Gospels, at least in terms of overall pattern and some details. What he omits is omitted largely for the very good reason that he is concerned in this first plague sequence with the 'signs of the End' and not with the ultimate manifestations of evil and good. The account of the 'desolating sacrilege' (Mark 13.14–19; Matt. 24.15–21) or the 'desolation' of Jerusalem (Luke 21.20–24) represents the ultimate activity of evil, which is presented by John in terms of the beast and Babylon the harlot (Rev. 13, 17 and 18). Such is the relationship of apocalyptic thought to historical events that the climax of evil is not necessarily re-presented by the same event in successive writings; so in Revelation one should not be misled by the reference to the siege of Jerusalem in 11.1–2 to place the centre of gravity there, under Lucan influence. Secondly, there is a measure of repetition, for the sake of emphasis, in the Synoptic accounts with regard to warnings against false prophets;[16] this theme is presented in a different way in Revelation, both in the Seven Letters and in the picture of the second beast (13.11–17). But there may be an allusion to it in the substance of the first seal. As for the third divergence, the manifestation of good in the triumphant coming of the Son of Man, with its sequel in the actual vindication of the elect (Mark 13.26–7; Matt. 24.30–1; Luke 21.27–8), is deferred until its proper place in the Seer's extended sequence of events (Rev. 19ff.), although John's account of visionary experiences provides anticipatory glimpses of this reality.

When the author of Revelation is so dependent upon the apocalyptic tradition used in the Synoptic Gospels, the possibility that he has used this material for substantially the same reasons as the Evangelists and for a similar purpose is worthy of serious consideration. It is by no means inevitable, in the light of the constant reapplication of apocalyptic material, but one should see whether in general terms it stands up to investigation.

Of Mark 13 Beasley-Murray wrote: 'It has long been recognised that the discourse holds a significant place in the Gospel of Mark, in that it forms both a conclusion to the teaching ministry of Jesus and an introduction to the passion narrated immediately afterwards.' R. H. Lightfoot commented that its position

>   immediately before the passion narrative, but altogether independent of it, suggests that at the time of the composition of this

[Mark's] gospel the church had not yet found it possible to define satisfactorily the relationship between the crucifixion and the expected final consummation. ... By means, perhaps, of traditional Jewish material as well as by reflection on the church's experiences, the teaching set forth in this chapter with regard to what must come to pass *before* the glory is revealed is already permeated with the thought of suffering. But the climax is still the coming of the Son of man; and in connexion with this, there is no note of suffering.

C. K. Barrett points out that 'Mark's own understanding of the matter' of suffering ('Jesus first suffers on behalf of others, and departs in death; later his disciples will suffer persecution in their service to him') is 'a neat rationalization but one that scarcely does justice to the traditional material Mark himself preserves, though within the new framework forced upon him by the actual course of events'.[17]

Just how closely Mark related the tradition to actual events is open to debate – much depends on whether the 'desolating sacrilege' of 13.14 refers to the episode of Caligula's image in A.D. 40 or to a prophecy of the fall of Jerusalem. Matthew does not make such an historical connection any more explicit; while following Mark 13 closely in ch. 24, he makes his own distinctive contribution in the series of parables presented in ch. 25, where they are applied strictly to the context of Mark 13.33–7. They function as 'instruction to the disciples about the demands on them while waiting with the church for the Parousia'.[18] It is Luke who has made the historical reference deliberately clear by applying the apocalyptic tradition to the past event of the fall of Jerusalem (Luke 21.20ff.). He also clarifies the relationship between the crucifixion of Jesus, the present circumstances of the Christian Church, and the expected final consummation. According to Conzelmann's summary of his own argument, the delay of the parousia is explained 'by means of the idea of God's plan which underlies the whole structure of Luke's account'.[19] 'The whole story of salvation, as well as the life of Jesus in particular, is now objectively set out and described according to its successive stages.' 'As the End is still far away, the adjustment to a short time of waiting is replaced by a "Christian life" of long duration, which requires ethical regulation.' This 'ethical teaching is coloured by the fact that persecution now prevails'. 'The virtue of *hupomonē* ... is viewed from the standpoint of martyrdom.' There are two overriding emphases in this context: one is the note of warning, taken over from Mark, presented as an exhortation to adjust to the long period of persecution which will be a fact of church life (Luke 21.12ff.); the other is the encouragement, distinctively Lucan, which is offered to the faithful now and in the future (Luke 21.15, 28).

If the author of Revelation is in any real sense an heir to this tradition, then we would expect his work to contain a reapplication of these ideas to a new set of circumstances subsequent to the composition of the Synoptic Gospels. The seals should indicate these circumstances which are basic to the author's experience, perhaps with reference to particular historical events where appropriate. The central theme of suffering should be related to the present situation of the churches and also be part of a total perspective which extends from the crucifixion of Christ at the one end to the final cosmic vindication of Christ at the other. We might also expect as a dominant idea, motivating the author's presentation, either the note of warning, or the note of encouragement, or a combination of the two. In the sense that C. H. Dodd's redefinition of the material from Mark 13 as 'a *Mahnrede* ("warning speech") in apocalyptic terms rather than an apocalypse proper' [20] reflects an important emphasis, it may be appropriate to extend this insight to the particular utilization of this material in Revelation itself.

Now that we have established in these points a kind of 'blueprint' for the treatment of the seven seals, on the assumption that this section represents a development of the apocalyptic tradition in continuity with the Synoptic Gospels, it is time to look in more detail at this section, and to draw some general conclusions from it, for comparison with this 'blueprint'.

It is important to recognize what Paul Minear called the

> extraordinary pains to show the continuity between the picture of worship in heaven (chs. 4, 5) and the opening of the seven seals (chs. 6, 7). Since it is the Lamb who will open each of the seals, it is his qualification to do so which forms the burden of chs. 4, 5.[21]

'Worthy art thou to take the scroll and to open its seals, for thou wast slain and by thy blood didst ransom men for God from every tribe and tongue and people and nation' (5.9).

As Paul Minear says,

> We must not neglect this clue to the meaning of the whole vision. It is a description of the operation of forces which were released by the single event of suffering and victory. ... The prophet is seeking to describe the repercussions, the echoes, the continuing effects of the passion story.

We can see already how in the terms of this symbolic vision one of the requirements of our 'blueprint' is met; the Seer expresses very precisely the fact that his perspective begins with the crucifixion of Christ.

So the victorious Lion/Lamb opens these seals. At this point we encounter a practical problem as to how the Seer envisaged the document, and the seals which had prevented access to its contents. This is not merely an academic issue in the debate between those who translate *biblion* as 'book' and those who prefer to translate it as 'scroll'.[22] For the solution of this problem may affect the way the 'seal visions' are interpreted: are these the subject-matter of the book which only the Lamb can open, or are they incidental features of the opening process so that the main burden of the contents is still to be revealed?

The logical modern attitude may require the latter view and look for the contents of the book later in the Apocalypse, perhaps in the trumpets or the bowls, on the grounds that the normal procedure of sealing documents, either books or scrolls, would prevent access to the contents until all the seals are opened. But at no stage in the subsequent chapters is there any indication to the reader that he is now being presented with the contents of this unsealed book – the trumpets have their own, and different introduction, and by the time of the interlude in ch. 10 we have encountered another document, a *biblaridion* (10.2). It is conceivable that the author's symbolism does not always follow the requirements of strict logic, and that in the seal visions he is presenting aspects of the book's contents. The symbolism permits him an artistic exposition of the elements, stage by stage, building up to a climax while ensuring, through the significance of the number seven, that each aspect forms part of the whole.

Sir W. M. Ramsay[23] suggested that the closest parallel is the Roman will or testament, a legal document in book form, traditionally sealed with the seven seals of the witnesses. This gives a fuller sense to Rev. 5.1; the *scriptura interior*, the writing inside the sealed book, is preserved in secrecy while the seals are attached; the *scriptura exterior*, a summary of contents on the outside has a practical usefulness but no legal worth. The frequently cited Old Testament parallel (Ezek. 2.9) has a quite different emphasis; the scroll written 'on the front and on the back' is spread before Ezekiel to emphasize how numerous are the 'words of lamentation and mourning and woe'.

If the sealed book is the precise model for Revelation, then it could represent God's 'will' in the sense of what Caird calls 'God's redemptive plan ... the world's destiny, foreordained by the gracious purpose of God'.[24] Ramsay himself believed that the contents of the book were a record of the Covenant between God and man, and that the opening of the book was to be understood either as a forensic or a prophetic act. In the present context in Revelation a prophetic/eschatological interpretation seems preferable; and the idea of the plan fits better than the idea of Covenant with the atmosphere of secrecy appropriate for Apocalyptic; the exposition of the legal theme of judgement is more suited to the other books, including the book of life, which are opened at Rev. 20.12.

The Lamb opens this book not only because he is the official legally charged with the duty of disclosing its contents, but above all because he himself has inaugurated the final stage of this plan; by the beginning which he made in the Cross he has ransomed men for God. This plan and purpose of God cannot be revealed to men until Christ makes it known. In the context of the Apocalypse of John, this plan of God revealed by Christ can be represented more extensively as the subject-matter of the work as a whole (cf. Rev. 1.1–2); but it is also concentrated within the circumstances of the opening of this sealed book. The relationship between the seven seals and the actual contents of the book can therefore be seen as an ambivalent one. The seals are the testimony of the witnesses of the 'will' to the secrecy which has been preserved until the proper time for the book to be opened. But the seals of the witnesses are also the symbols of the witnesses themselves, witnesses to the contents of the 'will'. So, even if we apply modern logic to the interpretation of the Seer's vision, there is a sense in which the loosing of the seals represents a releasing of the witnesses, to reveal the contents of that 'will'.

This exegesis further illuminates the perspective of the seals sequence. Beginning from the crucifixion of Christ, this perspective, which is itself a revelation of God's plan, includes a range of individual pictures, each of which can testify to the reality of that plan, for those with eyes to see and insight to understand the ultimate purpose.

> The natural assumption is that the opening of the scroll, by which its contents are both revealed and put into effect, follows immediately on the victory by which he (Christ) acquired the right to open it. This means that from John's standpoint some at least of the contents are already past.[25]

This suggests that John is an heir to the prophetic tradition of the Old Testament as he interprets events of the past, present and immediate future to demonstrate the overriding purpose of God. Even in situations of despair, in woes and tribulations, the prophet's followers can be shown how God makes use of the most unlikely agents to further his plan, and how the woes themselves are 'signs of the end' and therefore indications of the ultimate triumph of God's purposes.

These broad lines of interpretation can be confirmed or disproved by an examination of the actual visions introduced by the opening of each seal. What do these pictures represent? We should recognize that four of them, the four horsemen, are variations on a traditional theme which can be traced back to the prophet Zechariah. The derivation of this material from a special tradition within the Old Testament is not of course incompatible with the view that the whole framework is derived from the apocalyptic tradition of the Synoptic Gospels. There are many illustrations in Revelation of the author's skill in combining traditional elements from several sources.

Whereas in Revelation it seems to be the riders who are important, while the colours of the horses are symbols associated with the significance of the riders, in the two visions of Zechariah (1.8–15; 6.1–8) only the leading rider in the first vision is even mentioned, although it is usually assumed that the other horses had riders. For Zechariah the individual characteristics and separate identities of these patrols or messengers seem unimportant, but in each vision their dependence upon the commands of Yahweh is stressed: in 1.10, 'These are they whom the Lord has sent to patrol the earth',

and in 6.5, 'These are going forth to the four winds of heaven, after presenting themselves before the Lord of all the earth.'
The Hebrew text of the first vision (Zech. 1) does not suggest a large colour range for the horses, and probably these colours had no special significance at this point. The Hebrew of Zech. 6 represents the origin of the significant range of colours, probably according to some traditional ascription of colours to the four winds (6.5) or the four quarters of the heavens. The Septuagint translators, keen to preserve the colour symbolism, were responsible for introducing the same symbolism into Zech. 1 to harmonize with Zech. 6. The author of Revelation borrowed three suitable colours, white, red and black, directly from Zech. 6 to match the pictures he was drawing. The fourth colour, *chlōros*, is not so much a natural colour for a horse as an attempt to represent the bilious yellow-green of sickness.

It is difficult to say how much of the remaining context is carried over with the basic imagery into the pictures of Revelation. The functions of horses and chariots as servants of Yahweh are compatible with the view that has been taken of the seal visions as elements in the revelation of God's plan. There may well be some irony in the reapplication of Zechariah's 'peaceful patrols' and 'messengers of promise' to the subject-matter of the Apocalypse. It seems likely that John has worked up the details of the picture far more deliberately in his symbolism than was the case with this imagery in its original context in the visions of Zechariah.

One feature of the first vision (Zech. 1.8–15) which is carried over into Revelation is applied, not to the pictures of the horsemen in the first four seals, but to the fifth seal and its vision of the martyr-souls. It is reasonable to conclude that the meaning of Zechariah's vision centres on the lamentation formula 'How long?' (1.12) and the direct response from Yahweh, the 'gracious and comforting words' of 1.13.

Although outward events do not seem to indicate God's working, he is intervening on behalf of his people and Jerusalem. Some of Zechariah's contemporaries no doubt saw in the upheavals [at the accession of Darius I] a sign of hope that national independence was at hand. Zechariah's answer, in accord with the teaching of earlier prophets, is that judgment and deliverance are the prerogative of God.[26]

This theme, with its cry and encouraging response in terms of God's long-term purpose, is directly applicable to the fifth seal in Rev. 6.9–11.

Zechariah's two visions have provided John with the pattern for the four horses and their riders who appear as the first four seals are opened. The account of each of these four seals is shaped to conform to a basic model; the colour of the horse (the element supplied by the tradition) and the symbol associated with the rider (either the object he carries or the name by which he is known) both suggest the character and purpose of what is happening. The brief description is concluded by a statement which interprets the activity of the rider. In the light of Zechariah's emphasis on the fact that horses and chariots operate in obedience to Yahweh, it is significant not only that all four of Revelation's horsemen appear in response to the action of the Lamb and the word of command of the four living creatures, but also that the activity of the rider is similarly controlled. This is indicated by the use of the impersonal passive 'was given' in the first, second and fourth descriptions (6.2, 4, 8),[27] and by the location of the voice which utters the command about the third rider's activity (6.6). What powers these riders possess are given and restricted by God.

How would John's readers have understood these four characterizations of horses and riders? Is it possible to achieve a consistent interpretation which could be said to reflect the author's intentions? Let us begin with the possibility that the author is offering a prophetic reinterpretation of the contemporary situation and recent events.

It is the third seal which is most obviously linked to the contemporary situation. Clear evidence is cited by Rostovtzeff[28] that Asia Minor was subject from time to time to corn shortage and even famine. While Rome monopolized the corn produce of Egypt for the capital's needs, other cities of the Empire also relied upon imported grain; the cities of Asia Minor 'were unable to live on the import from South Russia, as its production continued to decrease and much of the corn grown there was used by the imperial armies of the East'. The Roman government could not afford to let the eastern provinces starve, and so measures were taken to encourage the production of corn and to limit the culture of vines and olive trees, since wine and olive oil tended to over-production in the East and the West.

Because of the seriousness of the situation, an edict was issued by Domitian in A.D. 92[29] forbidding the planting of more vines in Italy and requiring that at least one-half of the vineyards in the provinces be cut down, so that the ground could be used for growing corn. This drastic remedy was bitterly opposed in the vine-growing areas, including Asia Minor, and does not seem to have been enforced rigorously everywhere; an embassy from Asia Minor headed by the orator Scopelianus of Smyrna was able to obtain remission for the vineyards of the province. Domitian's measure is open to more than one interpretation: S. Reinach believed that it was a rather drastic means of protecting the livelihood of Italy's vine-growers.[30] This may have been an additional motive, but Rostovtzeff's argument that the real reason was to stimulate corn-production at the expense of vines appears to fit the evidence of the situation, even if it shows up the edict as a theoretical solution, rather than one dictated by practical considerations of agriculture.

Rostovtzeff associated the edict with evidence for a serious famine in Asia Minor at this period. 'The spectre of famine now hovered continually before the Greek cities: ... the vivid picture in the Revelation of St John ... is proved to refer to a widespread famine in Asia Minor by a Latin inscription of A.D. 93,[31] discovered at Antioch of Pisidia.' Under famine conditions the Roman legate L. Antistius Rusticus took emergency action by requisitioning grain to be sold at fixed prices to the public corn-buyers of the city.

The third seal in Revelation introduces the situation of famine with the symbol of the pair of scales in the rider's hand (cf. Ezekiel's prophecy of famine – 4.9ff.).[32] The colour chosen for famine is black – the colour of crops in the field blackened with blight. While the 'fair price' fixed during the famine at Antioch was one denarius per modius – and this was double the price current before the famine[33] – the prices named in this picture of severe famine in Revelation are one denarius per *choinix* (between 1½ and 2 pints or ⅛ of a modius) for wheat, with barley a third of the price. In human terms this means that a day's wage for a labourer (Matt. 20.2) will only buy enough wheat for his average daily consumption.[34] But there is no rationing of wine and olive oil, nor must the abundance of these commodities be restricted. It is this feature which corresponds most closely to the situation of Domitian's edict. Admittedly, there is no record of the decree being applied to olive-growing, but the olive trees and vines are undoubtedly in a comparable situation, requiring so many years to achieve maturity that their destruction could mean lasting ruin. Ramsay pointed out that it was an unwritten law of Eastern warfare that these crops should be spared.[35]

Do the other seals comparably reflect issues of current concern or events of the recent past? Most debate centres on the interpretation of the first rider; there could not be a greater contrast between the identifications proposed. Is he, as Irenaeus thought, the figure of Christ himself, or a symbol of the victorious course of the Christian Gospel (cf. 19.11–16)? Or is he a figure of evil, Antichrist himself (cf. the figure of Gog in Ezek. 39.3); or a Parthian king invading in the way Rome dreaded (as the bow is a Parthian weapon and white is the sacred colour of the Persians); or a Roman general riding in triumph; or another symbol of triumphant militarism?[36] There are arguments against all these interpretations.

There remains an interpretation which seems to do justice to all elements in the picture of the first rider and may also prove to be satisfactory in the total context of Revelation. It was Gunkel[37] who, in his *religionsgeschichtlich* interpretation of the four horsemen as four world gods, transformed into plague spirits, identified the first horseman as originally a sun-god. The white horse corresponds to the white horses of Mithras in the Avesta, where Mithras is the genius of celestial light who crosses the firmament in his chariot. Mithras is often depicted as a mounted deity, particularly as an archer on horseback; at Dura Europos he is shown riding a horse at a gallop and shooting arrows from his bow like a huntsman, and according to one Roman relief he appears to have possessed a bow from birth. The type of representation seems to have varied with the locality, naturally enough in the interests of identifying Mithras with local traditions. So Mithras is a horseman in Eastern representations, particularly those from Syria; similarly the sun-god is represented as a horseman in Asia Minor, indicating a local variant on the traditional theme of the chariot of the sun.[38]

Although Mithras is more frequently shown wearing oriental costume and a Phrygian cap, he does appear with a radiate crown when he is identified with the sun-god. The final aspect of the picture in Revelation, the statement that the rider 'went out conquering and to conquer', also finds a parallel in the description of Mithras; he is called 'unconquerable' or 'deus sol invictus'. Furthermore, if Rev. 6.8b does refer to all four horsemen, and 'wild beasts of the earth' relates to the first rider, this too has a Mithraic explanation. The focal point of Mithraism as a mystery religion, and therefore of the Mithraea, was a representation of Mithras killing the bull. This was the celebrated exploit of the god, commemorated in the gruesome ritual of the tauroctony, which imparted great benefit to the initiate. It would be appropriate to the author's irony if he equated the 'bull-slaying' ritual of Mithras with the murderous plague 'by wild beasts' of traditional expectation.

This is a possible – and indeed a very suitable – background to the thought of Revelation, not least because it is widely believed that Asia Minor was a highly significant region for the development of Mithraism, from its Indian and Persian inspiration, into the mystery cult which spread through the Roman world. Mithras was an important god for the Achaemenid kings and for Antiochus I of Commagene; his 'mysteries' were known to the Cilician pirates as well as to the Parthians, so that in the first century B.C. it may well have seemed that Mithras was the god who led the opposition to the Romans. The cult had penetrated to the heart of Rome by the end of the first century A.D. Statius in A.D. 79 has seen representations of Mithras, the god who 'twists the unruly horns beneath the rocks of a Persian cave'.[39] A vitally important stage has been reached for the worship of Mithras. In origin he was a warrior god 'whom the heads of the countries worship as they go to the battlefield ... whom the warriors worship at ... the manes of their horses'; in the Roman world the cult of Mithras followed the march of the Roman armies to the outposts of the Empire. It is reasonable to suppose that in Asia Minor, much nearer to his home, Mithras the god of soldiers and battle, unconquerable as the sun, was already presenting a serious challenge to the much less belligerent religion of Christianity.

Just as the author of Revelation depicts the situation of famine in terms of the current concern with Domitian's edict, so he draws the first rider with the features of Mithras, the warrior-god whose cult was well known in Asia Minor but is now perhaps becoming more closely identified with the presence of the Roman army. In this way he can take up the theme of 'wars' in the apocalyptic tradition of the Synoptic Gospels and apply to it the highly appropriate symbolic figure of a popular warrior deity. We have no means of knowing in what way this rival religion or cult of war impinged most directly on John's thinking, but we can conclude that it was a real issue in the contemporary situation. It could be suggested that rivalry had reached sufficient heights to justify the Seer in demonstrating this in the form of a parody (6.2 over against 19.11ff.). At least the idea of a parody does justice to the connection between these passages which falls far short of any positive relationship. And there is a sense in which this parody may be applied in the same way as the warning against false Christs in the synoptic apocalyptic tradition – a warning against religious 'saviour figures' with a superficial similarity to Christ.

The second and fourth seals need not occupy so large a space in our consideration because their features are more readily apparent. The second horse is red, an appropriate colour for bloodshed and slaughter, and this function of the rider is confirmed by his explicit commission 'to take peace from the earth, so that men should slay one another' (6.4) – these are 'the complementary sides of war-fare'.[40] This rider is given 'a great sword' (6.4); this *machaira* is most probably the bent sword or sabre appropriate for use by a horseman who cuts with slashing strokes from a lofty position, contrasted with the straight sword or *xiphos* suited to the thrusting strokes of a foot-soldier.[41]

The *Pax Romana* had brought prosperity to western Asia Minor, and seems to have limited fighting west of the Euphrates to the pacification of the Cietae from the mountainous regions of Cilicia. But east of the Euphrates the situation was very different. 'Rumours of wars' would be a constant feature of reports from the Eastern frontier, where Roman and allied troops were in action against 'the constant inroads of barbarians',[42] whether these were Parthians or raiders such as the Alans and other Caucasian tribes. Much nearer to the Seven Churches, there occurred in about A.D. 89 an event which demonstrated Domitian's despotic cruelty, when Civica Cerialis, the proconsul of Asia, was put to death by his command.

The ground for this act of violence was alleged participation in a conspiracy to overthrow the Emperor. If, as has been supposed, the procurator Gaius Minicius Italus, who 'by command of the Emperor' governed Asia 'in place of the deceased proconsul', was made acting-governor on the occasion of Cerialis's death, a step so unusual as the appointment of a personal agent of the emperor to the governorship of a senatorial province suggests that there was indeed a situation which necessitated vigorous action.[43]

Events such as these could be represented by the 'sword' of the second horseman, and a parallel drawn with the description of the conditions of the period offered in Sib. 4.142ff.: 'Great wealth shall come to Asia, wealth which once Rome, having gained it by rapine, stored in a house of surpassing riches, but anon she will make a twofold restitution to Asia; then there will be a surfeit of strife.'

The fourth horse is described as *chlōros*, a bilious colour more suitable to vegetation than to a horse,[44] but not inappropriate in the context of sickness and pestilence. The fact that it is not strictly a natural colour for a horse would not have prevented John from using it for its symbolic significance. It is better to understand the medical use of *chlōros* as 'yellow, bilious-looking', following Liddell and Scott, than to be influenced by prior considerations of Rev. 6.8 into classifying this use with the exclusively poetic usage of *chlōros* in contexts such as the pallor of fear and death, and thus rendering it as 'pale', with Bauer (Arndt and Gingrich). *Thanatos* is used in the same sense as in the Septuagint, where in thirty-four instances it translates *debher*,[45] and as an equivalent of *loimos* in the Lucan version of the synoptic apocalyptic tradition. This specialized use of *thanatos* by the author also explains the otherwise tautologous expressions with *apokteinō* in 2.23 and 6.8b, as well as the inclusion of *thanatos* in a list of plagues (6.8b, 18.8), without preventing the normal meaning of the Greek word in other contexts. In 6.8 therefore the name of rider and the colour of horse combine to provide a vivid symbol of pestilence.

Pestilence, like famine, was a recurrent problem in Asia Minor. A widespread epidemic of plague is recorded in the reign of Nero, which affected Rome itself in A.D. 65. Because of the greater detail available, it is worth noting the disastrous outbreak of pestilence which followed the victory over the Parthians in A.D. 165 'and which, it was generally believed, was brought back by the troops'.[46] This plague, sometimes identified with smallpox, spread westwards to Italy, Rome and Gaul; in western Asia Minor its ravages were described by Aelius Aristides and there is an inscription from Smyrna in praise of the river Meles for deliverance from 'pestilence and evil'.[47] There is also evidence at the same time for a widespread failure of harvests causing a devastating combination of famine and plague. While this is obviously too late to provide the setting for Revelation, an earlier occurrence, either as recorded in the time of Nero[48] or an unrecorded outbreak in the time of Domitian, perhaps combined with the known famine, would present a compelling background for John's imagery. The frequent occurrence, and persistence, of major outbreaks that are recorded makes it reasonable to posit others, perhaps less widespread, that were not recorded in the far from comprehensive historical accounts of the period. The suggested source of the outbreak after A.D. 165, in the troops returning from the Eastern frontier, may have been the origin on other occasions too; the troops would naturally transmit the contagion back through Asia Minor.

It is difficult to escape the conclusion that John, after creating this symbol of pestilence, the most economical of his creations since it consists only in a colour and a name, proceeds to exploit the ambiguity which remains in the word *thanatos*. In the realities of the ancient world one sense of *thanatos* (pestilence) most frequently led to the other sense (death). This transition is smoothed within the author's description by the introduction of Hades 'who is the natural companion for the personified Death'.[49] Hades, in accordance with the general line of New Testament thought, receives the souls of the dead for as long as his authority lasts. His is only an interim authority, for he must deliver up the dead at the resurrection; then Death and Hades are finished and 'thrown into the lake of fire' (Rev. 20.13–14). This transition to a figure representing death as the 'interim' end, enables the author to recapitulate the immediate consequences of these four aspects of the local situation that are issues of concern. In each case it is a matter of killing – 'to kill with sword and with famine and with pestilence and by wild beasts of the earth' (6.8b). For this John has utilized a traditional Old Testament motif of four plagues,[50] God's 'four sore acts of judgement', and he quotes from the version summarized in the words of Ezek. 14.21 ('sword, famine, evil beasts, and pestilence') and described in more detail in the preceding verses (12–20).

We have seen four issues of current concern, four aspects of the immediate situation in Asia Minor, presented by the author under the imagery of the four horsemen, derived from Zechariah, and summed up in terms of God's 'four sore acts of judgement' in the tradition represented by Ezek. 14. These two traditions reinforce the viewpoint that such actions are controlled and limited by God; he originates the activity and is the source of the riders' delegated authority. Their influence is restricted 'over a fourth of the earth' (Rev. 6.8b); this proportion also indicates the stage which has been reached in the progress of God's plan, compared with 'a third' affected by the Trumpet sequence, and the total destructive effect of the Bowls, while in the flash-back represented by Rev. 11 the proportion is 'a tenth' (11.13). The four horsemen introduce God's interim judgement, comparable with the judgements on Jerusalem of which Ezekiel spoke. But because of the present context, where this tradition of 'judgements' is subordinated to the horsemen tradition, the emphasis falls not on the individual judgements as God's punishment of his rebellious people and of his enemies, but on the concept of judgement as expressing God's authority and jurisdiction in the contemporary situation.

What is true of these four seals is equally true of what follows when the fifth seal is opened. We have seen, in the comparison with the Synoptic apocalyptic tradition, that the fifth seal would correspond to the section on Christian witness and persecution. But, as Charles points out, there is a difference of application: in the context of Jesus' words 'persecutions and martyrdom are foretold; in our text they are in part already accomplished'. The presence 'under the altar' of 'the souls of those who had been slain for the word of God and for the witness they had borne' (6.9) clearly indicates that their martyrdom was in the past when the Seer saw his vision. Charles concludes that 'the martyrs are incontestably Christian martyrs ... the martyrs of the Neronic times', while Caird agrees to the extent that 'prominent among these martyrs would be those who had died in the persecution of Nero, but all others are included from Stephen to Antipas'.[51]

But the recognition of an historical reference is only part of the lesson of this vision. The cry of the martyrs is answered in terms which leave no doubt that martyrdom is not only past fact but also present and inevitably future experience; in Kiddle's words, 'A great martyrdom lies before the Church.'[52] The author's own experience is sufficient evidence for a limited persecution, if only of individual Christians, at the time of writing, and the expectation of much more. In Rev. 1.9 he writes: 'I John, ... who share with you in Jesus the tribulation ..., was on the island called Patmos on account of the word of God and the testimony of Jesus.' It is likely that John saw the threat of much worse to come, and composed this work to meet that threat.

Such martyrdoms, past, present and future, are the continuing evidence for the working out of God's plan. The way in which this strong element of martyrdom corresponds to God's plan, and the means by which it furthers that plan, are indicated by the author in the terms of a Jewish tradition about the completion of the full number of martyrs. This tradition is found in a comparable, and late, form in the words of 4 Esdras 4.35f.: 'Did not the souls of the righteous in their chambers ask about these matters saying: "How long are we to remain here? And when will come the harvest of our reward?" And Jeremiel the archangel answered them and said, "When the number of those like yourselves is completed." '

With the opening of the sixth seal the perspectives have altered. No longer is the subject-matter concentrated on the special circumstances of the Asia Minor congregations, but a cosmic dimension is opened up for the first time by the description of the great earthquake and the cataclysmic portents in the heavens. The pattern is substantially that of the Synoptic apocalyptic tradition, with the qualification Charles noted, namely that the earthquake has been placed in the context of a cosmic, rather than a local, cataclysm.

The majority of the cities of Asia, specially mentioned by John, had abundant experience of earthquakes. Laodicea had been rebuilding at her own expense after the earthquake of A.D. 60. Sardis may have lost much of her citadel in the earthquake of A.D. 17. There are hints in the sixth letter also which are reminiscent of the slow recovery of Philadelphia, a city which lived under such a constant threat of earthquake that many of her inhabitants preferred to stay in the surrounding countryside. This was a region particularly vulnerable to earthquake tremors, and it is still true of the area today. But the traditional earthquake imagery which John uses, although it requires, for its effect, some experience or understanding of earthquakes on the part of his readers, is not restricted in scope as an allusion to a particular earthquake. Instead it builds upon experience and warns of an even more horrifying prospect, that of a great earthquake which shakes the world. That this is John's meaning is clear not only from the fact that he has presented as one big earthquake what Mark described as 'earthquakes in various places' (13.8), but also because of the further aspect in 6.14

– 'every mountain and island was removed from its place' – and the context where sun, moon and stars are affected as well.

John's picture of these cosmic phenomena is related to the Synoptic tradition and, like that tradition, is derived ultimately from aspects of the Old Testament pictures of the Day of Yahweh. John has applied to his picture some of the original colours, using, for example, the blood-red appearance of the moon from Joel 2.31, the rolling up of the heavens like a scroll from Isa. 34.4, and from Hos. 10.8 the call to the mountains 'Fall upon us!' Is this Day of Yahweh, the day of wrath and the end of the world, seen as a reality here and now? Are there earthly circumstances in John's time with which these traditional cosmic expectations could be identified? As with the earthquakes, so with the whole cosmic cataclysm it seems likely that any earthly phenomena would be inadequate to support the tremendous weight of this imagery. Charles therefore concludes: 'These woes are still in the future. They are not in our author the immediate heralds of the end, as in the Gospels.' [53]

With an awareness of the context in Revelation, where this description occurs in ch. 6 as the sixth element in the first of three plague sequences, so that there is much more to happen before the final judgement, it would be unreasonable to conclude that this is a sign of the immediate end. Even if the temporal obstacle is removed by recourse to some form of the Recapitulation theory, there would remain an obstacle of substance in the wealth of material which the Seer employs before he comes to describe the actual day of judgement. Has, then, the function of this material in the Synoptic tradition been forgotten? Equally it is reasonable to say that the presence of this element within the first sequence should mean that the cosmic cataclysm is closely linked with the material of the first five seals, even if the dividing line between the present and the future, representing the time of writing in an historical/apocalyptic sequence, has been crossed between the fifth and sixth seal. Does this mean that the author is emphasizing to his readers how imminent the end is to their present situation?

Luke 23.28–31 uses the quotation from Hos. 10.8 in a context which may assist in showing how the tensions inherent in John's picture of the sixth seal may be held together without contradiction. Hosea's words, first applicable to the historical situation envisaged as leading to the fall of Samaria, subsequently available for use as part of a picture of cosmic disaster, can be reapplied to an apparent prophecy of the fall of Jerusalem in A.D. 70. In the last context a commentary is provided by the sentence: 'If they do this when the wood is green, what will happen when it is dry?' This expresses proverbially the truth of two stages in the inexorable progress towards disaster, whether this is related by Luke to the crucifixion and the fate of Jerusalem, or to the destruction of the city as an historical stage in the eschatological process.

If the passage where John utilizes the same tradition, derived ultimately from Hosea, can be read in a similar light, two important aspects emerge. Firstly, the present situation as exemplified in the first five seals should have demonstrated to Christian eyes the operation of God's plan. Soon the realization of this truth will be brought home to the whole world. The situation will be so self-evident that all classes of society will be terror-stricken; they will make frantic attempts to escape from the judgement of God and the wrath of the Lamb.[54] In the words of God through Haggai, 'Yet once more I will shake not only the earth, but also the heaven' (2.6; as quoted in Heb. 12.26), on which the writer to the Hebrews commented that this 'indicates the removal of all that can be shaken ... in order that what cannot be shaken may remain' (12.27). The relationship of seals 1–5 and seal 6 is sequential like the dry wood to the green; the readers are therefore prepared for the next stage in the process of God's plan, and prepared for something on a different scale from what has gone before.

Secondly, we can recognize that God's judgement 'when the tree is dry', and the circumstances surrounding that event, are the main burden of the Seer's book. Therefore the Seer's aim, at this early stage in the seals sequence when God's plan is being outlined, is to show how closely the elements of this plan are linked to the current situation experienced by the Churches. In this way the seals are both realistic (in referring to actual circumstances) and symbolic (in indicating the outcome of these events). This means that the sixth seal vision can have points of contact in those portents, and in particular the earthquakes, of local experience; but also from this stage onwards, once the cosmic dimension has been introduced, the symbolism refers not so much to particular events as to the ultimate consequences which these events prefigure. In a very real sense the sixth seal is a 'sign of the end', applied within the limits of the Synoptic tradition, but it is a sign given while the wood is still green, while the Lamb is revealing the extent of God's plan.

That there is a delay, in real if not in symbolic terms, is shown by the restraining of the four winds, recorded in Rev. 7.1. There may be a significant allusion here to the mention of the four winds in the apocalyptic tradition of the Synoptic Gospels. The context of Mark 13.27 and Matt. 24.31 is that of the gathering of the elect from the four winds at the time of judgement when the Son of Man has come in glory. This triumphant coming, with the final vindication of the elect, is deferred until Rev. 19ff.; therefore this special activity of the four winds is held in check and there is a lull as the winds are restrained by God's angels at the four corners of the earth. The same idea of a lull is taken up again, after the Interlude in which the elect are sealed, by the silence in heaven which lasts for half an hour (Rev. 8.1). After this significant pause, which is the first element of the seventh seal, the angels with the trumpets are introduced and the author moves rapidly to an exposition of the seven trumpet plagues.

It is time to relate what has been said about the seals to the suggested 'blueprint' drawn up from the apocalyptic tradition of the Synoptic Gospels. What emerges clearly is a further justification for the original comparison of the seals sequence with the Synoptic material; the evidence leads to the conclusion that the seals represent a reapplication of the tradition to the new circumstances of the Church in the years following the fall of Jerusalem. Each of the first five seals relates to an issue of concern for the churches of Asia Minor. The various forms of suffering which the communities have experienced are associated closely with events and circumstances of the reign of Domitian. By virtue of the image of the sealed book John presents all these elements as part of God's total plan; the revelation of this plan was inaugurated at Christ's crucifixion and proceeds to the point at which the cosmic 'signs of the end' are anticipated. It is also clear that the perspective of John's work, intended for the churches of Asia, is controlled by two factors: firstly, the need to prepare his readers to realize what is happening and about to happen, to enable them to 'read the signs of the time', so that they are forewarned of the gravity of the situation and of the demands placed upon the churches; and secondly, the need to offer encouragement and reassurance, so that his readers may receive confirmatory evidence of God's continuing activity and controlling power in the events of their days, and be uplifted by sharing in the Seer's visionary experiences which reveal the triumph of heaven and God's measures to preserve his elect.

A comparison between the seven seals and the other plague sequences, the trumpets and the bowls, reveals some important points of parallelism. Several features emphasize the fact that God is the originator of all these 'plagues' and therefore they take place under his ultimate control. The setting for each series of manifestations is clearly established; against the background of activity in heaven or, more precisely, as a direct result of that activity, the horsemen ride out, the blast of the trumpet heralds a cosmic event, and the bowls are poured out on the world.

We have seen the significance of the picture of worship in heaven (Rev. 4, 5) as establishing the unique qualification of the Lamb to open the seven seals. He inaugurates and reveals the extent of God's plan. There is a similar emphasis on the setting in 8.2–6 which prepares for the sounding of the trumpets. The seven angels 'stand before God' and receive their trumpets; they sound them as a sequel to the action of the angel with the golden censer. A comparison of 5.8 with 8.3 shows that 'the prayers of the saints' are an element in both situations, even though there is some uncertainty from the imagery whether they are the incense itself, or are added to it. We may speculate that the prayers in Rev. 5 are 'in tune with' the song which the elders and the living creatures sing (5.9–10); in ch. 8 the prayers ('upon the golden altar') may echo the cries of the souls 'under the altar' (6.9) that God may 'judge and avenge our blood'. God acts in response to this cry although the response is not necessarily a direct answer to the prayer: in 6.11 the souls are 'given a white robe and told to rest a little longer'; in 8.5 the angel picks up the same censer that had offered the prayers to God and, using it for a different purpose, he gives a symbolic demonstration of God's judgement by throwing the censer full of fire onto the earth. The scale of this gesture shows that it is not the final judgement, but it is a warning of what is to come, a warning reiterated by the blasts from the angel's trumpets.

Just as the worship in heaven and the prayers mingled with the incense in the angel's censer are significant for the first two sequences, so the 'portent in heaven' and the conquerors standing by the sea of glass, singing the 'song of Moses', are important as the setting, described in Rev. 15, for the plagues in ch. 16. In this vision the conquerors have received the heavenly reward such as was promised in the Seven Letters, and they sing the 'song of Moses' celebrating God's triumph over his enemies, and the song of Christ's triumph – the 'song of the Lamb'. Then the angels appointed specifically for this purpose come 'out of the temple' ('in heaven') and receive the 'seven golden bowls[55] full of the wrath of God' from one of the four living creatures (15.6, 7). It is stated explicitly that the outpouring from these bowls will complete the sequences of plagues and will represent the final working-out of the wrath of God upon his enemies (15.1). In this setting, therefore, God's promises are fulfilled and God's judgement is executed: the punishments are administered in accordance with the warnings so often given but repeatedly ignored. This vision expresses in symbolic terms the same truth conveyed by the Pauline doctrine of the Righteousness of God; Justification has its counterpart in Wrath (cf. Rom. 1.17–18).

Not only are the plague sequences as a whole under the authority of God, so that each sequence embodies his will and purpose, but also the individual features of the plagues are controlled by him. In the seventh plague in each sequence there is an element which reminds the reader that the origin of the sequence is in heaven: after the seventh seal is opened there is silence in heaven; when the seventh trumpet sounds, there are loud voices in heaven worshipping God and declaring his Kingdom to be a present reality; and as the seventh angel pours out his bowl, there is a 'great voice' from heaven 'out of the temple, from the throne, saying, "It is done!"'

We have noted already how the four horsemen in the seals sequence are summoned and controlled; this view was supported by the use of *edothē* in 6.2, 4 and 8 and by the occurrence of the 'voice in the midst of the four living creatures' in 6.6. A comparable restriction or control over the scope of the other plagues is indicated by the accounts of the fifth trumpet and the fourth bowl. Of the locust/scorpions it is said 'they were allowed (*edothē*) to torture them for five months, but not to kill them' (9.5). Those who received the seal of God on their foreheads (7.3ff.) are protected by God, so that they are not exposed to this limited torture of humanity (9.4). Again, in 16.8 it is said of the sun 'and it was allowed to scorch men with fire'. Those subjected to the scorching heat of the sun are those who also 'cursed the name of God who had power over these plagues'. This last phrase is an explicit attribution of authority, even though it is put into the mouth of God's enemies.

The progressive stepping-up of the severity of these plagues sequences is represented, not so much by the description of fresh horrors, each more ghastly than the last, as by the indications of their range and intensity of application. In the seals sequence, the four horsemen are given 'power over a fourth of the earth'. Again and again in the trumpet sequence it is emphasized that these plagues affect 'a third'; while this restriction is made for the first four and the sixth trumpets, there is a temporal limit of five months set to the torture after the fifth trumpet. The precise significance of this period is uncertain,[56] but the context implies a restriction comparable to the proportion of one-third. Finally the effect of the bowls is total, although the punishments inflicted by God's wrath are confined to those areas characterized by hostility to himself. Within those areas there is no suggestion of only partial affliction – as 16.3 testifies, 'every living thing died that was in the sea'. In addition to these points, account should be taken of the change to a cosmic dimension in the sequences of plagues. This must involve some aggravation of the plagues by increasing their range.

We have seen how the cosmic dimension is introduced in the sixth vision of the seals sequence; it was argued that, although the imagery of the sixth seal has points of contact in, for example, the local experience of earthquakes, nevertheless its main object is to symbolize a great earthquake and portents with cosmic significance, in expectation of the great earthquake of the seventh bowl (16.18). For similar reasons it can be said, anticipating our conclusions for the moment, that the whole sequences of plagues represented by the trumpets and the bowls are envisaged in cosmic rather than purely local terms. It is suggested that the author sets out, in describing the seals sequence, to relate events and factors in the contemporary circumstances and the recent past to God's ultimate plan, with his control of the present situation and his use of events to reveal his purpose and his judgements. The congregations of Asia Minor can see the 'signs of the end' in what is happening to them; the author reinterprets the Synoptic apocalyptic tradition to express this truth.

After the fifth seal, in which the martyr-souls are commanded to wait until the full number of martyrdoms has been completed, the description of the sixth vision links the present closely with the future and anticipates the cosmic dimension which is the outcome of the 'signs' within the local situation. Although it is vitally important to the author's argument that this connection of present and future, local and cosmic, should be made, the distance remaining between the current situation and the ultimate judgement and vindication is expressed by the motif of the restraining of the four winds. There-after this distance is covered rapidly as the author's work is built up, thoroughly but expeditiously, to its cosmic climax; explanations are given in the form of 'flashbacks' to smooth the path of the rapid development. The second and third plague sequences are seen to belong within this process: they indicate that critical stages have been reached in the working-out of God's plan. That their place is within the enlarged cosmic dimension, anticipated by the author, but actually belonging to the immediate future of his expectations, is shown both by the range of subject-matter of the sequences and also by particular features comparable with the ideas of the sixth seal.

As a conclusion to the portents of the sixth seal, John sees 'four angels standing at the four corners of the earth, holding back the four winds of the earth' (7.1). Comparable with this, but clearly not to be identified with it, is the reference at the beginning of the sixth trumpet vision (9.14) with its command: 'Release the four angels who are bound at the great river Euphrates.' The balance between these two passages serves to indicate that the action has advanced. The sixth seal represented an anticipation, and the restraining of the winds by the angels showed that this was reserved for the future. The sixth trumpet, like the other trumpets, is cosmic in scope (although using traditional ideas which could convey a locally restricted meaning) and demonic in characterization; that a later stage has been reached in the author's schematic representation of God's plan is shown by the action of releasing what has been bound (or reserved) for this moment. Significantly, part of this theme of the sixth trumpet vision is resumed in the description of the outpouring of the sixth bowl in the sequence of 'last plagues'; the area affected by this sixth plague is 'the great river Euphrates', with the result that the water is dried up, 'to prepare the way for the kings from the east' (16.12). Again, the theme of invasion from the East, with its local reference to the natural frontier of the Euphrates, is applied to a cosmic setting, this time the mustering for Armageddon. The use of the word 'prepare' could carry with it additional and deliberate eschatological connotations. But in any case the action is seen to have progressed to a further stage at which the Euphrates itself is dried up: God's activity, associated in Old Testament tradition with the Exodus and the Second Exodus, is applied finally to the drawing up of the opposing forces for the ultimate conflict. The sequence of ideas between these three visions, the seal, the trumpet and the bowl, emerges very clearly and presents an emphatic denial of any form of Recapitulation theory.

While such parallels and comparisons between the three sequences of plagues are highly significant in exegesis, the contrasts are also important, not least the difference in the source material used by the author between the seals on the one hand and the trumpets and bowls on the other. We have seen that the sequence of seals is substantially a reinterpretation of the apocalyptic tradition of the Synoptic Gospels. While acknowledging a significant debt to the book of Joel,[57] it can be said that the principal 'inspiration' for the material of the other two sequences is the traditional narrative of the Egyptian plagues. There are explicit references to the first, second, sixth, seventh, eighth and ninth plagues as given in the account in Exod. 7.14–12.36:

1 (Exod. 7.20f.) Rev. 8.8f., 8.10f., 16.3, 16.4

2 (Exod. 8.5f.) Rev. 16.13f.

6 (Exod. 9.8f.) Rev. 16.2

7 (Exod. 9.23f.) Rev. 8.7, 16.21

8 (Exod. 10.12ff.) Rev. 9.3ff.

9 (Exod. 10.21ff.) Rev. 8.12, 16.10

When applied specifically to this context of a relationship between the tradition of the Egyptian plagues and the trumpet and bowl sequences, the form-critical analysis offered by H. P. Müller in his article 'Die Plagen der Apokalypse' offers further illumination. On the basis of the seven bowls, Müller isolates five motifs (not all of which occur in each instance):

1 The empowering (angels given the bowls, commanded to pour them out);

2 The exercising of authority (stereotyped expression as when the angel empties the bowl);

3 Consequences – apocalyptic 'creative energy'. Formula using *egeneto* (cf. clumsy expression in 16.19);

4 Effect on living creatures in each area;

5 The response of men to God.

Müller also finds the majority of these motifs applicable to the first four trumpets (as well as to a few other passages in Revelation) and to the Exodus narratives of the Egyptian plagues. Martin Noth, in his commentary on Exodus,[58] describes the section 7.8–10.29 on the Plagues of Egypt as 'a formal entity' which 'is built up in a most symmetrical way and represents an independent whole even in content'. The present narrative is directed towards the account of Passover night which forms the logical climax (11.1—13.16). Despite its present symmetrical structure, 'it is ... evident that even the set of plague stories is not a well considered literary product but is derived from living oral tradition'.

The Passover tradition embodies the conviction that Israel is freed from Egypt by the miraculous intervention of its God.

The reason for this event being preceded by plagues which were shown before Pharaoh ... is that Yahweh wished to 'multiply' his 'signs and wonders' in Egypt. This is said expressly in 7.3 and ... 11.9. ... Whenever in the Old Testament summary references to the mighty deeds of God at the beginning of the history of Israel speak in an apparently stereotyped phrase of the 'signs and wonders' at the Exodus from Egypt ... it is the plagues that they primarily have in mind.[59]

In the 'living oral tradition of the mighty acts of God towards his people ...' it is 'intended to lay special stress on the fact that it was the wonderful power of Yahweh alone which was at work in the Exodus from Egypt without Israel having to, or even being able to, do anything of itself'.

Such a schematic enumeration of plagues occurs in a variety of contexts within the Old Testament. It seems reasonable to see here a process of development from the formative traditions of the Exodus and in particular from Yahweh's 'signs and wonders' in Egypt. Once applicable to the historical situation of the Exodus, the tradition is celebrated by the Psalmist (Pss. 78, 105), reapplied by the prophet as he exhorts the nation to repent (Amos 4.6ff.; Isa. 5.25ff.; 9.8ff.; Joel 2.12f.), and systematically formulated as a programme of curses, representing God's punishment for sin (Lev. 26; Ecclus. 40.8ff.; Testament of Benjamin 7.2f.; Pirke Aboth 5.11). The numbers seven and ten are both associated with the Egyptian plagues, but it is the former which becomes significant in subsequent applications, particularly in Yahweh's 'sevenfold vengeance'. The development of this tradition has made it eminently suitable for the use to which John applies it. Two separate emphases can be conveyed: the prophetic note of warning and the reiteration of the need to repent; and, in the legal context, the systematic justice of the punishment administered by God. The significance of the number seven in this context is appropriate for John's requirements of number symbolism; this may be influential in determining the form of all three plague sequences. And there is a further emphasis in the Egyptian plagues tradition, exemplified in the interpretation offered by Philo (*Vit. Mos.* 1.17–26) which seems to have appealed to John. He applies the first four plagues of the trumpets and the bowls sequences systematically to four elements of the created order – earth, sea, fresh water, heavenly bodies.

In conclusion, it is necessary to draw together the main features of Revelation's sequences of trumpets and bowls and to show what special contributions they make to the development of the Egyptian plagues tradition. A fundamental question concerns the time references of these two sequences. One of the difficulties in the interpretation of apocalyptic imagery is to determine at what point the action, depicted in symbolic terms, ceases to be a representation of past and present and becomes a projection into the future. It is by comparison of the subject-matter with the known course of historical events that scholars interpreting the book of Daniel have located this dividing line of the time of writing between 11.39 and 40 in that book's sustained description of the last vision. The narrative of the Book of Revelation is not so obviously continuous, and so the location of this line causes greater difficulty. But attention has already been drawn to the sixth seal as an important indicator of events of the imminent future, 'signs of the end' which will lead to the ultimate climax after a short delay.

According to this argument, the line between present and future is prepared for by the fifth seal, with its view of past and future martyrdoms, and is actually drawn between the fifth and sixth seals. The natural corollary to this is the interpretation of the trumpet and bowl sequences as future expectation, viewed either literally or symbolically. The fact that the Egyptian plagues tradition has been reinterpreted within the Old Testament in terms of events subsequent to the Exodus, and, moreover, in terms of future punishments, would facilitate this. Such a conclusion in the exegesis of Revelation is supported for several reasons: namely, the interpretation of all the elements of the sixth seal within their context as an anticipation of the cosmic dimension, and the parallels drawn between the sixth seal and corresponding features in the other two sequences which support this idea of temporal development; the continuity between the seal and trumpet sequences which suggests some kind of temporal succession; and the nature and range of the subject-matter of trumpet and bowl sequences which seems to fit most happily within the cosmic dimension, anticipated by the sixth seal.

It has already been remarked that most natural disasters, and phenomena likely to be viewed as portents, pale into insignificance when compared with the Seer's descriptions of the sixth seal, the trumpets and the bowls. Local experience as well as folk memory may contribute to the description, but the narrative is heightened intentionally and given a cosmic dimension appropriate for this order of future expectation. This is true of the fifth trumpet vision where the 'natural' element of the locust plague is only one of several basic ingredients set within the supernatural context of a fallen star, smoke rising from the abyss, and the identification of Abaddon/Apollyon as king over this locust/scorpion cavalry. Not even the suggestions of commentators, such as Theodoret's 'If one carefully considers the head of the locust, he will find it exceedingly like that of a horse',[60] can preserve a naturalistic context for these locusts, who are to attack mankind and not their natural targets of grass, any green growth and trees (9.4).

A similar point can be made, and more of the author's method and intention can be observed, on the basis of the sixth trumpet and sixth bowl, also referred to earlier. The theme of invasion from the East, from beyond the Euphrates, appears to have been a regular expectation within this part of the Roman Empire. This much is a realistic element from the historical situation, utilized in the Seer's imagery. But the picture he paints goes beyond the bounds of even the most symbolic representation of Parthian invasion. The hosts are mustering for Armageddon. At this point the author's conviction about, or artistic use of the theme of, Nero's return with support from the East, destructive of the power of Rome, merges with the concept of the final battle between good and evil, between God and his enemies, developed within the Old Testament tradition.[61] While John combines these traditions for spectacular effect, juxtaposing the theme of invasion from the north, out of Israel's tradition, with the current feelings about invasion from the east, appropriate to the Asia Minor situation, his method is applied carefully, so that the dominant element is distinguished either by the force of the imagery or by the context in which it is placed. Otherwise the difficulties would be insuperable in trying to distinguish an historical element presented in mythological terms from a mythological element presented in historical terms.

A final question concerns the destination of these two sequences of plagues and their function and purpose within God's plan. The trumpet plagues appear to be destined to affect mankind in general, although it is explicitly stated of the fifth trumpet that its process of five months' torture will not affect those whom God has sealed on the forehead (9.4). In contrast, the plagues from the bowls have very precise destinations;[62] they are poured out so as to affect all who are God's enemies or in any way involved with the beast. So the first plague affects the beast's worshippers and all who bear its mark (16.2, cf. 13.12–17); the second, the sea which is traditionally personified as the power of chaos and opposition to God's creative order, and in Revelation is the place of origin of the beast (16.3, cf. 13.1); thirdly those who 'have shed the blood of saints and prophets' are given 'blood to drink' (16.6, cf. 17.6); fourthly those who are scorched by the sun are those who 'blasphemed the name of God' and such blasphemy is characteristic of the beast (16.9, cf. 13.6); the fifth bowl is poured on the throne of the beast itself (16.10); the sixth prepares the way for the 'kings from the east', who are associated with the beast and identified with his ten horns, to march to defeat at Armageddon (16.12,16 cf. 17.12–14); the seventh affects Babylon, the great city, which is 'split into three parts' (16.19).

The trumpet plagues which are to be the general experience of mankind are interpreted most satisfactorily in the same context as the prophetic use of the plague tradition, with its emphasis on a call to repentance. The associations of the trumpet itself, as G. B. Caird has summarized them,[63] support this line of interpretation. The precise background may be the synagogue ritual of Tishri 1 ('a remembrance day of trumpet blowing', Lev. 23.24) with the recital of the scriptural verses Malkiyyoth, Zikronoth and Shopharoth.

Whether the anthologies of verses preserved in the Rabbinic writings go back to the first century, we have no means of knowing, but the practice is certainly an old one. John must have been accustomed to hearing, along with the synagogue or temple trumpets, verses which spoke of the kingship of God, of God's remembering his people, and of the blowing of trumpets.

Within this sequence of trumpet plagues John tells his readers clearly that the trumpets are 'a proclamation of the divine sovereignty, and a summons to general repentance'.[64] But the outcome of this prophetic call to return to God also has similarities with the experience of many Old Testament prophets. 'The rest of mankind, who were not killed by these plagues, did not repent' (9.20). The plagues are a warning to mankind, a warning which is unheeded; but for those who have been sealed by God this sequence offers reassurance in the proclamation of God's sovereignty and also, in the Interlude (10.1–11.13), a further insight, retrospectively, into God's plan. Because the warning is unheeded the pace of events moves rapidly onto the appearance of Antichrist.

The bowls 'of the wrath of God' poured out by the angels against all who are involved with the beast, are best understood in the light of the 'sevenfold chastisement' that is evolved within Jewish legal theology as a scheme of punishment for disobedience to God. These plagues 'are the last, for with them the wrath of God is ended' (15.1). Warnings have been given to those who worship the beast and have persecuted the saints and the prophets: the main warning and challenge to repentance was in the sequence of trumpet plagues; subsequently there was the announcement of the eternal gospel (14.7) proclaiming the hour of God's judgement. Now the punishments are administered comprehensively within the areas of opposition; man is involved right at the outset of this final sequence of plagues on the Egyptian model; as Swete says, these plagues 'are not tentative chastisements, but punitive and final'.[65]

These two sequences of Egyptian plagues have presented, in turn, the two emphases which we examined in the development of the plague tradition – the call to repentance and the systematic punishment. It seems that this presentation is consistent and deliberate; it can only convey the impression of the process of God's judgement moving towards its climax. If these two sequences are taken in association with the earlier sequence of seals, which combined warning and exhortation in the context of the revelation of God's plan, seen to be operating through the contemporary situation, then what emerges is no system of recapitulation, but a consecutive account of the history of salvation and judgement.

It is then reasonable to conclude that the apocalyptic tradition of the Synoptic Gospels is influential for our author's presentation, not only because it provided the model for the seals sequence in the way that the Egyptian plagues tradition provided the model for the trumpets and the bowls, but also because its programme for the three traditional stages of apocalyptic expectation is followed through in the three plague sequences of the Apocalypse. The *thlipsis* of contemporary events and circumstances is represented in the seals sequence, with the sixth seal fulfilling a similar function to Mark 13.8 in looking ahead to the next stage. The *ōdines* are the cosmic woes, the supernatural portents comparable to the material of the trumpets, heralding the end. Revelation introduces at this stage the strong emphasis on a call for repentance. This feature, which is a product of the Seer's prophetic approach to the circumstances of his own time, also influences the order of events in the last stage. The *telos* is presented in the first instance as a judgement with systematic punishment, and then as a triumphant vindication.

4

The Two Witnesses

Rev. 11.3–13 poses a problem of identification and interpretation in miniature. Who are the two witnesses on whom this brief episode is focused? The brevity of this passage, and its apparent independence from other themes of the book, serve to increase the enigma. The multitude of identifications of the two witnesses, both as proposed by early commentators and as current in modern exegesis, can be classified under three broad headings. The symbolism may refer to actual historical figures and the traditions associated with them; it may be the imagery of prophecy concerned with figures belonging to the last days; or it may not represent actual people but rather a general truth, such as Christian witness or prophecy.

The passage about the two witnesses occurs within the structural framework of the plague sequences. It forms part of what Paul Minear describes as an 'Interlude'. But this term should not be understood as belittling the importance of the passage; in fact because of its context, in a sequence moving towards its climax, 'because of the rise in dramatic intensity . . . the reader's attention is drawn all the more strongly to the seemingly extraneous interlude'.[1]

It is necessary to recall the parallel structure of the two sequences of the seals and the trumpets. There is a clear break in the literary structure after the first four elements in each sequence: the four horses in ch. 6 and the four trumpets in ch. 8 are set apart by their brevity and symmetry. The fifth and sixth elements in both sequences are presented at greater length and without any clear regulating pattern other than the basic requirements of their own sequence. Both the sixth seal and the sixth trumpet are followed immediately by a highly significant interlude which also serves to increase the dramatic intensity of the sequence by delaying the seventh element.

The account of the opening of the sixth seal (6.12ff.) is followed by the episode of the sealing of the 144,000 'out of every tribe of the sons of Israel' (7.4). It may be debated what precisely these servants of God are being 'sealed' against, but it is clear that they are being protected, so that, in 9.4, for example, the locust/scorpions would not now touch them; a pause is made in the sequence of terrible events in order that this sealing may be accomplished. At the same point in the trumpet sequence, after the sixth trumpet has been sounded, there is another action with a similar motivation of protection against calamity. This is the measuring 'of the temple of God and the altar and those who worship there' (11.1) which precedes the account of the two witnesses. The references to the 'temple of God' (11.1) and 'the court outside' (11.2), coupled with the place-reference, 'where their Lord was crucified' in 11.8, are indicative of the Jerusalem temple. The two interludes, then, share not only a common theme, but also an 'atmosphere' which is so Jewish[2] that some scholars have sought here for traces of originally Jewish apocalypses.

To complete the account of the parallel structure we should look at the seventh seal and the seventh trumpet. At the opening of the seventh seal 'there was silence in heaven for about half an hour' (8.1); apart from the description of the angel with the golden censer (8.3–5), the pace of the narrative then moves swiftly into the account of the seven trumpets sounded by the angels (8.2, 6ff.). The episode which follows the sounding of the seventh trumpet is also set in heaven; but instead of silence 'there were loud voices' making triumphant statements about the present reality of the Kingdom of God (11.15–18). There is a close parallel between the description in 11.19b of the accompaniment of the opening of God's temple in heaven, and 8.5b with its account of the consequences of the angel's action in throwing the censer on the earth. And in the trumpet sequence, like the seal sequence, the seventh element points ahead rapidly. It is not intended that we should pause long on the scene in heaven, except to gain reassurance from what is said, just as there is reassurance in 8.4 in the fact that the prayers of the saints have been heard in heaven. Rather, the seventh trumpet heralds the beast from the sea, who appears at 13.1, after the account has been given in ch. 12 of the reasons for his appearance.

The interlude between the sixth and seventh trumpets is a long one (10.1–11.13). It is introduced by a 'mighty angel' (10.1) who heightens the expectation of the seventh trumpet by solemnly declaring that when that trumpet is sounded there will be no more delay, but 'the mystery of God, as he announced to his servants the prophets' will be fulfilled. In this way the reader is prepared for the coming of Antichrist (13.1ff.), for the proclamation of God's kingdom (11.15ff.) and the speedy intervention of God to destroy Babylon (14–19). We are also told that this 'mighty angel' 'had a little scroll in his hand' (10.2); it is this scroll which the author is invited to take and eat (10.8ff.). Just as the awaited revelation of the seventh trumpet would be a mixture of woe and triumph both for the prophet and for the world, so this scroll 'was sweet as honey in my mouth, but when I had eaten it my stomach was made bitter' (10.10).[3]

But this parallel does not by any means require that the scroll is to be identified with the message of the seventh trumpet. This would be cumbersome and would convert the 'interlude' into a proleptic revelation to the prophet of what is still to come. It is unlikely that the 'mighty angel' would both promise the revelation by the medium of another angel and also have the text of it open in his own hand. Therefore it is natural to relate the 'little scroll' to the material in the remainder of the interlude (11.1–13). The vision of the scroll is a way of introducing this special unit of material; the author digests its contents and is then told to make those contents known (10.11). The relationship, then, between the bitter/sweet contents of the scroll and the woe/triumph of the seventh trumpet is a similarity of essential characteristics, perhaps amounting to an intrinsic connection, where the one episode is seen as a foretaste of what is later fulfilled, a microcosm presented in anticipation of the macrocosm.

There could be a significant contrast between the *biblaridion/biblion* of 10.2, 8ff. and the *biblion* of 5.1. In ch. 5, the scroll is 'sealed with seven seals' and can only be opened by the Lamb/Lion; in ch. 10, the scroll is 'open in the hand of the angel'. The open scroll requires no special agency to make it available; according to the figurative language of the author, he readily absorbed its contents. There appears to be a convention in apocalyptic writing that a book is sealed when it relates to the distant future.[4] As the events referred to draw near, the contents of the 'prophecy' are made available; up until then the seals have preserved the book from misuse. By this convention the scroll of 5.1 refers to the events of the present and the immediate future. Conversely one could argue that a scroll which is already lying open is one which has served its purpose in the past. The events to which it refers are past events, for which it offered an interpretation. In certain circumstances such a scroll might still offer 'food for thought' and the material from it could be used in a subsequent reinterpretation.[5] This argument need not be applied literally, unless circumstances demand it; by itself it is no more a warrant for the theory that the material of ch. 11 derives from an earlier apocalypse than is the convention of a sealed book any assurance that the prophecy was actually composed in the way that the 'pseudonymous' tradition of authorship asserts. But it can be a pointer to a 'flash-back' in apocalyptic writing, in the same way that the unsealing points to a prophecy for the immediate future.

From such an examination of the context three main points emerge which could serve as criteria for an interpretation. They are the Jewish 'atmosphere' of the material, the association with the final appearance of Antichrist, and the suggestion that the author is interpreting a significant event of the past. We should now explore the possibilities of this historical context and begin by looking at the setting of the first two verses in ch. 11.

It is usual to interpret 11.1–2 (the measuring) and 11.3–13 (the witnesses) closely together as associated ideas within a single theme, even though several commentators have argued that they were originally derived from different sources. In their present context they are bound together by the framework of the contents of the little scroll, as well as by the shared allusions to time (42 months=1260 days) and place (Jerusalem). It is the present context which is of importance from the point of view of identifying the references and interpreting the author's meaning. But some of the speculation about origins may be suggestive in indicating the possible terms of reference of this kind of material in the author's day.

Perhaps the most favoured theory, propounded by Wellhausen, Bousset and Charles, is that which sees in 11.1–2 a fragment of a 'Zealot pamphlet'.[6] It represents a prophecy, written during the siege of Jerusalem and before A.D. 70 while the Zealots were still in occupation of the inner court of the temple; the assurance of such a prophecy is that the temple itself will not be destroyed even when the city is occupied. The difficulty with theories of this kind is that such prophecies prior to A.D. 70 represent disappointed hopes in the harsh realities after the fall of Jerusalem. R. H. Charles concludes that the author of the Apocalypse can only have reinterpreted these ideas in terms of a preservation from spiritual danger.[7] Thus the majority of commentators offer symbolic interpretations. Such exegesis is usually so general that it evades any detailed argument which might lead to its refutation; but it does seem that so general a meaning could have been conveyed by the author without the precise description which is a feature of this passage.

But there remains a further way in which the author could have made use of material with a definite historical reference, and this supports the suggestion that here is a clear reference to past events. Either he uses a quotation from a familiar source, such as the 'Zealot pamphlet' may have been, or he composes for himself a verbal picture with recognizable allusions. And so he introduces an historical 'flash-back' to the temporally distant, but undoubtedly significant, situation of the siege and fall of Jerusalem. Two aspects of the situation are referred to: the 'measuring' of the temple, and the surrender of the outer court to the nations who are trampling the holy city (cf. Luke 21.24). Apart from these references, the main function of the allusion seems to be to set the scene briefly for the appearance of the two witnesses.

The author is not necessarily concerned to emphasize, as his primary point, the failure of the original prophecy, if such it was. Instead he wishes to draw attention to the complex situation leading up to the destruction in A.D. 70, and to illustrate this by two aspects, the optimistic and the pessimistic, corresponding to the sweetness and bitterness of the scroll (10.9–10). On the one hand there was the attitude of religious enthusiasm coupled with zeal for the preservation of all that Jerusalem represented for the Jew; on the other hand there were the 'outsiders', those who trampled over the holy city and those who collaborated and surrendered the city to them.

It may be that the author is making use of an essential ambiguity in the notion of 'measuring the temple' and intends the thoughtful reader to recognize this point. It is usually assumed, as has already been indicated, that the measuring is for the purpose of preservation from calamity. This would be the most natural sense in an original prophecy, set against the trampling in v. 2, and is supported by the 'one full line to be spared' referred to in 2 Sam. 8.2b;[8] but that context also refers to 'two lines he measured to be put to death' (2 Sam. 8.2a),[9] where the measuring is clearly with a view to destruction. A third possibility is that of measuring with a view to rebuilding and restoring (cf. Ezek. 40.2ff.; 41.13; Zech. 2.1ff.; Jer. 31.39). In the context of Ezekiel 40—2 the measuring is associated with the vision of the ideal temple of the restoration; it has been suggested by Bornkamm that the context in Revelation is similar, in so far as the measuring of the temple is a prophetic anticipation of the measuring of the city of New Jerusalem (21.15ff.).[10]

If the author is exploiting this ambiguity in the idea of measuring, he could be saying that the measuring in the original prophecy was understood to preserve the actual sanctuary in Jerusalem, but in the event the outcome was quite different and the sanctuary was destroyed; but this should certainly not be viewed in an entirely pessimistic light, because the essential significance of Jerusalem, its religious heart, was indeed preserved and revivified by the experience. And, in accordance with the interpretation of ch. 12, the religious 'Remnant', the spiritual reality which is preserved and will be restored, is found within an area of Judaism as well as within the Christian Church.

The historical 'flash-back' to the siege and fall of Jerusalem sets the scene for the two witnesses who are introduced in 11.3. The relationship between the two episodes is expressed with precision by the juxtaposing of the two equivalent time references in vv. 2 and 3. In 11.2 the trampling of the holy city is said to last for forty-two months; as S. Giet pointed out, this is approximately the period of the Flavian war, from the spring of A.D. 67 to 29 August 70, during which time Jerusalem was 'profaned', but in the sanctuary the sacrifices continued uninterrupted, until at the end the sanctuary was destroyed by fire.[11] One can agree with Giet that the historical identification of this period of forty-two months and an allusion to the Danielic period of $3\frac{1}{2}$ times ($3\frac{1}{2}$ years=42 months) are by no means mutually exclusive. Indeed it seems likely that Daniel's prophecy of the duration of 'the shattering of the power of the holy people' (Dan. 12.7) has been reinterpreted in terms of new historical circumstances in which it seems to be fulfilled. It may well be that confirmation of this is available in a similar interpretation, combining traditional and historical elements, for the identical period, expressed as 1260 days, which is set for the prophecy of the witnesses in 11.3. We must now consider in turn the main features of the account of the witnesses to establish the various criteria which must be satisfied by any complete interpretation.

'And I will grant my two witnesses power to prophesy' (11.3). In the Greek the construction is Hebraic and the wording, if not the idiom, is parallel to the preceding sentence in 11.2. This parallelism may be contrived, as Austin Farrer suggested, in order to express more clearly and emphatically the connection we have observed already between the episode of the measuring and trampling and the episode of the witnesses.[12]

The development of the usage of the Greek word *martus* in Christian contexts has been discussed at length in a large number of articles and monographs.[13] Arndt and Gingrich summarize the uses under three classifications: the literal meaning is in the legal sense (Deut. 17.6; 19.15; Matt. 18.16; 26.65//; Acts 6.13; 7.58; 2 Cor. 13.1; 1 Tim. 5.19; Heb. 10.28); the word is used figuratively of anyone testifying to anything (of God, especially in the formula of calling upon God as witness to vouch for the truth of something (Rom. 1.9; 2 Cor. 1.23; Phil. 1.8; 1 Thess. 2.5, 10); of human witness in general, often in the relatively inert and passive sense of being a spectator (1 Thess. 2.10; 1 Tim. 6.12; 2 Tim. 2.2); and in the particular and active sense of the exertion of men who are messengers of God); and the third classification is the specialized meaning within the context of the persecuted Church, a 'martyr' dying for his testimony.

It is clear that the usage is not restricted to the legal meaning, either literally or in a precise metaphorical application; nor is a witness necessarily an 'eyewitness' of the event to which he can testify. Even in non-biblical Greek, *martus* and its cognate words referred 'not merely to the establishment of events or actual relations or facts of experience on the basis of direct personal knowledge. It signifies also the proclamation of views or truths of which the speaker is convinced.' 'The development of the distinctive Christian use is the result of' the application of these words 'to the content of Gospel proclamation and to the circumstances in which this took place'.[14]

It was in the context of the witnessing by Christians to Jesus, despite the persecution of the Church, that the word *martus* underwent a semantic change and acquired the distinctive Christian sense of 'martyr', defined by Origen as 'one who of his own free choice chooses to die for the sake of religion and prefers to die rather than deny his religion and live'.[15] The first problem lies in establishing at what stage this adaptation in meaning took place, such that the word could be used without qualification in the sense of 'martyr'. In 1 Clement 5 the participle *marturēsas* is used of both Peter and Paul who are cited as apostolic examples of those who 'contended unto death'. J. B. Lightfoot[16] understood this, in the circumstances, as a reference to their martyrdom, but not all scholars would agree, especially as regards the technical sense of the verb. The description of Peter refers only to his sufferings; Paul in the same way is shown as an example of endurance and his preaching of the Gospel is described in terms of the verb *didaskō* and the noun *kērux* and not by the repetition of the verb *martureō* or a cognate. It seems likely, then, that *marturēsas* refers to martyrdom rather than to Christian witnessing in this context. But at this stage the context, not the word itself, is decisive for the technical sense; 1 Clement 38.2 and 63.3 show that the words *martureō* and *martus* can still be used in a general sense. That the meaning 'martyr' is still not widely established is suggested by the complete absence of this technical term in the Shepherd of Hermas, where martyrs are 'those who suffered for the sake of the name',[17] and in the writings of Ignatius which are otherwise full of the ideas of martyrdom.

After the middle of the second century, *martus* and its cognates are used absolutely in the sense of martyrdom. Examples are found from the church of Smyrna in the Martyrdom of Polycarp (cf. 19.1), from Melito of Sardis (in Eus. *h.e.* 4. 26.3) and from Polycrates of Ephesus in his letter to Victor of Rome about the paschal question. Strathmann concludes from the origin of these references that 'the sphere in which the martyr concept developed was the church in Asia Minor' since 'elsewhere at this time no traces of the later concept are to be found'; he associates this fact with 'the first clear steps . . . taken towards such a development' in the Book of Revelation, which is also linked with the churches of Asia Minor.[18]

In the Book of Revelation the word *martus* occurs five times. In 1.5 and again in 3.14 'the faithful *martus*' is applied to Jesus Christ himself. The significance of this is seen most naturally in the light of the opening words of the Book (1.1–3) with the carefully structured account of the Book's authority – 'the word of God and the *marturian* of Jesus Christ'. God's revelation is transmitted in and through Jesus Christ, who has reliably fulfilled this task; he is worthy to be described by the Messianic title from Ps. 88.38 (LXX).[19] But Arndt and Gingrich classify this usage of *martus* under the heading of 'martyr' on the grounds that 'the death of Jesus was early regarded as the first martyrdom'. More cautiously, Strathmann states that the 'reference to the revelation' 'does not exhaust the meaning of the term'; he quotes John 18.37 and comments: 'He showed Himself faithful to this calling by dying'.[20]

A similar title 'my *martus* my faithful one' is applied to Antipas at

2.13. The information about him is meagre; we are told that he 'was killed among you' that is, in Pergamum. The reference implies that the faithfulness of his witness is demonstrated in his death; because of the parallel title there is some recognition of the fact that 'the crucified Lord is the model of the Christian witness'. If the technical term for 'martyr' is not yet established, this is the situation out of which that usage was born. A similar context, although set out in more general and figurative terms, is suggested by the description of the woman Babylon as 'drunk with the blood of the saints and the blood of the *marturōn* of Jesus' (17.6). According to R. H. Charles, *martus* here, as in 2.13, means 'martyr'; 'for since the Seer expects all the faithful to seal their witness with their blood (13.15), the word *martus* in our text is a witness faithful unto death, and therefore a martyr'.[21] Strathmann does not agree, because there is also a reference to 'martyred' saints as well as this supposed reference to martyrs. He thinks this passage deals with two distinct categories: 'those who suffer death for their evangelistic witness are mentioned as well as those who are killed simply because of their faith'. I suspect that Strathmann with his distinctions and Charles with his 'tautologous clauses' are both being too precise; the author is not trying to classify those who have suffered at the hands of Babylon, but he is describing them as 'saints' and *martures*. Whether *martures* means 'martyrs' depends on the development of usage; but this is certainly a context in which that special sense becomes a real possibility.

The ambiguity remains in the reference to 'my two witnesses' in 11.3; these two bear a prophetic witness, and are then put to death by the beast. The suffering of the Old Testament prophet is part of the Seer's picture, although by no means necessarily an integral part of the term *martus*.[22] Johannes Munck seems to base his identification of the witnesses as Peter and Paul on the predominantly Lucan use of *martures* for Apostolic witnesses, and in particular on Acts 22.15; 26.16 for Paul and 1 Pet. 5.1 for Peter.[23] While it is true that the Apostles, in both the narrowest and the broader senses of the term, are described as *martures*, the converse does not hold true, even for Revelation itself. This argument cannot, then, stand on its own; in identifying the witnesses of ch. 11, the possibility is not excluded of a reference to the Apostles in general, or to Peter and Paul in particular, but such a solution is by no means demanded.

It is possible that Clement of Rome used the verb *martureō* of martyrdom, and this is before the end of the first century and not so long after the date of Revelation. J. B. Lightfoot, commenting on this development of the technical sense, wrote: 'Doubtless the Neronian persecution had done much to promote this sense, aided perhaps by its frequent occurrence in the Revelation.' [24] The earliest instances of witness by the major figures of the Christian Church, witness made complete in death, were likely to have a significant effect on the terminology of witness. Perhaps Munck's argument about Peter and Paul's martyrdom is more significant on this point than he was prepared to recognize. As a tentative conclusion to this survey of the significance of *martus* in ch. 11, it is a valid possibility that the word is indicative of the consequences in suffering and martyrdom as well as of the action of bearing witness. If a Christian example is being given, it could be that of Paul and Peter, not because they were apostles, but because they were martyrs.

The witnesses are identified as 'the two olive trees and the two lampstands which stand before the Lord' (11.4). The imagery here is derived from Zech. 4 but there are differences in the way it is applied. In Zechariah's vision the two olive trees are seen, one on the right and one on the left of a single lampstand (*luchnia* = *mᵉnorah*), which carries seven lamps (*luchnos* = *nēr*). The seven lamps are described as 'the eyes of the Lord, which range through the whole earth', and the two olive trees 'are the two anointed who stand by the Lord of the whole earth'. Certainly the lampstand with seven lamps and the two trees are distinct from one another, not equated as are the two trees and the two lamps in Revelation. The rather obscure text in Zech. 4.12 may mean that the two trees supply the lamp directly with oil.

According to P. R. Ackroyd, the interpretation of Zechariah's vision 'points first to the seven eyes of God, ranging throughout the whole earth, expressive of the omniscience of God and the range of divine rule'. 'A second stage of interpretation describes the olive trees as "sons of oil" (RSV "anointed") representing Zerubbabel and Joshua as the two agents of the divine purpose.' A third element in v. 12 'represents an extension of the basic idea, pointing to the function of the two leaders in contributing to the well-being of the community'.[25]

Because the author of Revelation seems to have used this imagery freely, there can be no certainty that he will have interpreted it in the same way as in Zechariah's vision. The seven lamps are also a feature of the vision in Rev. 1, and, according to the interpretation in 1.20, are identified with the seven churches. G. B. Caird follows this idea through and accordingly interprets the two lampstands in Rev. 11 as 'a proportion of the church in all parts of the world'.[26] Some commentators, like Zahn, are emphatic that John has used the imagery creatively, with disregard for the context in Zechariah. Others would follow the speculative suggestions, considered by Bousset, that this imagery may belong to a broader tradition, interpreted by Zechariah in a specialized way, or, as considered by Charles, that links in the development of thought from Zechariah to Revelation are missing. Identifications of the two olive trees within Judaism ranged widely; according to Rabbinic exegesis, deriving a spiritual interpretation from the context of Zechariah, they represent priesthood and monarchy.[27]

The author of Revelation has collected a number of images which he can apply to the two figures of the witnesses. He seems to have treated the symbols from Zechariah's vision with freedom so that he can apply them directly to his own subject. There were two witnesses; this number may simply represent actual circumstances, but it must also be significant that the legal requirement is for two witnesses to validate a testimony.[28] To describe his witnesses further, John utilizes the imagery from Zechariah; the olive trees are readily available and in the right number. As he also wishes to use the idea of the lamps he must modify the number to make it applicable.

If the two olive trees originally represented Zerubbabel the anointed king and Joshua the anointed priest, the fulfilment in Zechariah's day of the prophecy of Jeremiah (33.14–26), then it is possible that the reapplication of this imagery refers to those who exercise royal and priestly functions within the Christian Church. In fact, as John addresses the seven churches of Asia at the start of his work, he ascribes glory to Christ who 'made *us* a kingdom, priests to his God and Father' (1.6, cf. 5.10; 20.6). Such a reference in terms of ch. 11 could apply generally to the Christian churches, or, if a more specific reference is possible, then to individual Christians, perhaps two notable examples, who have been martyred and share 'in the first resurrection' (20.4–6).

What fresh idea could be added to the picture by the modified imagery of the lamps? One possibility is that outlined by Caird – this is the proportion of the church to suffer martyrdom; but it is a weakness of this theory that no satisfactory account can be given of why precisely two-sevenths is the selected fraction. When the seven-branched lampstand (or seven lampstands) is such a potent representative symbol of the unity and diversity of the churches, the force of the imagery here seems to be limited so arbitrarily merely to bring it into line with the pairs of witnesses and trees. If the imagery was to represent an aspect of the universal Church, one feels that the picture could have been drawn to include the seven lamps.

Another interpretation would correspond more closely with the original spirit of Zechariah's vision and the imagery of the olive trees. In Zechariah the lamps are the seven 'eyes of the Lord which range through the whole earth', expressive of the extent of divine rule. If this is reinterpreted in terms of the work of God within the Christian Church, and its missionary outreach to the known world, then it is possible to see how this universal reference can be expressed meaningfully in terms of the figure two, rather than the original symbolism of seven. The allusion could well be to the Early Church situation represented by Paul in these terms – 'I had been entrusted with the gospel to the uncircumcised, just as Peter had been entrusted with the gospel to the circumcised (for he who worked through Peter for the mission to the circumcised worked through me also for the Gentiles).' (Gal. 2.7–8.) Peter and Paul had divided the world between them in God's service. John could then be referring very precisely to these two notable Christian martyrs who had been 'the eyes of the Lord' to the world.

'Heirs to the crowns of Zerubbabel and Joshua, the witnesses are to succeed also to the rod of Moses and the mantle of Elijah.' [29] These words of G. B. Caird provide a connecting link to the third area of consideration, that is the power which the witnesses possess. There is little doubt that 11.5–6 depicts the two witnesses as exercising Elijah's power as 'a man of God' to call down fire,[30] and sharing in Elijah's ability to prevent rain and Moses' reputation for turning water into blood, as the one 'who smote the Egyptians with every sort of plague' (1 Sam. 4.8). What is much more open to debate is the significance which such attributes can have when applied to the two witnesses; is this a genuine apocalyptic tradition about Moses and Elijah which has found currency in a Christian context, or is it another element, alongside the imagery from Zechariah, which goes to make up a larger and radically different picture?

Jeremias identifies the two witnesses with Moses and Elijah. 'The two witnesses of Rev. 11.3ff. are the prophet like Moses (Deut. 18.15, 18) and the returning Elijah (Mal. 3.23).'[31] He discusses the return of 'the suffering Elijah'; 'in only one New Testament passage (Rev. 11.3ff.) is the expectation that Elijah redivivus has still to come in the future plainly advanced as a doctrine of the early Christian community'. This expectation is in conflict with the Gospel tradition which believes that Elijah has already come in the person of John the Baptist. Jeremias concludes that Rev. 11.3ff. must therefore belong to a pre-Christian apocalyptic tradition which treats of the return of Moses and Elijah and their suffering. Mark 9.12f., with its prophecy of suffering for both the Son of Man and Elijah, can be taken to support this conjecture, assuming that the reference is to an extra-canonical tradition, which has been expunged from later Jewish writing for reasons of anti-Christian polemic. This tradition, although lost in Judaism, is preserved within the early Christian traditions about the Antichrist which Bousset described and documented.[32] Jeremias also quotes from the Coptic Apocalypse of Elijah,[33] which appeared in Steindorff's edition of 1899 (subsequent to Bousset's work):

> When, therefore, Elijah and Enoch hear that the shameless one has displayed himself on the holy place, they come down and fight with him, saying ... The shameless one will hear it and become angry and will fight with them in the market place of the great city and will make war with them for 7 days and they will lie dead for 3½ days on the market place in view of the whole people. But on the fourth day they will rise again ... On that day they will rejoice to high heaven as they shine forth and the whole people and the whole world sees them.

Elijah and Enoch appear again directly before the parousia of the Messiah: 'They lay aside the flesh of this world and put on their heavenly flesh; they prosecute the son of lawlessness and kill him.'

There are important points of agreement with the tradition in Rev. 11 (the death of the two witnesses, the exposure of their corpses for 3½ days, the Resurrection and Ascension), but there are also significant differences (Enoch in place of Moses, the appearance of Antichrist prior to the witnesses, the purpose of the coming of the witnesses) which point to an independent tradition, although perhaps a neighbouring one. Here Jeremias is effectively reiterating and reinforcing the original arguments of Bousset. The conclusion of the story in the Elijah Apocalypse with the return of the witnesses might be, Jeremias suggests, the original conclusion of this tradition, modified in Revelation because there it is Christ who overcomes Antichrist (19.17ff.).

Johannes Munck is critical of the work of Bousset on which Jeremias relies, and is particularly critical of Bousset's presuppositions in reconstructing a tradition earlier than and independent of Revelation from material later, often much later, than Revelation.[34] He supports these general criticisms by a detailed consideration of five points of variation from the tradition of Revelation which Bousset held to support the independence of the tradition he had reconstructed.

It is clear from Munck's discussion that the traditions are by no means as homogeneous as Bousset thought, and that the variety of individual differences tends to destroy the force of his argument on the basis of five main differences. And without substantial evidence for a tradition of the two witnesses, independent of Revelation, that could lead back to a Jewish tradition older than Revelation (but instead there is argument for Revelation as the source of these traditions) Jeremias' account of the apocalyptic tradition of 'the suffering Elijah' loses much of its immediate support and significance. For Munck also argues that the Coptic Apocalypse of Elijah represents a confused rendering of Rev. 11, and not an independent tradition from Jewish sources.[35] Nor is Mark 9.12f. an adequate indication that 'the idea of a suffering forerunner is not strange to the contemporaries of Jesus'.[36] V. 12 does not say that Elijah will suffer as the Son of Man will, and v. 13 can be explained as a Christian interpretation in the light of the death of John the Baptist. Without the support either of Bousset's thesis or of evidence from the Gospel tradition, Jeremias' other references cannot sustain his argument.

Is the tradition of suffering any better supported in the expectation about Moses? According to Jeremias' account of 'The Second Moses as a Figure of Suffering' in Rabbinic writings 'elements of suffering are constantly linked with this figure'.[37] This is natural because the historical Moses 'was regarded as the great example of patience', and, at least in the third century, 'atoning efficacy was ascribed to his death and burial in the wilderness'. In the Assumption of Moses (3.11) he is described as the sufferer, who 'has suffered much in Egypt, at the Red Sea, and in the Wilderness, through forty years'. In the New Testament also Moses is depicted as a figure of suffering (cf. Acts 7.17–44; Heb. 11.24–26). And there are verses where, according to Jeremias, the expectation of a 'prophet like Moses' (Deut. 18.15, 18) is 'construed as an intimation of the suffering Messiah' (Luke 24.27, 44ff.; Acts 26.22f.). But this emphasis on the elements of suffering is explained in the light of the Moses/Christ typology where 'the reality of the second Moses determines the view of the first'.

But the picture cannot be drawn as sharply as these first impressions suggest. Jeremias' own account emphasizes the problems and obscurity about any Jewish typology involving Moses. If the second Moses is part of popular Messianic expectation, then the ideas of suffering may well belong to the realities of the situation facing the Messiah, rather than being intrinsic to the expected figure of Moses (cf. the range of parallels in Rabbinic typology cited by Jeremias, where the reference to suffering involves the whole people and not just the second Moses: 'Like Moses, the Messiah will lead the people into the wilderness to undergo a period of distress and suffering.').[38] This judgement would be supported by Jeremias' conclusion from the New Testament use of this typology, if the passages Jeremias cites can sustain such a typological construction. But it is more likely that these passages should be taken literally with reference to the fulfilment of the Old Testament (the books of Moses and the prophets). Finally neither Acts 7.17–44 nor Heb. 11.23–28 is designed to present the picture of the Suffering Moses; the latter offers an example of faith, in that Moses, instead of enjoying the wealth of Egypt, chose to share in the common sufferings of his people.

The expectation of a Suffering Moses, like that of a Suffering Elijah, then, seems to derive almost all of its original support from Rev. 11. It would therefore be more realistic to examine more critically what this passage says about Elijah and Moses; does it make use of any earlier traditions apart from the allusions to the Old Testament in 11.5 and 6? Although there are no grounds that we know of for deriving the suffering of the witnesses from any expectation of such suffering figures, it is possible that the account of their powers and activity may owe something to traditional expectations.

The expectation of the return of Elijah is based on the prophecy of Mal. 3.23–4; if this is taken with Mal. 3.1f. then he is the messenger and precursor of Yahweh himself (cf. Ecclus. 48.10, Str.-B. 4.782–4). Elijah is expected as the forerunner of the Messiah, either together with Enoch or alone.[39] It is possible that the expectation of Elijah was also identified with the expectation of the eschatological high priest which is rooted in Zech. 4.1ff. and developed in the Testaments of the Twelve Patriarchs and Talmudic literature.[40] In accordance with this it could be maintained by the second century A.D. that Elijah would anoint the Messiah.

The expectation of Moses is of a different order. There are few references to the return of Moses himself in the last time, and these are associated with the problem of the fate of Israel's wilderness generation, for whom Moses' death would have atoning power. Nowhere in the older Rabbinic literature is there any idea that the returning Moses will be the Messiah. But instead Moses came to be seen as a type of the Messiah; the reference to a 'prophet like Moses' (Deut. 18.15, 18) is variously applied, and sometimes associated with the Messiah (cf. John 1.21, 25; Acts 3.22) although not necessarily equated with him, except in Samaritan and occasionally in Christian theology; and the typology of the first and the final redemption became a frequent principle in Rabbinic writing ('as the first redeemer (Moses), so the final redeemer (The Messiah)').[41]

The tradition of two forerunners of the Messiah is not found in older Rabbinic literature, but appears within the apocalyptic tradition, beginning with 1 Enoch 90.31 and is expressed more generally or allusively in 4 Esdras 6.26. It is possible that this tradition is reflected in the story of the Transfiguration at Mark 9.4–5//s where Moses and Elijah appear with Christ. But outside the New Testament by far the most usual identification of these forerunners is with Enoch and Elijah, chosen because they were both translated to heaven while still alive (4 Esdras 6.26). If Mark 9.4f. and Rev. 11.3f. represent evidence for another tradition in which Moses replaces Enoch, then perhaps this tradition was supported by a belief in the translation of Moses.[42] But might it not be more likely that the Gospel tradition of the Transfiguration modifies the existing popular hope, in order to depict Moses and Elijah, the embodiments of 'the Law and the Prophets', as the 'supporters' of Christ? Then the author of Revelation either for this or for his own good reason retains the imagery of the two figures of the Transfiguration. But meanwhile Jewish expectation is perpetuating the tradition of Enoch and Elijah, and writers in the Christian apocalyptic tradition, and even early commentators on Revelation, preserve this identification of the two eschatological figures, despite the allusive intentions of the author of Revelation.

As far as we know this specific pairing of Elijah and Moses in eschatological expectation is unprecedented outside the Christian tradition. But in the Gospels there are two relevant passages. The discussion of the identity of John the Baptist (John 1.20–1) involves three figures, Christ, Elijah and the 'prophet like Moses', which may reflect popular expectation.[43] The Transfiguration, in its Marcan form (Mark 9.4–5), introduces 'Elijah with Moses ... talking to Jesus', which even corresponds to the order of the allusions in Rev. 11.5–6 (although this order reverts to the more natural and historical order 'Moses and Elijah' in Mark 9.5 and in the Matthaean and Lucan versions). In default of other evidence it seems likely that the author of Revelation has in mind this latter episode in the Gospel tradition, when he records the words of the heavenly voice about 'my two witnesses'. As we have seen, the element of suffering and death does not appear as an integral part of the traditional expectation, nor is it present in the words of the Gospel traditions. It seems reasonable to conclude that this element is added by the author of Revelation on the basis of experience. He is offering a reinterpretation of ideas about Elijah and Moses, and he identifies them with two notable witnesses who have suffered and died. It is possible that the evidence of the martyrdoms of Peter and Paul provides the material for the suffering in the story of the witnesses.[44]

Why might the author of Revelation choose to present Peter and Paul in terms of Moses and Elijah? There is no doubt that the ideas of the prophet whose return is expected, and the awaited 'prophet like Moses' were suitable for application to the pioneers of the Christian mission. Christian evangelism could be described in terms of prophecy,[45] and its principal exponents would readily be seen by their enemies as 'two prophets' who 'had been a torment to those who dwell on the earth' (Rev. 11.10). The popular expectations that existed about Elijah and Moses were ripe for reinterpretation, and the Elijah theme had already undergone a Christian interpretation in terms of John the Baptist; further reinterpretations were possible within the endeavour to achieve an eschatological understanding of the Christian Church. Each popular expectation offered scope in terms of the awaited appearance, and for Elijah, and probably for Moses too (in some circles at least), there was the potentiality inherent in translation or assumption to heaven. As Farrer observes, 'The ascension of the witnesses shows them once more in the parts of Moses and Elias.' [46] The potentiality of these figures is reapplied by John in terms of death and resurrection and then ascension to heaven, a sequence which deliberately parallels the example of Jesus Christ himself. The martyrs die as their Lord died, 'and like him they have their Easter Day',[47] although the tradition of 'the third day' is adjusted to correspond with the $3\frac{1}{2}$ days (or half-week) of Daniel's prophecy. There is tremendous assurance in the thought that these early martyrs have been taken up to heaven to their Lord.

Perhaps it is the author's intention to offer a bold reinterpretation of the Transfiguration tradition in terms of Paul and Peter with their Lord. There is a certain appropriateness in the description of Paul (like Elijah) as the 'prophetic troubler of Israel', and of Peter (like the Mosaic figure) as the 'legal prophet', especially since this also corresponds very neatly with the division of labour set out in Gal. 2.7–8, and already discussed in terms of the Zechariah prophecy. An interpretation in terms of Peter and Paul can then offer an explanation, relying on a creative combination of ideas from traditional expectation and Old Testament material, which does greater justice to the situation than theories about conjectural earlier traditions on which the author is dependent. Peter and Paul hold together the pairing of Moses and Elijah and the association with suffering and death at just the points where our evidence about contemporary and earlier traditions is in danger of letting these ideas fall apart.

The two witnesses/martyrs will be allowed to complete the prophetic element of their testimony (11.7a) before the intervention of the Beast (cf. Mark 13.10; Matt. 24.14). The beast is *to thērion*, the same word which is used in 13.1 of a beast with seven heads 'rising (*anabainon*) out of the sea', and in 17.3, 8ff. of the beast on which the harlot sits, the beast which 'was, and is not, and is to ascend (*anabainein*) from the bottomless pit'. In 11.7 it is also described as 'the beast that ascends from the bottomless pit'. Since 'the bottomless pit' (*abussos*) can be used of the underworld, in the sense of the primeval depths filled up with the ocean or waters of chaos, these three descriptions can be taken as identical, and the beasts regarded as one. The antecedents of this beast figure, and its connection with the Antichrist tradition, are discussed in detail in the later chapter devoted to the beast. For our present purposes, it is important to see what effect the interpretation proposed for the beast in Rev. 17 has upon the understanding of the role of this same beast in Rev. 11.

The use of the present participle *anabainon*, with the repeated definite article in the Greek of 11.7, suggests that it is a description of a characteristic of the beast, rather than a reference to a particular event, where the participle replaces another main verb. This admits the possibility, natural enough in a panoramic view of the activities of Antichrist, that he can appear on more than one occasion. In the ultimate manifestation described in chs. 13 and 17 the beast is to be understood in terms of the 'Nero Redivivus' legend, applied to the circumstances of the worship of the Roman Emperors. The Antichrist legend can be applied to particular historical figures as, for example, to Antiochus Epiphanes in Daniel, and to the Roman general Pompey in Ps. Sol. 2.29. In a rather different metaphor, Nero himself was described as *thērion* by Apollonius of Tyana, according to Philostratus (*VA* 4.38). It would therefore maintain the continuity and essential identity of the beast imagery if the beast of ch. 11 were Nero himself, and the beast of chs. 13 and 17 were 'Nero Redivivus'. Exactly this interpretation is possible if the two witnesses represent Peter and Paul, who traditionally were martyred in the reign of Nero.

The Antichrist legend has a long history, both in its politico-religious and even more in its theological manifestations; the word 'Antichrist' is itself relatively late, first being known in Christian writings, but the ideas to which it was applied are much older. They can be traced back to Daniel's vision of the beasts and to the 'contemptible person' of Dan. 11.21, and further back to Ezekiel's account of Gog and Magog (chs. 38, 39). The ideas are probably older still, and may derive from the Creation Myths, in the conflicts of the creator with Tehom or Tiamat, or with Leviathan. Naturally enough for a nation which so orientated itself on Jerusalem that the capture of Jerusalem represented a cataclysmic experience for the nation, the final conflict with Antichrist is also centred on Jerusalem or its neighbourhood (e.g. Dan. 11.45 'between the sea and the glorious holy mountain'; 2 Baruch 40.1f. 'they will take him up to Mount Zion'). So in the apocalyptic elements within the Gospel tradition, the 'desolating sacrilege' is linked with a prophecy of the destruction of the Jerusalem temple (Mark 13), a theme which is historicized by Luke in terms of the siege and fall of Jerusalem (Luke 21.20).

It is reasonable to look for an association with Jerusalem in the application of the Antichrist imagery in Rev. 11, especially if, with many scholars, one detects an earlier Jewish or Jewish-Christian apocalypse, preserved at this point in Revelation. At first sight the connection with Jerusalem is clear: 11.1–2 provides the context of the siege and fall of Jerusalem; 11.8 describes the setting, where the witnesses' bodies lie, as 'the street of the great city ... where their Lord was crucified'; and thirdly, by a more recondite argument from 11.13, if the figure of seven thousand killed in the earthquake is a strict continuation of the decimation of the city, then a total of 70,000 inhabitants might be an appropriate figure for Jerusalem.[48] So the most obvious reference of the location in 11.8 is to '*that* Jerusalem which had killed the prophets and crucified the Messiah' (Matt. 23.29–31, 37f.; Luke 13.33f.; 21.20–4).

But 11.8 offers two further designations of the city which are intended to be understood *pneumatikōs*, that is, spiritually; this must refer to a deeper meaning than the surface, or literal, one (cf. the use of *sarkikōs* in Justin *dial*. 14, and the contrast *kata sarka*, *kata pneuma* in Rom. 1.4).[49] These names are 'Sodom' and 'Egypt'. In Isa. 1.9, 10 Jerusalem and its rulers are compared with Sodom and its rulers (cf. Isa. 3.9; Ezek. 16.46ff.; Martyrdom of Isaiah 3.10; Rom. 9.29). Sodom's reputation of rebellion and moral degradation and the utter ruin that resulted are presumably in mind (cf. 2 Pet. 2.6, Jude 7). In the Gospel tradition Sodom is compared favourably with Capernaum in its response to Jesus (Matt. 11.24), and with the cities of Israel who reject the Christian missionaries (Matt. 10.15; Luke 10.12). Although the comparison is applicable to Jerusalem at its worst, it is also employed more widely in contexts of rebellion against God and judgement on evil. Egypt is naturally understood in Israel's tradition as a place of captivity, and the recollection of the Exodus from Egypt could be employed by Deutero-Isaiah, to bring hope in a subsequent situation of captivity, in Babylon. 'It is virtually certain that by John's day Egypt had become a typological name for all anti-theocratic world kingdoms' (cf. R. Jose b. Chalaphta – 'All kingdoms are called by the name Egypt because they enslave Israel'; cf. Str.-B.3.812). There are precedents also for the combination of references to Sodom and Egypt as examples of evil. Amos 4.10–11 couples punishments like the plagues brought against

Egypt with the punishment of Sodom. There are allusions in Wisd. 19.10ff. to similar themes.

The city is called *hē polis hē megalē* (11.8); in every other instance in Revelation 'the great city' refers to Babylon (identified as Rome) – 16.19; 17.18; 18.10, 16, 18, 19, 21. If this expression refers to Rome in every other instance, while Jerusalem, old and new, is described as 'the holy city' (11.2; 21.2, 10; 22.19) or 'the beloved city' (20.9), it is reasonable to suppose that 11.8 also refers to Rome, especially when the examples of parallel usage of *megalē* for Jerusalem, cited by commentators, are not reassuring.[50] Perhaps we ought to look again at the total identification made in 11.8: the only literally applicable name is 'the great city' or Rome; the other three names, 'Sodom', 'Egypt', and 'where their Lord was crucified' (i.e. Jerusalem in the evil context of that event) all follow that important word *pneumatikōs*. Therefore these three names, each in their own way symbolic of an evil, are applied to Rome, which, in the personification of Babylon the great harlot, epitomizes evil for the author.

The Antichrist legend, although its final working-out was located in or near Jerusalem, had for some time been associated also with Rome, as Rome had supplied the particular identifications of the general personification of the figure of evil. What seems to have happened in Revelation is a reapplication of this tradition in such a way that Rome's evil is 'brought home' to her, and results in her own destruction. The destruction of Jerusalem associated with this expectation in the Gospel tradition is now an historical fact; but the course of the 'just war' against evil has moved on – perhaps feelings aroused by Rome's participation in the destruction of Jerusalem have contributed to the zeal with which that war is undertaken – so that it must now work itself out in the anticipated destruction of Rome (Rev. 18). Rev. 11 could represent, both historically and thematically in the mind of the writer, the transition stage in this reapplication. The historical context is set by 11.1–2, with its reference to the siege and fall of Jerusalem. But now the expectation about Jerusalem is being transformed into a future hope about the glorious New Jerusalem, the holy city of Rev. 21, 22. It may be that Jerusalem will still provide the setting for a final conflict, but this is only expressed in terms of a survival of the Gog/Magog tradition set around 'the beloved city' (20.7–10). Within the main theme of the book, the last and most awful manifestation of Antichrist, in the beast of chs. 13 and 17, is linked indissolubly with Rome, personified as Babylon the harlot.

This shift of location which brings Rome's evils home to her is accomplished very neatly, and it is the two witnesses who, by virtue of their origin and identification, provide the focus of this reorientation. The witness who 'came up with Jesus from Galilee to Jerusalem' and the witness who saw the vision of Christ on the Damascus road, these two who, according to tradition, came to Rome and were martyred there in the reign of Nero, in themselves supply the connecting link. The Lord, crucified in Jerusalem, is the model of the Christian witness; Peter and Paul, in following this example, carried their witness to the heart of the Roman Empire. The Seer, in recalling this episode at this point, sets the scene for his account of the last manifestation of Antichristian bestiality by the power of Rome; and the record of Nero prepares the way for the expectation of 'Nero Redivivus'.

Most of the arguments for the setting of Rev. 11.3–13 in Jerusalem rather than Rome (such as those raised by Charles)[51] have already been answered, at least by implication. The reference to Jerusalem in 11.2 fits well in our present account. A connection between Moses and Elijah and Rome would admittedly be strange, but the imagery used of these Old Testament figures has been reapplied to a new situation which connects up with Rome as well as with Jerusalem. The expression 'those who dwell on the earth' (11.10), far from limiting the reference to one country (Israel) refers to the non-Christian world (cf. 3.10; 6.10; 8.13; 13.8, 12, 14; 17.2, 8) who are 'from the peoples and tribes and tongues and nations' (11.9). The relevance of the figure of seven thousand in 11.13 is highly debatable, and it has not been proved to be exactly one-tenth of Jerusalem's estimated population. The most important aspect of this feature of the story may be the affected proportion ($\frac{1}{10}$) compared with one-quarter (the fourth seal – 6.8) and one-third (the trumpet plagues – cf. 8.7). If the force of this progression can be pressed, this would indicate an event which actually preceded the opening of the seals, thus supporting the argument for a 'flash-back' in ch. 11. Finally the argument from an original document preserved in this passage, while opening up possibilities for further consideration in connection with the suggested reapplication of the Antichrist legend, is too speculative to carry much weight, and in any case need not affect a judgement on the final author's intentions.

We can now draw together the main points discussed. From the context of ch. 11 come the indications, firstly that here is material with a Jewish 'atmosphere', especially in the measuring of the temple in 11.1–2; secondly that this material is closely linked with the final appearance of Antichrist; and thirdly it is suggested that the author is interpreting a significant past event. All these points are borne out in the proposed solution which, in turn, satisfies five principal requirements from the text itself. In this situation the word *martus* can begin to indicate the consequences, in suffering and martyrdom, as well as the action of bearing witness; it is then possible that a Christian example is presented of Peter and Paul as martyrs. The imagery from Zechariah refers to those with a royal and priestly function within the Christian Church and in particular to a pair of key figures who were 'the eyes of the Lord' to the world. Peter and Paul represent the foundation on which the association of Moses and Elijah in a context of suffering and death can be built. There is continuity and essential identity between Nero, as the beast of ch. 11, and 'Nero Redivivus', as the beast of chs. 13 and 17. And finally the combination of the symbolic 'cities' behind the setting of Rome represents the result both of the historical activity of Peter and Paul and of the reinterpretation of the Antichrist tradition.

The scroll open in the hand of the angel introduces the 'interlude' and provides an occasion for an historical 'flash-back'. The scene is the siege and fall of Jerusalem, the forty-two months of the Flavian war from A.D. 67 to 70 which the Seer reinterprets in accordance with his overall theme. Then the scene changes, moving further back, but pausing at the closely related episode of the witness of Peter and Paul in Rome, their witness and their martyrdom in the 1260 days from A.D. 64 to 67/8. Within this account, with its traditional and historical allusions, there is also a reference back to a more distant event, the Crucifixion in Jerusalem, an event which provided the example that Christ's martyrs are following. The 'interlude' ends with the earthquake,[52] and then the seventh trumpet sounds. But the third woe, the manifestation of Antichrist, is anticipated by a triumphant assertion of the reality of God's power; this offers reassurance that, however dark the hour of Antichrist may seem, in truth all power is vested in God and this is the moment he has chosen for 'the kingdom of the world' to 'become the kingdom of our Lord and of his Christ, and he shall reign for ever and ever' (11.15). Before the beast actually rises from the sea, the

Seer provides further explanation, in historical and in cosmic terms, of the circumstances which have brought about this final and most bitter earthly manifestation of Antichrist. So John introduces the portent of 'a woman clothed with the sun'.

5

The Woman Clothed with the Sun

Rev. 12 has often been used as a source-book for comparisons with other religious traditions, as was indicated in my introduction. It has also provided two other areas of debate: a comparison with the Qumran Thanksgiving Hymn 1QH3, and a persistent identification, largely by Roman Catholic and Eastern Orthodox scholars, of the Woman with the Virgin Mary. It would be desirable, therefore, to establish at the outset some principal criteria which must be satisfied for any interpretation to be viable.

The identification proposed should be consistent with itself, unless the text indicates that the symbols are ambivalent, and the overall picture should be true to that of the text, without blurring any clear distinctions, or destroying any emphases. The text should be interpreted as it stands, unless there is weighty textual evidence to the contrary, and the concepts expressed should be 'in period' and credible for the writer's situation. Only as a last resort, and then on the basis of adequate evidence, should any part of the passage be passed over as an example of traditional material incorporated without reinterpretation by the apocalyptist, and assumed, therefore, to have no meaning in the present context. Once this method of exegesis, favoured by R. H. Charles,[1] becomes authenticated, there is the real danger that it may merely provide the easy way out in a difficult passage.

If an Old Testament theologian were to produce a parallel volume to P. S. Minear's *Images of the Church in the New Testament*,[2] a significant portion of the work would have to be devoted to the picture of Israel as a woman. This is conveyed in a variety of ways, from the expressions 'daughter' or 'virgin daughter' of Zion, Jerusalem, Judah, or 'my people',[3] to the view of God's covenant with Israel as a marriage bond.[4]

The imagery can be extended by referring to the sufferings of the people as those of a woman in childbirth.[5] It appears that the Septuagint as well as the Dead Sea Scrolls enlarged on this figure of Israel as a woman; this seems to show that the imagery was increasingly popular towards the end of the Old Testament period. The imagery of passages such as Isa. 7 and 9 may be brought into association here, although there is no evidence that these were understood in any corporate sense, of the nation as a whole, in their original context; the references require an individual woman, whether one from current history or an ideal figure in the future, by whose agency the all-important sign is given, in the child who is born.[6]

Nowhere in the Old Testament is there any clear indication that the figure of Israel as a virgin daughter falls into any category of thought about the 'one' and the 'many', of a deliberate transference of ideas from a corporate to an individual sense, so that the 'virgin' people would one day be represented by one particular Virgin Daughter still to come. At one stage removed from this is the thought of the ideal Israel as a Remnant, perhaps preserved and embodied in a special community, a thought such as can be demonstrated from the Qumran Hodayoth. The image of childbirth with its pains is one of a complex of confused and interwoven images describing the sufferings of Israel in 1QH 3.[7] The setting suggests the emergence of a redeemed Israel through such trials and suffering, which are a description of persecution (whether by the Seleucids or by Rome). Even if the comparison between 1QH 3 and Rev. 12 is drawn no more positively than this, it can be said that Revelation represents an extension and further development of imagery from the Old Testament tradition, applied to the true Israel and its place in God's purpose. As some measure of confirmation that the Old Testament is a source of at least part of this imagery, Rev. 12.2–5 contains allusions to Isa. 66.7 and 26.17f.

There is of course far more to the picture of the woman in Rev. 12 than her being in labour and bearing a child. The first feature to note is that the woman, like the dragon, appears as a sign in heaven; it is not necessary to assume from this that all subsequent action takes place there. The earth is brought in specifically in the casting down of the dragon; it is probable that the desert also is on earth, to judge from v. 14 if not from v. 6. The casting of Satan from heaven to earth is a significant feature of the chapter, and the introduction of the characters 'in heaven' may merely serve to heighten the effect. Satan, as the book of Job (1.6f., 2.1) shows, originally had a place in heaven. The fact that the woman also appears in heaven might, but does not necessarily, indicate a divine or semi-divine person; it

could equally well mean that an ideal, rather than an actual historical, figure is indicated. Further, since in the context of the book as a
whole and in the theology of the Christian Church, although not in
this chapter as it stands, the most significant feature is the birth of
the child, the heavenly origin of this child could be expressed by
introducing the mother as a figure in heaven.

What is the meaning of the description of the woman in terms of
the sun, moon, and stars? The obvious first comment is that these
are appropriate decoration for the woman who is introduced as a
sign in heaven. The twelve stars could be symbols corresponding to
the twelve signs of the zodiac,[8] but in a context where Old Testament reminiscences are more than possible, they could stand for the
twelve tribes of Israel. One is reminded of the account of Joseph's
second dream in Gen. 37.9 where he sees the sun, the moon and the
eleven stars bowing down to him. The Hebrews were conscious of
the dangers of worshipping the heavenly bodies (Deut. 4.19), but
this did not mean that they disregarded them; as potent symbols
they were subordinated to the worship of Yahweh (e.g. Pss. 19.1–6;
104.19; 148.3f.). There are passages which display an inclination to
decorate ideal or representative figures with the imagery of the
heavenly bodies (e.g. Test.N. 5.3–4; Song of Sol. 6.10). God himself is described as 'sun and shield' (Ps. 84.11) – this idea is
expanded in Rev. 21.23 and 22.5; and of the Christ in triumph, in
the vision of Rev. 1, it is said 'and his face was like the sun shining in
full strength' (1.16 – this being a quotation from Judg. 5.31 where it
is applied, as an image, to the friends of the Lord God).[9] These ideas
would seem to be quite possible in a description of the nation of
Israel, in an idealized form, playing the role purposed by God.

To say this is not to deny the possibility of other influences on the
creation of this picture, for our immediate interest is with the
author's application of this material within the context of his own
thought. It is credible that he should have depicted Israel in these
terms. He may conceivably have chosen these images to paint some
ideal picture which his readers could contrast with, or recognize as a
striking parody of, the trappings of worship of the Emperor and the
spirit of Rome, or religious cults of Greek or Eastern origins, in
particular the local cult of Artemis of Ephesus, the mother goddess.
He may well have used some source for this chapter, possibly of
pagan origin, perhaps because he wished to point a lesson from a
myth familiar to his readers. These questions warrant investigation,

although it is probable that evidence is insufficient for anyone to do more than express a preference. What is important for the moment is the tracing of a line of interpretation that may represent the primary intention of the author in using this material. According to computer studies it appears that this chapter, alone in the book, may not owe its written form to the author of the book. Such an assessment may only represent a difference in degree from what might be said about other material in the book, in that here the author has taken over a block of tradition ready-cast from another source, whereas in other cases traditional ideas may have been handled by the author, but cast in their present form by himself.

Whereas it may not be either Jewish or Christian thinking to refer to the Mother of the Messiah as 'clothed with the sun', it is at least possible that material, expressed in a foreign manner, can be understood in a Jewish or Christian way, because the concepts employed can find some echo in Jewish or Christian ideas.[10] This would seem to be the reason why the author made use of them, because he found that what he wished to say at this point could be expressed through them.

When we turn to consider the statement about the birth of the child, it is equally true to say that this passage is not understandable as material of Christian origin, if it passes over the life and death of Christ, moving directly from the birth to the taking up of the child to God and his throne.[11] Despite the intervening quotation from Ps. 2.9, it hardly seems to do justice to the Jewish Messianic hope either. But we should be prepared for just such a lack of clarity in expression, and a picture which does not correspond precisely with what we might expect in the light of Christian theology; yet, to explain its use by the author, there are points which can carry Christian ideas, imperfect and inadequate though the forms of expression may be. It seems reasonable to conclude that the birth of Jesus Christ is intended by the figure of the birth of the child, and, because of the nature of the material, the bald reference, and the idea of the dragon's hostility, have to stand for the reality of the Incarnation. The taking up of the child to God can represent the immunity of Christ to the temptations of the devil, and, if the link with thoughts such as those of the Fourth Gospel is sufficiently strong, it may also suggest the exaltation of Christ in glory on the cross,[12] as well as his Resurrection and Ascension.

It might be possible to interpret the birth as other than the human birth of Christ (e.g. as the birth of the Messiah in heaven, in anticipation of the Parousia)[13] but unless such theories can offer a far better explanation of the material, it seems reasonable to conclude that the figure of birth represents the Incarnation, Christ's birth among the Jews, the chosen people of God. The Gospels do not dispute that Jesus was in his earthly life a full Jew; Matthew and Luke are both concerned to trace his descent through the royal Davidic house with which Messianic hopes were associated (Matt. 1.1ff.; Luke 3.23ff.). So Jesus' coming to earth can be depicted, in summary form, by the symbol of a divine birth from the ideal mother, the daughter of Zion. It is open to debate as to how far one can assimilate the woman, as the ideal picture of Israel, to an individual, historical woman, Mary, who was chosen as the mother of Christ. In the circumstances of this chapter, one cannot expect to find references to Bethlehem, or the details of the Gospel records of the Nativity.

It has been argued that the birth is a torment, as here depicted, and therefore this cannot represent any physical birth through Mary, since such a picture would not agree with the New Testament teaching about the Virgin Birth and its subsequent theological development. This argument may have some validity, but it would be dangerous to press it, since one may be guilty of reading back ideas that belong to a later, more precise stage of doctrine. It is, however, possible to do justice to the imagery of the birth woes, in terms of the national, rather than the individual, interpretation. One might observe, without necessarily placing much weight upon it, that the birth pains and the act of giving birth are separated in the narrative by the account of the dragon's appearance. The woes could be regarded as one of the characteristics of the woman, like the crown of stars, employed as pointers to her identity, because of their Old Testament associations. Israel is seen in her heavenly characteristics and her sufferings – 'heavenly' in the ideal form of God's plan; 'sufferings' in the actual historical setting of the moment under foreign domination. Or it may well be that the basic theological picture of Israel is not merely the image of a woman, but actually the image of a pregnant woman, which would indicate both her potential in God's purpose and the inevitability of suffering (the Messianic woes) in the execution of that purpose.[14] From a Christian viewpoint it may also be said that the birth can be torment for Israel, the old 'chosen people'. The birth of the Messiah for whom they had hoped brought them distress; he was not as they expected, and so in blindness they rejected him, and have given up their prerogatives as God's chosen people in favour of the new Israel, the Church.

The second character in the heavenly vision, the great red dragon, must be considered with due regard to its association with the beast of chs. 13 and 17. A fairly close connection must be assumed, because of the features common to all the descriptions. At the same time, account must be taken of the identifications provided within this chapter, particularly in v. 9. It might still be argued that the material in this chapter has been derived from more than one source (as R. H. Charles did in his commentary).[15] But whether a source is used in this chapter or not, whether the material comes from one source or several, the very fact that these ideas were associated together by the author, when he grouped them in his book and allowed the connecting links to be apparent, must mean that an interpretation is justified in taking these ideas together, where the links exist.

The dragon is, according to Rev. 12.9, 'the devil' or whatever other name one may choose to call him. The point of v. 9 is to blend together the various names and characteristics by which he has been known in tradition, and is recognized in human life, and to add to this a further and immediately relevant characterization. Just as Satan was at work throughout the Old Testament, from the activity of the serpent in the garden of Eden (Gen. 3), so he is now very much at work in the current, or anticipated, hostilities to the Christian Church. His diabolical powers have taken as their current disguise, or have been delegated in a certain form to, the beast as the symbol of the Roman Empire. The relation between dragon and beast appears closer and more intricate than the simple relation of chief devil to subordinate demon, and more like the merging of one diabolical image or manifestation into another; this is demonstrated by the close parallelism of their attributes (12.3; 13.1; 17.3).

The association of the serpent (*ophis* – in LXX a land creature)[16] with water in the concept of the sea-monster (*drakōn*) offers further scope for mythological ideas to develop, since there is little doubt that the Hebrews agreed with the common tradition that the seas represent the powers of chaos, though the extent to which they applied this tradition can be exaggerated. The monster from the sea is a personalization of the impersonal powers of the waters. This it is which Yahweh is believed to have subdued, in accordance with the tradition of the conflict between the deity and the dragon of chaos. Perhaps it is in this context that the stream of water disgorged from the serpent's mouth in v. 15 is to be understood. It is noticeable how the variation between 'serpent' and 'dragon' in vv. 13–16 maintains the synthesis of v. 9.

In the New Testament there appears to be no substantial distinction between the words *diabolos* and *Satanas*, in spite of their difference in origin.[17] There hardly seems to be any particular reason for the alternation of the terms in the Fourth Gospel and Revelation, beyond the feeling that by such variation the fullness of the ideas might be expressed. The Old Testament idea of the Satan as the accuser in heaven, shown by the book of Job (1.9ff., 2.4f.), is in the background of the present thought, in that the theme of this chapter is the fall of Satan from such a justifiable post of responsibility ('the accuser' – Rev. 12.10) to a situation where he terrorizes the earth. The final title 'the deceiver of the whole world' again may refer to the serpent of the Fall, although the verb used is *planaō* rather than *apataō* which seems more usual in the Fall context (LXX – Gen. 3.13).[18] But the use of *planaō* introduces a special significance to this expression, because of its later-Jewish and in particular its apocalyptic background. Deception – the leading astray of those buoyed up with eager expectations – is a characteristic feature of the Last Days (cf. Mark 13.6//s; 2 Thess. 2.11).

An illuminating parallel to this whole passage can be traced in Isa. 26 and 27. The quotation in Rev. 12.2 of words from Isa. 26.17f. has already been noted. Not only does this section make use of the image of childbirth, and the next section refer to the idea of hiding for a little while, until the wrath is past (like the woman who is carried by the eagle to safety in the wilderness), but also the following verses at the start of ch. 27 provide a comparable variety of names for the creature of evil whom the Lord will punish: 'In that day the Lord with his hard and great and strong sword will punish Leviathan the fleeing serpent, Leviathan the twisting serpent, and he will slay the dragon that is in the sea.' It is, at the least, possible that the current arrangement of ideas in Rev. 12 may owe something to this section of the collected prophecies of Isaiah. This is an example of how these various ideas could be associated.

The section comprising vv. 7–12 has the general appearance of being an extended parenthesis. This impression is given by the disjointed effects at the beginning and end of the section; by the uncertainty as to where the war in heaven might fit in the historical phases outlined in the remainder of the chapter; and by the recapitulation of v. 6 in v. 14, as if there was a danger that the connections of thought might have been severed by this apparent digression. Austin Farrer sees vv. 7–12 as an extended comment on the previous verses and in particular on the sky-raking in v. 4.[19] These points are not central to the myth which is being utilized, the myth of the birth of the child, but are none the less significant and deserving of development in that they set the main theme against a larger background. They serve to show the broader effect that the principal sequence of events has on Satan's sphere of operations.

Satan loses his position in heaven because of Christ's Incarnation and its consequences, which set up a new relationship between man and God, that could effectively bypass Satan's role within the heavenly council, as the Old Testament understood this. In New Testament thought there was no place for an independent Director of Public Prosecutions! This change in attitude towards man's relationship with God, particularly with reference to the concept of the Last Judgement, was expressed in terms of the banishment from heaven of Satan and his henchmen. It was intelligible that Satan should be angry at the loss of this sphere of power and authority, and this would inevitably cause repercussions in such spheres of authority as remained open to him. So not only does the earthly activity of Christ bring about Satan's fall,[20] but also Satan's fall itself brings about the persecution threat to the woman and her seed, in circumstances where Satan's power and sphere of authority is manifested under the guise of the enforcement of Emperor-worship. Such, in outline, is the relationship of the account of the Fall of Satan to the sequence of events in this chapter, which explains why this theme is introduced here. But we must emphasize that this theme is not developed merely within this particular sequence of events; if it were, it could be set down in terms of the child, rather than Michael, casting down Satan to the earth, and be treated as just one more phase in the sequence. But this would leave mankind as the victims of Satan's anger; Christ's victory would be accomplished, and only heaven would be affected by its realization.

But the victory in heaven is won by Michael and his angels, not directly by Christ.[21] This represents a transitional stage in which the devil's anger is increased, simply because he knows that he has only a little time left to him (v. 12). This passage is applied optimistically by the present author, because he moves on from here to the final stage, the ultimate victory of Christ (Rev. 19 where the Messiah and his hosts conquer the beast and the kings of the earth). Thereby the victory is realized for earth as well as heaven. In Apocalyptic literature the Archangels, frequently referred to under a variety of proper names, are made responsible for carrying out definite aspects of the divine will. So here Michael, quite consistently, accomplishes the first stage in Satan's repulse. It could be said that this restriction of Satan's activities occurs simultaneously with the birth of Christ. Satan loses this power as a result of the child's birth, and because he failed to prevent or annul it. This is the divine purpose, part of which Michael has executed.

A significant feature of the description of the dragon at his first appearance (v. 4) is the manner in which he sweeps a third of the stars from heaven with his tail. The background of this idea may well be in the goat's horn (Dan. 8.10) which casts some of the host of stars to the ground and tramples on them, but there may also be a measure of irony in the description, because in the setting of this chapter the dragon anticipates, by his activity, his own defeat – the stars which fall from heaven could correspond to Satan and his angels.[22]

A review of this section cannot be concluded without a brief consideration of vv. 10–12. The great voice from heaven utters what could be described as a hymn. Passages of this type are scattered through Revelation. What seems most notable about this one is its apparent inappropriateness in this particular context; were it not for v. 12, which reads like a strenuous attempt to bring the material round to the subject-matter in hand, the passage would be far more relevant in the context of the final victory in ch. 19. It is true that 12.10 refers to Satan the accuser; but the reference is not made explicitly to the War in Heaven. The themes expressed certainly serve as an introduction to the chapters which follow; it is not unusual for these hymns to be placed, because of the reassurance they offer, in anticipation of what they celebrate, but in that case v. 12 points back again rather abruptly to the immediate situation. One would hardly expect a hymn, celebrating the achievement of Michael, that would cut across monotheistic preconceptions. But v. 11 does not even seem applicable to Michael, but rather to the Christian martyrs who have resisted the worst that Satan can contrive. If we conclude that this hymn is appropriate to the theme of Revelation as a whole, it would be possible to say that it is applied here in the midst of mythological material, because this kind of hymn of praise seemed to be demanded by the context.

The woman encountering the serpent could stand as the personification of Israel, the daughter of Zion, the counterpart of Eve. It seems possible for this figure to be identified with Mary the mother of Jesus; but the evidence falls short of proof either that the theme of the representative woman had been developed in this way, or that the earliest Church saw Mary in this light.[23] It would be possible to go further, if the Early Church saw Mary as the ideal representative of themselves; but this would be to make of the woman a kaleidoscope of interpretations, when such fluctuations are scarcely indicated by the text.

The first question should surely be whether it is possible to make consistent sense of the woman as a symbol for Israel, the nation from which Christ came, throughout this chapter. It is certainly possible to say, when the Christian Church is first introduced as the 'rest of the woman's seed' in v. 17, that this corresponds to historical reality, since the Church, like the Christ in his earthly life, had physical origins within Judaism. One might say that this is a late stage in the development of the themes of this chapter at which to introduce the Christian Church. But it certainly serves well to lead into the following chapters, and, in the context of an historical introduction setting the scene for the final stages of persecution of the Church, it fits admirably.

What sense can we then make of the woman as carried into the desert by an eagle, preserved by God from the dragon, protected from the dragon's river that threatens to sweep her away? We must first look at the details of the picture. The eagle in the Old Testament was a symbol of swiftness, of God's protection of his people, or an expression of what is unattainable to man, yet within the control of God. In the ancient world generally the eagle has associations with, or acts as a symbol for, deities (e.g. Zeus uses an eagle as a messenger).[24] An attractive interpretation based on the Old Testament background is that here is a kind of Exodus from a power even fiercer than the Egyptians – 'You have seen what I did to the Egyptians, and how I bore you on eagles' wings and brought you to myself' (Exod. 19.4). Like (or as) Israel, the woman was carried on an eagle's wings to the safety of the desert. It might also indicate a transplantation for political purposes (cf. Ezek. 17.3ff.) by an agent of the divine plan (the king of Babylon).[25]

The woman's destination ('the place' – 12.14) seems surprisingly precise; the definite article serves to refer the reader back to the place mentioned in 12.6 – this is 'a' place, but it is a place prepared by God, and therefore a precise reference. The only other occasion in the New Testament on which the words *hetoimazō* and *topos* occur together is in John 14.2f. (but cf. 1 Chron. 15.1 – LXX); it is not necessary to conclude that the place prepared by God for the woman must be in heaven, and that therefore this is an indirect reference to the Assumption of Mary. Previously this chapter has referred to an exaltation to heaven as being 'taken to God and his throne' (v. 5); if a comparable 'rescue operation' were here envisaged one might expect similar terminology.

The woman is to be cared for in her place of refuge for 'a time, and times, and half a time' or 1260 days. This 3½-year period, expressed in these ways, and as forty-two months (the period also of the trampling of the holy city by the nations in Rev. 11.2) is a common feature in apocalyptic literature (cf. Dan. 7.25; 12.7) as an expression for the time of tyranny until the end comes, and also for the period of the earthly glory of the righteous until God draws all to a close, in short for the period of eschatological crisis. If the Exodus motif is important here (cf. the eagle), then the 42-month period might also correspond to the forty-two years of Israel's wilderness wandering.

We should note that this period starts when Satan tries to attack the woman, is prevented from this, and in disappointment goes off to persecute the rest of her seed, the Church. This, presumably, is the last short period of earthly activity which Satan is allowed. And throughout this period the woman is shielded from his attacks. In effect this points a contrast between the woman and the Christian Church, within the context of Revelation as a whole. The Church suffers Satan's attacks, but the woman is shielded from them; the woman is preserved from the ordeal, while the Church submits to it, but is prepared for it, and sealed by God, so that she will not be harmed spiritually. God calls some at least of his Church to martyrdom; it is in view of this apparently inescapable fact that the author writes his message of exhortation to the Church.

The fourth detail of this passage to be examined is the river of water from the serpent's mouth. We have already seen that water could be associated with the power of evil, particularly in the figure of the sea-monster; from this it is a credible development that one way for the monster to express hostility would be to spout water, aiming to overwhelm his enemies. An Old Testament passage, to which allusion may be made in v. 16, is Num. 16.32 (the episode recalled is the swallowing up of Korah's rebellious faction by the earth). Interesting, from the point of view of Exodus imagery, is the possible anachronistic allusion to this episode in the Song of Moses (Exod. 15.12). The real point of contact in the Old Testament imagery could only be that God so protects his people from danger, by not allowing them to be engulfed by the waters.

R. H. Charles recognized that if the source for the narrative at this point were Jewish, then the reference would be to the flight of Johanan ben Zakkai and other notable Jews to Jabneh, shortly before the Fall of Jerusalem.[26] Jabneh became the major centre of Jewish authority and scholarship in the years which followed Jerusalem's destruction. But Charles also said that if the source were Christian then the allusion would be to the flight of the Christian community in Jerusalem to Pella at about the same time. In both cases, he asserted, these verses are devoid of significance in their present context. The passage is a meaningless survival from an older source, because what was relevant to A.D. 70 now admits of no intelligible reinterpretation.

But might it not be conceivable that an author, quite possibly using an older source not of his own composition, wishes to include a passage, not merely out of an antiquarian interest in the preservation of old material, but because he can express his ideas thereby? If so, we must not surrender too easily in our search for a contemporary meaning in the work before us. It is also possible that the author may wish to make some historical reference, not confined to his present political situation, but tracing a pattern in past events as an introduction to the present. Furthermore, there have been already several indications, in an historical and theological sequence beginning with the birth of Christ, that the author's intention is to furnish some such historical introduction to the persecution of the Church in the period leading up to the Last Judgement. This last phase in which the author and his readers now find themselves had a definite starting-point, when the woman, pursued by the dragon, took refuge in the wilderness. If the material in this passage can be shown to have a relevance to A.D. 70, we are not bound to conclude that this relevance was confined to a previous source. At some time after A.D. 70 an author could look back upon the destruction of Jerusalem as the prelude to the final eschatological phase.

The identification of the woman's flight with that of the Christian community from Jerusalem to Pella has been supported by some commentators. But this does not provide a satisfactory solution; the Church at Jerusalem was not the mother of the Messiah, nor does it appear that the authority of the Jerusalem church in the early days, as suggested by the narrative of the Acts of the Apostles, persisted throughout the New Testament period, or was accepted by the other churches to the extent that they would refer to the Jerusalem church as their mother. The sentiments implicit in Gal. 4.25–26 may well represent a widespread Christian attitude which would preclude this possibility. The destruction of Jerusalem in A.D. 70 seems to have marked a significant decline, if not actually the end, for that Christian community. From a viewpoint perhaps twenty years on, it seems unlikely that an author would look back on the Pella settlement in the way that he looked at the flight of the woman.

Recent discoveries and theories about the sectarian character of Judaism suggest some candidates for the representative true Israel that has taken refuge in the wilderness, to escape the corruption of 'modern life', and the rule of Rome. The difficulty of making an identification with any one sect in this way is that, in all probability, only the sect itself would regard itself as the true Israel. One could not expect rival sects to agree on this. How, then, can one conceive of a writer in the Christian tradition, in which the relationship with the sectarian milieu of Judaism is to say the least debatable, choosing one sect to identify in this way, confident that all his readers would be able to share his feelings and interpret his allusion correctly?

This difficulty does not arise if the identification is made with the flight of the Jewish scholars to Jabneh. Because it was the private property of the Roman Emperor, R. Johanan ben Zakkai asked Vespasian or Titus for permission to go there; he favoured it since it was Roman property and already had the traditions of an independent Sanhedrin by virtue of the city's special government.[27] With the new influx of scholarship it became the widely acknowledged centre of Judaism in exile, and the Sanhedrin continued to meet there up till the outbreak of the second Jewish Revolt in 132. The school of Jewish learning there was regarded as having great authority; Johanan and his fellow teachers seem to have succeeded in their aim to reconstruct there the spiritual fortress of Judaism.

'Jewish tradition long regarded Yohanan's settlement there as the crucial nexus in the orderly transmission of the authority of the Sanhedrin in Jerusalem to the rabbinical courts of later ages.'[28] It may be significant that the Sanhedrin met at Jabneh, in the time of Johanan, in a vineyard. This is usually interpreted figuratively: 'the Sanhedrin sat in rows similar to vines in a vineyard',[29] but a possible meaning, apart from the literal, geographical one, could be that they were conscious of a direct link with the Israel of the Old Testament (bearing in mind the symbolism of the vine in the Old and New Testaments).

After the revolt in A.D. 70 the official Roman attitude to the Jews was surprisingly lenient: 'people shrank from declaring war on the Jewish faith as such, and from driving the far-branching Diaspora to extremities'.[30] It is true that Jerusalem as a political and religious centre had suffered severely, and that Jewish losses in the revolt had been staggering – although the figures given were doubtless much exaggerated, they indicate the impression made upon contemporary observers. What Dio Cassius said of the later revolt – 'All of Judaea became almost a desert' – may well be applicable here, and is an interesting parallel to the imagery of Revelation at this point. But in spite of all this the Jews were far more fortunate than they might have expected, by virtue of the traditional Roman tolerance towards them and their religious customs,[31] and the Roman sense of justice which saw that the revolt had not been based on much more than the violent agitation of a minority.

Certainly the Jews were as vulnerable as the Christians to the extremism of an Emperor like Domitian, should he choose to enforce the action of sacrificing to the Emperor's genius as a test of loyalty; 'an emperor who demanded worship from his subjects might one day, like Gaius, demand it from the Jews too and revoke existing edicts of toleration'.[32] Both Jewish and Christian traditions claim Flavius Clemens and Domitilla as victims for their religion. Another Jewish tradition records that *c*. A.D. 95, when the Senate were debating a decree that would expel all Jews from the boundaries of the Empire within thirty-six days, R. Gamaliel II with some friends made a hurried winter journey to Rome, presumably to avert the threatened persecution and plead for the Jewish cause.[33] Nevertheless, as a general rule, the Jews were far more secure from such persecution, because of Roman toleration, than were the Christians who were, more and more obviously, no mere sect of Judaism, and consequently cut adrift from the protection Judaism could afford in these circumstances.

One can interpret Rev. 12.13–16 in the light of this background. The woman, as Israel, represents the nucleus of the nation, salvaged from the ruins of Jerusalem, which had built the new spiritual home of the nation at Jabneh. This is the place appointed in God's plan in which the Jewish nation, at least as a religious unit, can recover some of its strength.

The situation of Judaism after the revolt was a desert existence, set over against the glories of Jerusalem, their true religious home, around which all future hopes had centred. But the desert as a place of refuge is an Old Testament symbol from the Exodus tradition. Within that tradition the eagle is an appropriate symbol for the military might of Rome. It can function as a contemporary political agency (a king of Babylon) for the divine plan, conducting the Jews to an exile in Jabneh. In this place of refuge, with the continuing Roman policy of toleration, they were safe from the worst of hostility and persecution which Rome was to throw at the Church through the Satanic and bestial activities of Emperor-worship.

When under Domitian the threat of this kind of persecution loomed large again for the Jews, there was to hand some means of warding it off. Perhaps one may interpret the stream from the serpent's mouth as this kind of threat. Whether the picture is formed from traditional mythology, or perhaps from the natural imagery of a winter cloudburst which drains into the earth just in time before devastation is caused, it could symbolize some such event as R. Gamaliel II's hurried winter journey to Rome to plead that the threat might be averted. This measure was only made possible because of the divine plan that had preserved the continuity of the authoritative leadership of Judaism at Jabneh, and nourished it in difficult years.

This protection is offered to Judaism for as long as the phase of persecution for the Christian Church will last, until the period of crisis ends in the Final Judgement. Compared with some other parts of the New Testament, and with some interpretations, notably that of Eduard Schweizer,[34] placed on Revelation itself, this exegesis represents the author as holding quite an enlightened and tolerant view of Judaism. But in a Book which depicts the Christ in glory it is appropriate that the best and truest, the ideal remnant of Israel, the chosen people of God, represented in the image of the mother who gave birth to Christ on earth, should not come to an ignominious and unworthy end. The ideal figure of Israel (unlike those who claim to be Jews and are not, but are nothing less than agents of Satan) has a worthy place in the divine plan. In this respect, then, the author of Revelation agrees with Paul that God has by no means rejected his original chosen people; rather 'all Israel will be saved', when the full number of the Gentiles has been gathered in (Rom. 11.1, 25–6).

6
The Beast and the Harlot

That the historical method of interpretation for the symbolism of the Book of Revelation is unfashionable is nowhere more apparent than in most recent writing on the topic of the beast with seven heads. I am not sure that other methods of interpretation, taken by themselves, always lead to an improvement in exegesis, even if they do spare the reader from a total absorption in *gematria* and similar riddles, and indicate that there are broader issues involved in this imagery. In some instances the neglect of historical clues can be a definite change for the worse; the reader is left pondering general truths, divorced from the realities of a particular situation, so that even his natural questions about what prompted this piece of writing remain unanswered. Therefore, a reconsideration of the beast in Revelation should be alert to any real possibilities of historical reference suggested by the evidence, without becoming totally preoccupied with the search for historical slots into which to fit the material.

We need to recognize the full range of beast imagery employed in Revelation. It is clear that there are actually three beasts: the dragon, the beast from the sea, and the beast from the earth. In this chapter we are concerned chiefly with the second beast, whose identification remains problematic. But it is necessary to say something briefly about the other two beasts and their interrelationship.

The third creature, with two horns, is the traditional false prophet of the Last Days. He is given this title in Rev. 16.13 and 19.20. The form of the creature is probably derived from the two-horned ram of Dan. 8.3, although there is nothing in that context to suggest a false prophet. It may be, as Austin Farrer suggested,[1] that John merely adopted the next 'visionary creature' of Daniel after the fourth beast of ch. 7; but the ram-like appearance was suitable dress for a false prophet, in the light of Matt. 7.15, where the false prophet comes in sheep's clothing, although inwardly he is a ravening wolf.[2] The first creature, the dragon, is explicitly identified as 'that ancient serpent, who is called the Devil and Satan, the deceiver of the whole world' (Rev. 12.9). He is the accuser whose place is in heaven, but he has been thrown down to the earth, where he proceeds to make war on all those who bear testimony to Jesus.

These three beasts must not be distinguished too sharply without recognizing the kinship which exists between them. All three share in, and are motivated by, a power and authority which they have in common. This is why, according to Paul S. Minear, they all have horns, to symbolize this power. It is clear that the kinship does not consist merely in the common purpose and activity described in the visions of the Book of Revelation. There is a common mythological form of a bestial figure with seven heads which underlies the two distinct conceptions of Antichristian power in the dragon and the beast from the sea in chs. 12 and 13. And it is this figure of the beast which is treated in ch. 17 as a riddle which demands a solution. We may be able to learn from this example something about the author's method of handling his symbolism; he sketches the basic picture with broad strokes, and then highlights that part of it on which he wishes his readers to focus their attention.

The Greek word for 'beast' in this context in Revelation is *thērion*;[3] its original meaning is that of a 'wild animal' or an 'animal living wild'. The figurative use – what Liddell and Scott euphemistically call a 'term of reproach' – came quite easily to the Greek. Tit. 1.12 shows that it could be something of a proverbial expression, applied to Cretans – 'always liars, evil beasts, lazy gluttons'. In the Sibylline Oracles Nero is described as *thēr megas*, and Pliny the Younger refers to Domitian as *immanissima belua*. Apollonius of Tyana, according to Philostratus, called Nero a *thērion*.[4] The context shows that he was thinking of the metaphor of a beast of prey with claws and teeth, a carnivorous animal such as a lion or a panther. But the mere fact that the term could be used metaphorically, or even that it was used of a Roman Emperor, in particular of Nero, is not, by itself, any proof that the beast with seven heads in the Book of Revelation has to be Nero. It cannot, however, be excluded as a possible line of thought which may have influenced the author, if there were circles in which the term could be applied to a person, a figure of historical importance, even a particular Emperor.

Beasts and dragons are almost universal features of mythology. The beast with seven heads, rising from the sea, as described in Rev. 13, most closely and naturally recalls the vision of the four beasts in Dan. 7, but the imagery can undoubtedly be traced back much further than this. Heaton and Bentzen in their commentaries on Daniel, following up ideas derived ultimately from Gunkel, believe that the author draws heavily in ch. 7 upon the imagery of the Creation myth in its Babylonian form.[5] Other references to the Creation myth within the Old Testament are important for this background, especially Pss. 74.13ff.; 89.9ff., in which Leviathan and Rahab are understood to represent the primeval monster Tiamat of the Babylonian myth. Beasts coming from the sea signify the powers of Chaos as distinct from God's creation; in Ps. 74.13–14 God's triumph over the beasts is described as a major part of the activity of Creation. The Greek word *drakōn* is the usual rendering of 'Leviathan' in the Septuagint (Job 41; Pss. 74.14; 104.26; Isa. 27.1; but not Job 3.8). This would have seemed a more suitable Greek word for a sea-monster than *thērion* which was usually restricted to an animal based on land. Even if the Septuagintal choice of words were taken as decisive for the author of Revelation this would not, of course, exclude the Leviathan material from a consideration of the mythological background at this point. It is clear that, although there are two distinct episodes, two different contexts in Rev. 12 and 13, none the less there is a common mythological form behind the dragon and the beast from the sea, and what illuminates one may well shed some light on the other.

Where the Leviathan material could be especially helpful is with the description of both beast and dragon as having seven heads. Admittedly the beast of Revelation combines the features of all four beasts in Dan. 7, and the sum of their heads is seven. Yet Leviathan also has more than one head (Ps. 74.14); he is specifically described as seven-headed in Canaanite mythology, if we may assume that the material of this tradition can be traced back to the Ras Shamra texts, and the name 'Lotan' there corresponds to 'Leviathan' in the Old Testament. In the Baal myths of Ras Shamra, Anat tells how she 'muzzled the dragon' and has 'slain the crooked serpent, the foul-fanged with seven heads'. Later in the same myth it is said of Baal himself: 'Though thou didst slay Lotan the primeval serpent, didst make an end of the crooked serpent, the foul-fanged with seven heads.'[6] The identification of Leviathan with Lotan is reinforced by a comparison of this latter passage with Isa. 27.1 where the same qualifying adjectives are used: 'In the day the Lord ... shall punish Leviathan the primeval serpent, even Leviathan the crooked serpent, and he shall slay the dragon that is in the sea.'

One direct approach to the question of an historical identification of the beast is through the background to the riddle posed by the Seer in Rev. 17. V. 10 appears to furnish a precise clue to the dating of the book, or at least of this passage within it. But it would hardly be surprising if the detective work in following up this clue failed to produce any conclusive evidence. The one thing which the author did not need to tell his readers was the date at which he was writing; veiled hints from which they could recognize the facts of their own predicament would be all that was necessary.

One such hint is provided by the woman associated with the beast in Rev. 17.3; she is identified in v. 18 of the same chapter as 'the great city exercising kingship over the kings of the earth'. In v. 9 the seven heads which help to form a seat for the woman are identified as seven hills. This is a common feature of the Latin poets' description of the city of Rome. It seems, then, to be a reasonable assumption, from this cumulative evidence, that the woman represents the city of Rome; woman and city are otherwise referred to in Revelation as 'Babylon', and this corroborates the identification, as we shall see. It remains to be seen whether special reference is intended to any particular aspect of the city and its greatness. One consequence of this identification is the observation that, by this stage, the Antichrist tradition must have been severed from Jerusalem, where it was located at an earlier point within Judaism. (Rev. 11 may contain a remnant of this earlier tradition which has been reworked in a new context.) Now the Antichrist tradition is applied and reinterpreted in some relation to Rome and its anticipated destruction. The implication of this development, for the purposes of an historical dating of the Book of Revelation, is that Jerusalem has already fallen, and in the more distant past, so that it no longer figures in such an immediate way in the Seer's interpretation of eschatology (as it could in Luke 21.20).

The woman, Rome, relies on the beast with seven heads in the same way that the city rests upon its seven hills. But the text in 17.10 makes clear that the significance of these heads is greater than this. With this kind of material we need not be surprised if one symbol stands for several things, or several symbols have a single identification. The way that the symbols are handled in each particular context must be allowed to determine their special connotations. The heads are associated with the woman when they form a seat for her; but they must also be considered as what they are physically, an integral part of the beast. The heads bear 'a blasphemous name' (13.1), and the whole beast is described in 17.3 as being 'full of blasphemous names'. The natural historical interpretation of this blasphemy associated with Rome is in the context of Emperor-worship, where the names are the titles claimed or inherited by, or bestowed upon, the Emperor, names which could have religious overtones, or pretensions to divinity. If the author's thought is indeed working within this frame of reference, then the heads which represent 'seven kings' can most reasonably be identified with seven Roman Emperors. But, when this assumption is made, the problem of precise identification is only just beginning. None of the logical starting-points, on the basis of political history, for the counting of a sequence of seven Emperors is entirely satisfactory. It may help to tabulate the data in this way:

Julius Caesar	Augustus	Galba	Vespasian	Nerva
	Tiberius	Otho	Titus	Trajan
	Caligula	Vitellius	Domitian	Hadrian
	Claudius			
	Nero			

If the sequence starts from Julius Caesar, or Augustus, this would make Nero, Galba, or (if the unsuccessful rulers in the Year of the Four Emperors are discounted) Vespasian, the sixth in the sequence; but at such early dates one would not expect the reworking and diminution of the Jerusalem Antichrist tradition to have taken place. A start from one of the new dynasties (Vespasian or Nerva) brings a date that is really too late, on the grounds of other internal as well as external evidence for dating. If we start with Galba, Domitian can be the sixth; but the first of three unsuccessful claimants, in a year of civil war, does not seem a reasonable place to begin. If the author then does not count dynasties, and is hardly likely to produce a significant sequence by a process of random selection, the real possibility which remains is that he is counting 'Antichrist' figures, hostile to the Church, beginning from a particularly notable example. Nero would have the strongest claim for such an identification in this period, since, to judge from Tacitus,[7] he started a fashion in hostility, whether persecution of the Christians was then established on a legal basis or not. Each succeeding Emperor would presumably have to be counted in the sequence of seven, whether he was actively hostile to the Christians or not.

If Nero is the first, the sixth Emperor is Titus or Trajan, depending on whether the three 'pretenders' are to be included or omitted. There are arguments for and against including them; one can only be confident that either all or some must be included. It would be forcing the historical material to include only Galba, on the grounds that he was a 'Just Revolutionary', but to include two out of the three is impossibly arbitrary. Yet this would be required to achieve the 'correct' answer, that Domitian is the sixth Emperor who is now reigning as the author writes. External evidence for the dating of the book has generally followed the tradition of Irenaeus, that the Revelation 'was seen towards the end of' the reign of Domitian (Irenaeus, *haer.* 5.30.3). Is it possible, then, to make some kind of harmony out of the evidence and choose Trajan as the sixth Emperor of the sequence, taking Irenaeus as a somewhat inaccurate witness in favour of Trajan, since the end of Domitian's reign is nearer to the beginning of Trajan's than it is to the end of Titus' rule? Such a conclusion should not be adopted too readily without further evidence. The date of composition has been pushed on to the turn of the century. There is also an argument worthy of consideration that the later the date the more likely it is for a writer who is not too politically conscious to include the three 'pretenders' in his list of Emperors. These three did hold the office and title of Emperor, and could be given a place among the other Emperors by Suetonius, Josephus, and the Sibylline Oracles.[8]

In describing the first beast in ch. 13 the Seer writes: 'One of its heads seemed to have a mortal wound, but its mortal wound was healed' (13.3). If, despite the difficulties of particular identification that have been experienced, the general theory of the heads being Emperors is retained and tested against this aspect of the imagery, the implication is that one out of the succession of seven Emperors received a death-blow but has been restored miraculously to life. This, read in association with the ideas of 17.8 and 11, seems to provide a forcible reminder of the superstition that the Emperor Nero was not really dead but would return one day. A variety of commentators have believed that John was influenced by this Nero legend; but they differ in detail over the way they think he made use of it. H. B. Swete traced the explanation back as far as Victorinus of Pettau, the earliest of the Latin commentators.[9]

The wound, although at first in 13.3 it is assigned to one of the heads of the beast, is later, in vv. 12 and 14, assigned to the beast itself. But there could be such flexibility of reference if the beast symbolizes certain aspects of imperial rule and the beast's heads represent a succession of Emperors. The two may be interchangeable, because the imperial authority is vested in the individual Emperor. The heads being the successive members of the dynasties, the beast is actualized in only one of its heads at any one time; in the actual situation of a particular time the other heads need not exist for all normal intents and practical purposes; in fact they do not exist as Emperors, except in history and prophecy. The head which was wounded must be one of the first five, if the data from 17.10 can be utilized, since the wounding is represented as a past event. It would be a risky argument to say that, because in passages like Rev. 6.1 the author can use the cardinal 'one' to stand for the ordinal,[10] therefore to refer to 'seven heads' and 'one wounded' must mean that the first is wounded. But where hypotheses abound and arguments frequently are inconclusive, the apparent coincidence of the theme of 'wounded mortally yet returning', known to be associated with the figure of Nero and the fact that, independently, Nero was seen to be the most suitable starting-point for the sequence of Emperors, provides too promising a trail not to be followed.

Several factors contributed to the belief in a 'Nero Redivivus' – a superstition which flourished in the minds of many long after Nero's reported death: among them the circumstances of his death, with few witnesses; his personality, verging on the demonic, which made a profound impression; and his enthusiasm for the East, with his desire to transfer the capital of the Empire thither, a project supported by the prediction of astrologers that there would be a new, Eastern and almost Messianic, reign after his repudiation in Rome.[11] Following the report that Nero had cut his own throat with a sword at the villa of his freedman Phaon on 9 June 68, rumours spread that he had not actually died, but had somehow escaped to the East, from where he would soon return to regain his throne. Such rumours spread most quickly in the Eastern provinces, and often had a particular reference to Parthia (possibly fostered by that nation in its antagonism to Rome). The return of Nero from Parthia, with a huge army subduing all opposition, was envisaged: 'And to the west shall come the strife of gathering war and the exile from Rome, brandishing a mighty sword, crossing the Euphrates with many myriads.'[12] In these earlier stages the figure of Nero remains more or less human; there are records of at least two impostors who

appeared in the East, claiming to be the Emperor, and either
originating from, or encouraged by, Parthia. Tacitus records several
instances; Dio Cassius dates one in the reign of Titus, and Suetonius
may refer to the same one. In view of what we know about the early
Antichrist tradition, it is of interest that one account of the belief
states that Nero will make Jerusalem the seat of his new empire.[13]

The figure of 'Nero Redivivus' soon acquires supernatural attributes; at this later stage, his return from the abyss, with hordes of
demons, is awaited as an omen of the last days.

> There shall be at the last time, about the waning of the moon, a
> world-convulsing war, deceitful in guilefulness. And there shall
> come from the ends of the earth a matricide fleeing and devising
> sharp-edged plans. He shall ruin all the earth, and gain all power,
> and surpass all men in cunning. That for which he perished he
> shall seize at once. And he shall destroy many men and great
> tyrants, and shall burn all men as none other ever did.

He is seen as the 'dragon' having 'the form of a beast', and the
'terrible serpent' who would be borne through the air by the fates.
He was identified as 'Beliar the great king, the king of this world';
'he will descend from his firmament in the likeness of a man' and as
'Beliar of the Augustan house he will come . . . and raise up the dead
and perform many wonders for men'.[14] In this way 'Nero Redivivus'
has become assimilated into the mythology of Beliar and the serpent. Clearly these beliefs were still very much alive, and developed
in mythological directions, at the period when Revelation could
have been written, so that the author could apply the tradition to his
own particular purposes.

How can an actual physical wound, self-inflicted by Nero in the
past, affect the Empire now? How did Nero's death jeopardize the
power of the Empire, when he committed suicide as a fugitive and
an enemy of the state? Does not his death, far from threatening
imperial authority, in fact demonstrate the power of the state over
him? How can the rumours about 'Nero Redivivus' be said to have
enhanced the prestige of the beast and increased the worship of the
dragon, when, if anything, the legend of Nero's imminent return
from Parthia would have been seen as a threat to the empire and the
imperial dynasties? Minear finds such problems so destructive of
any historical interpretation in terms of 'Nero Redivivus' that he
writes: 'If we are to understand the wounded head, therefore, we

should look not so much for an emperor who died a violent death, but for an event in which the authority of the beast (and the dragon) was both destroyed and deceptively restored.'[15]

It is possible that these two events might still be equated, provided that the matter is not foreclosed, as it is by Minear, by an unexamined assumption that the beast would naturally be identified with the Roman Empire. The woman of ch. 17 stands, as has been seen, for the city of Rome set on the seven hills. But even that identification leaves open the possibility of a special reference to a particular aspect of the city and its greatness. The heads of the beast are seven emperors; but this does not make the simple and direct identification of the beast with the Empire obligatory, although it would be true to say that the city of Rome relies on her empire just as the woman sits on the beast.

If John is indeed depicting the Roman Empire as Antichrist, then his thought is diametrically opposed to the emphasis of Paul, in Romans especially, upon obedience to the powers that be – undeniably the Roman administration – as ordained of God.[16] It is not impossible that Paul and John should be in open disagreement, in the same way that it could be thought that Paul and James disagreed. The fashion of persecuting the Church, inaugurated by the Emperor Nero, would have brought about an almost complete change in the Christian environment, quite adequate to explain such a reversal of attitude. But there is another explanation which merits serious consideration, a possible harmonizing of these two apparently divergent views about Church and State, which does not need to emphasize the radical change in the historical situation to justify these opposing attitudes. It remains possible that Paul's and John's terms of reference were not identical, that Paul was concerned with the authority and political administration of the Empire, while John characterized as Antichrist that aspect of imperial organization most inimical to Christianity, the institution of Emperor-worship. In the situation of the last decades of the first century A.D. this institution would have been regarded as the concrete realization of the power hostile to God, the creation of Satan, a bestial parody, in the enforced worship of a deified man, of the only true worship of God through his Incarnate Son.

This more precise definition of the beast from the sea corresponds with two of the most distinctive aspects of the creature's characterization: the fact that, through the beast from the land, the false prophet, the inhabitants of the earth are made to worship the beast; and the description of the beast as 'full of blasphemous names' with 'a blasphemous name upon its heads' – the divine pretensions claimed by, or attributed to, the seven emperors. For the coherence of the imagery it would be equally true to say that, as the woman is supported by the beast, so the city of Rome is supported by the institution of Emperor-worship, or specifically by the worship offered to each of these seven emperors in turn, through which her empire is united in a common loyalty expressed in a common creed.

There are two aspects of Emperor-worship in the reign of Nero which are important for our purpose in understanding the symbolism of the Book of Revelation. The first is the notable contribution which Nero made to the development of Emperor-worship, especially as this was seen by the Christian Church. On these grounds Nero could be characterized as the figure of Antichrist or, more precisely, a major contributor to the historical realization of Antichrist, as the inaugurator of persecution of the Christians. And the second is the aspect symbolized by the wound. The suicide of the Emperor – and this self-administered and normally fatal blow recalls the historical circumstances which made it inevitable: the indecision and inaction, the artistic aberrations which alienated support – betrays an intrinsic weakness in this whole philosophy of Emperor-worship. Nero's suicide is the wound in the head; it is also the wound of the beast – the imperial cult – because it is the demonstration of a weak link in the chain, which shows how the institution contains within itself the seeds of its own destruction. And this weakness which Nero demonstrated applies not only to the weakness of character shown by the suicide, but also to the weakness, from the point of view of the cult instituted as a political instrument by Augustus, of artistic exaggeration, the affectation of the trappings of oriental despotism, and the tendency to megalomania, which would be as able as any physical weakness might be to bring the institution to destruction. And such a wound to the beast can also be regarded as a wound to the dragon who shares the characteristics of the beast, inasmuch as the beast's authority is derived from the dragon and any reversal suffered by the beast has similar repercussions for the dragon. So Satan and the powers at enmity with God are adversely affected by the failure of Nero, the condemnation of his memory, and the exposure of inherent weaknesses and blasphemous pretensions in the imperial cult. Because

Nero committed suicide as a fugitive and enemy of the state, he did not, it is true, jeopardize the power of the Empire directly. It can even be said that his death demonstrated the power of the Empire over him. But it did jeopardize that power indirectly; we have observed how this is true of the imperial cult in a way that is highly significant for our purposes; the truth can also be summed up more generally in the words of Rostovtzeff: 'Above all, Nero . . . entirely destroyed the prestige of the Augustan dynasty.' [17]

As Minear observed, in John's presentation it is the healing of the wound which enhances the prestige of the beast; it encourages the beast, leads to greater blasphemy, and impels men to worship the dragon. If the beast stands for the Roman Empire, it is certainly true that the rumours about 'Nero Redivivus' supported by Parthia, far from heightening the authority and power of the Empire, constituted an insidious threat to its supremacy. It threatened the security of Empire and Emperor, as events on the Parthian frontier had done for generations. But this is precisely the situation which seems to be symbolized in Rev. 17.16–17, in the vision of the destruction not of the beast but of the harlot by the ten horns of the beast. It is argued that a clear distinction must be drawn between the woman and the beast, while account is still taken of the relationship between them. While the woman represents the city of Rome and may be the patron goddess of the city, the beast stands for all that is worst and Antichristian in the power of Rome; in the figure of the beast a special reference is intended to the cult of the Emperor, with its blasphemous exaggerations and extravagances, and this identification is supported by the colouring given to the traditional mythology of the beast by the legend of 'Nero Redivivus'.

The original tendency to megalomania, through artistic or religious extravagance, which gave inspiration to this nightmare legend or dream, would be regarded as a serious flaw in the Imperial cult from the pragmatic Augustan point of view; but it could also be seen as the logical development and consequence of the mass hysteria accompanying the worship of a man as a deity. Thus not only is the 'Nero Redivivus' legend, from the historical point of view, an apparent healing of Nero's self-inflicted death-wound, so that the adulation of Nero, crushed by reports of his death and the damnation of his memory, is revived and exaggerated in this new fantasy; but also, from the point of view of Christian or other opposition to the cult, the legend represents the most natural and direct succession and extension of the abominable practices of Emperor-worship; this is the way such blasphemous pretensions would inevitably lead, especially when sought with enthusiasm and more than purely administrative motives. The wound represented by Nero's eventual failure was healed, and his glory enhanced, by the current rumours which affected all with dread, wonder and questioning, much more than by Vespasian's action in papering over the cracks in the Augustan policy of Emperor-worship.[18] This miraculously healed presentation of the principal blasphemies of the imperial cult in the Nero legend makes Emperor-worship a more terrifyingly bestial opponent and augments the power of Satan.

So the suicide of Nero, and its consequences, can be seen not merely as an historical event when 'an emperor ... died a violent death', but also as a symbolic event 'in which the authority of the beast (and the dragon) was both destroyed and deceptively restored'. And, although we accept such an historical interpretation, we need not exclude the possibility that the author is making, by these means, certain theological points which have been most valuable illuminated by those commentators who have largely rejected any kind of historical reference within the symbolism. So the historical symbol of the beast which has one of its seven heads bearing a fatal wound, yet miraculously healed, can still be treated as a grim parody of the Lamb, 'standing, as though it had been slain'. And the historical event of Nero's suicide does not necessarily preclude any further development in the symbolish of the sword which inflicted the wound, or of the wound itself (since the word translated as 'wound' in Rev. 13 is *plēgē* which is translated in all twelve of its occurrences in Revelation outside this chapter as 'plague'.)

> The sword is the symbol of God's wrath; the wound is a God-inflicted plague which simultaneously destroys the authority of head, beast and dragon. It is a wound from which the beast may recover only by using deception, by succeeding in his temptations, by making absolute his illusory claims to ultimate power over human destiny.[19]

Let us return to the sequence of Emperors represented by the seven heads of the beast. If the starting-point with Nero is now established more firmly, which is the sixth head which we are told is operative at the time of writing? We observed earlier that the two possibilities were Titus or Trajan, depending on whether the three 'pretenders' are included or omitted, and we saw reasons for caution before choosing Trajan, in our efforts to approximate to the 'correct' answer required by the external evidence (the tradition of Irenaeus that the Book of Revelation 'was seen towards the end of' the reign of Domitian). Let us examine the possibility that Titus could be the sixth emperor, the sixth head in which the Beast is fully realized.

Although Suetonius could call Titus 'the delight and darling of the human race'[20] and record the spontaneous mourning and affection which greeted his death, yet men had dreaded his accession because of earlier manifestations of his character. His concessions to the Senate and policy of mild tolerance did not stop the spread of discontent, particularly in the East. The Jews, of course, were prepared to ascribe an agonizing end to the destroyer of their temple. An important feature of the situation, at the time these chapters of Revelation were written, seems to have been the popular interest in 'Nero Redivivus'. Dio Cassius records that a false Nero appeared in the reign of Titus; there may even have been more than one of these impostors who appeared at this time in Asia Minor, giving fresh impetus to the legend. If Titus is the sixth, then the seventh head would be Domitian, whose succession was already assured, barring accident, since Titus had no male heir but only a daughter, and had declared that his brother should succeed him. His accession was probably dreaded even more than that of Titus, because of his known character and the demonstration of his ability in his 'first fling' in A.D. 69.[21]

Some scholars have held that the description of the seventh head and emperor as one who 'when he comes ... must [*dei*] remain only a little while' (Rev. 17.10) is more appropriate for Titus than for Domitian in view of Titus' actual brief reign. It is true that Titus only reigned from 79 to 81, but there seems to be little evidence for any popular knowledge of his ill-health, on which such a contemporary prophecy might be based; in fact, his death came as such a surprise that foul play was suspected. But the word 'must' in the description of the seventh emperor is not necessarily prophetic. The consequences of his reign for the Church, or even more likely, the timing of the new onslaught of the Antichrist as the eighth figure, would be adequate explanation of the use of the Greek word *dei*[22] to express the necessity, in the divinely ordained plan, of only a short reign for the seventh emperor.

Although the character of the beast is fully realized in each of the seven emperors in turn, it is regarded as achieving its ultimate bestiality only in the eighth manifestation, as the smitten head returning, that is, as 'Nero Redivivus' (Rev. 17.11). Then it is fully the beast 'which was and is not and is to come'. If Domitian proves to be the seventh emperor, then 'Nero Redivivus' is not totally identified with him. But then 'Nero Redivivus' hardly could be equated with a man known to the people from his youth as a potential political figure; instead, he is the one who comes after, or breaks into, the reign of the seventh emperor, cutting him short. This kind of situation would do justice to the reinterpretation of the Nero legend in terms of a supernatural figure. As time passed, and pretenders came and went, the only expectation worthy of consideration was that of the reappearance of a superhuman Nero figure, of Neronic manners and demonic power, in the belief that something like Nero, but infinitely more powerful and dangerous, must appear as suddenly and surprisingly as Nero had disappeared.

To regard the eighth as another emperor following the seven, who can therefore be identified with Domitian, is to misunderstand the real significance of the eighth position. For if the author had intended this, he could have expressed it by the symbol of a beast with eight heads. The use of a sequence of seven involves progression towards a climax, which accordingly places a special emphasis on the seventh position (this is perhaps most clearly demonstrated in the Book of Revelation by the handling of the seven seals). Suppose that the sequence is built upon Nero, who establishes the theme by his hostility to the Christians and his blasphemous exaggeration of Emperor-worship. Which would provide the more satisfactory climax to this sequence – Titus, admittedly the destroyer of the Jewish temple, but an emperor with a comparatively just reign; or Domitian, the successor of Nero in many ways recognized even by pagan writers, with his religious extravagances and, possibly, his hatred of the Christians expressed in a revival of persecution? [23]

The most satisfactory reconstruction of the historical application of this tradition symbolism, combined with the Nero legend, would seem to be the following: The sixth emperor, who is now reigning, is Titus. Current expectations and fears centre upon his brother Domitian, whose character is known and who has been designated as the next emperor. It is feared that he will provide the climax to the

sequence which began with Nero. If all these signs of the times are
fulfilled the Christians must pray to God that he will have mercy and
shorten the time, for the sake of the elect.[24] Domitian must not reign
long if the Church is to survive; and God reveals that it is ordained in
his plan that the sufferings and tribulations of the Church will be
brought to their terrible climax and then wound up, 'swallowed up
in victory' within the reign of Domitian.

In this way the eighth – the full diabolical power of the Roman
imperial self-assertion and blasphemy – as a 'Nero Redivivus' will
burst in upon the reigning seventh emperor. The eighth is not
himself an individual emperor, except by his characterization within
the legend based upon the first of the sequence. When this sequence
reaches its climax in the seventh the full venom breaks out; this is
the Satanic power of Rome which has already appeared in each of
the emperors, probably to varying degrees. Only as the Antichrist
figure, which goes beyond a single historical identification, does it
have what could be called 'a personal existence'. However great the
dread of Domitian as heir to the throne, the equation of him with
this demonic power would be unrealistic and unthinkable; rather his
reign will see its ghastly manifestation. This eighth figure is none the
less accurately described in the words of Rev. 17.11 RSV: 'it is an
eighth but it belongs to the seven', which the Jerusalem Bible,
recognizing the parallelism in the clauses, renders 'at the same time
the eighth and one of the seven'. This demonic power exercised a
major influence, recognized within an historical emperor, in the
reign of Nero, the first of the sequence, and it was this influence
which inspired the Nero legend, leading to the expectation of the
'eighth'.[25]

At the least this seems a possible solution to the complex riddle
posed by the symbolism of the beast. It offers support to that
method of exegesis which interprets the Book as an application of
traditional mythological ideas within an historical context. The
author seems to have included some sort of clue to the time of
writing in this section of his work. If the riddle has been solved
correctly, a surprisingly precise date has been achieved, from the
internal evidence, for this material, if not for the Book as a whole.

A date in the reign of the Emperor Titus, furnished by the author
in connection with the imagery of the beast, seems to conflict with
indications of a date in the reign of Domitian, detected elsewhere in
the book. Significantly, these pointers to a Domitianic date, which

correspond well with the external evidence, are to be found in those passages such as the seven letters and the seven seals which are most concerned with the contemporary situation of the Church in Asia Minor. But this apparent conflict over dates, important though it is, does not entail the rejection of the solution just offered to the 'riddle of the beast', either on the grounds of mistaken exegesis, or as concerned with what is merely an archaic survival, irrelevant to the main purpose of the author's current work.

The interpretation which attributed this material about the beast to the period of Titus also spoke of the expectations associated with Domitian's accession, including the view that his reign would see the irruption of 'Nero Redivivus' in all his demonic excess. These expectations, although formulated some years previously, were still supremely relevant for an author producing his full-scale Apocalypse during the reign of Domitian, under the local circumstances indicated elsewhere in this investigation. There was no call to up-date the prophecy, to modify the tradition again, as had been done so often with apocalyptic writings in the past. The author writes from a conviction that the present circumstances show 'the signs of the end', that the expectations now being realized in Domitian's reign show that these factors are fundamental to the working out of God's plan and, in particular, that the more extravagant the blasphemous pretensions of the Imperial cult become, the nearer draws the irruption of the full power of Antichrist, and the final defeat of that power by God.

As John builds up his total presentation, he uses recognizable pictures drawn from the situation in Asia Minor to indicate the immediacy of his prophecy. But he also uses older formulations, traditional motifs to give depth to his portrayal and to indicate its perspectives. These motifs are applied skilfully, being reinterpreted where necessary, to develop the main themes of his prophecy. We have seen how the traditional materials of chs. 11 and 12 are used in this way.

Because the author of Revelation made use of the Nero legend, this does not mean that he was necessarily a believer in the popular applications of it current in his lifetime, or that he had ever supported it for its own merits or campaigned on behalf of a pretender. Rather the upsurge in this belief at the time he was writing may have suggested it to him as a useful contemporary image to employ as a vehicle for his own message. He had drawn much of his material from the Old Testament, and particularly from the Book of Daniel, where this imagery had been used for much the same purpose, in a similar situation to that which he himself was facing, and from this material he fashioned a similar exhortation to endurance for the people of God.

Similarly John uses the beast, which, it is suggested, may well have been the author's own formulation (although on traditional lines), presented in the first instance during Titus' reign. The immediate effects of using this imagery now without modification are: to reemphasize a previous prophecy, stressing the continuity of the prophet's message and the immediate relevance of its expectations in the contemporary situation; to demonstrate again the principal theme of the working out of God's plan in numerous signs in the past as well as the present; and to show how apprehensions about Domitian, formulated as a warning, are being substantiated in present circumstances, in which they are rapidly reaching the climax of their realization.

Admittedly it is hypothetical to suggest that the author has spoken of the beast before and is now incorporating this prophecy within his present work. In justification it can at least be stressed that the formulation has an appropriateness on both occasions: for the reign of Titus, when this revelation of God's plan was first made known, and for the reign of Domitian, when there is every indication that this prophecy is approaching its complete fulfilment. One can only speculate about the original circumstances in which this prophecy was formulated; something can be gleaned from what has been said already about the influences and the variety of materials which contributed to its expression; perhaps, with a more adequate appreciation of the Jewish environment which conditioned so much of the author's thinking, one may recognize the incentive to such a prophecy in the bitter feelings against Titus as the conqueror of Jerusalem.[26]

E. Stauffer describes the author as a 'pitiless parodist' in the hate and scorn with which he treats self-glorified Rome.

A carnival procession sways past, the beauty parade of the great harlot sitting upon many waters, committing fornication with the kings of the earth, making the peoples of the earth drunk with the wine of her fornication, drunk with the blood of the saints. She sits upon a scarlet-coloured beast, arrayed in purple and decked with gold and precious stone and pearls, having in her hand a golden cup full of abominations and unclean things, and upon her fore-head the mysterious name, Babylon the Great, the Mother of the Harlots and of the Abominations of the Earth.[27]

The context of the Book does seem to demand the application of this picture to Rome. The questions remain as to what aspect of Rome is being considered beneath this imagery, and who was the model for the vivid picture presented.

The extent of the evil influence, the harlotry represented by Babylon, is indicated in chs. 17 and 18. 'All nations' are implicated: 'the kings of the earth have committed fornication with her, and the merchants of the earth have grown rich with the wealth of her wantonness' (18.3 – cf. 17.2; 18.9). A similar idea is contained in Isa. 23.17, where Tyre 'will play the harlot with all the kingdoms of the world upon the face of the earth'. The laments of ch. 18 – 'the kings of the earth ... will weep and wail over her when they see the smoke of her burning' (18.9) – these laments can be compared with those of Ezek. 26.16 ('the princes of the sea') and 27.29f. ('the mariners and all the pilots of the sea'). This is a very vivid way of expressing the extent of the harlot's influence, since those who are so distressed at her downfall betray the depth of their involvement in her practices. The variety of emotions expressed in Ezekiel's vision (particularly in 27.35, 36) show that grief is not the only reaction; this may well be true also for the vision in Revelation, since not only do the kings of the earth weep and wail but some – the ten kings represented by the ten horns – are in a sense the cause of the harlot's downfall as they unconsciously play their role in God's plan.

The first element in this picture to be considered is the use of the noun *pornē* (harlot) and the words cognate with it.[28] Frequently some link is made between harlotry and idolatry. In the letters to the seven churches there is a criticism of those who hold the teaching of Balaam, which sanctions the eating of food sacrificed to idols and the practice of immorality – *porneusai* – (2.14), and of the woman Jezebel who beguiles Christ's servants to practise immorality and eat food sacrificed to idols (2.20f.). This is reminiscent of the terms of the Apostolic Decree, recorded in the Acts of the Apostles (15.20, 29; 21.25),[29] which appears to set minimum requirements for Gentile Christians in place of the Jewish regulations. Because the Apostolic Decree is usually understood in a literal sense as ritual ordinances concerned with food and festivals, it does not mean that the references to Pergamum and Thyatira must be understood in the same way.

For in the Old Testament the literal sense of the term 'harlotry' is developed into a figurative expression for Israel's unfaithfulness to Yahweh. The use of this imagery is often coupled with an emphatic rejection of the literal practice of cultic prostitution (e.g. Jer. 2.20; 3.6; Hos. 4.12–14). This could be an explanation of the growth of the metaphor, if very frequently the unfaithfulness to Yahweh involved the practice of, or the condoning of, sexual rites in the worship of other deities. The first statement of these developed ideas occurs in the book of Hosea, where the prophet's personal experience is presented as a sign of Yahweh's relationship with Israel (Hos. 2.2f.; cf. Isa. 1.21; Ezek. 16.15).

The harlotry of Israel as described in the Old Testament is twofold: it is a vivid expression for idolatry, involving necessarily the desertion of Yahweh and the true sanctuary; it is also a political disloyalty to Yahweh, when the nation fails to trust in his providence but looks for support to Egypt, Assyria and other nations. Because of the close connection of politics and religion in Old Testament theology, these are but two aspects of a single attitude, a failure of wholehearted trust in the one God who controls all.

As well as a range of references to Israel in these terms, the imagery is applied to Tyre (Isa. 23.15f. mentioned above), to Nineveh (Nahum 3.4), and to Samaria the 'transgression of Jacob' (Mic. 1.5, 7). K. G. Kuhn makes a surprising comment on Isa. 23.15f. and Nahum 3.4 that 'in these two passages the harlotry does not denote idolatry, as normally in the Old Testament, but the trading activity of the city'.[30] This comment has more basis in Isa. 23.18 where there is specific mention of 'merchandise', 'food and fine clothing'; but there is no need to restrict this language to its literal meaning. It can well represent a sustained metaphor when selling oneself and selling luxury goods are linked; in the future both 'will be dedicated to the Lord' (23.18). The use of trading imagery appropriate for the subject does not preclude an understanding of harlotry in the sense of idolatry, of rejection of the Lord. In the same way the lament of the merchants in Rev. 18.11–19 is seen as supporting imagery within the total picture of Babylon the harlot.

Above all, chs. 3 and 4 of Jeremiah are important because of the similarity of ideas to the passage in Revelation about the great harlot. 'You have played the harlot with many lovers; and would you return to me? says the Lord. . . . By the waysides you have sat awaiting lovers . . . you have polluted the land with your vile harlotry . . . yet you have a harlot's brow, you refuse to be ashamed. . . . And you, O desolate one, what do you mean that you dress in scarlet, that you deck yourself with ornaments of gold, that you enlarge your eyes with paint? In vain you beautify yourself. Your lovers despise you; they seek your life. For I heard a cry as of a woman in travail, anguish as of one bringing forth her first child, the cry of the daughter of Zion gasping for breath, stretching out her hands, "Woe is me! I am fainting before murderers."' The harlot in Rev. 17 is described as dressed in purple and scarlet, bedecked with gold and jewels and pearls, and her name is written on her forehead. The other important point of contact between this passage in Jeremiah and the woman in Rev. 17 is the idea that the harlot's lovers will turn upon her and seek to kill her. So the ten horns and the beast hate the harlot (Rev. 17.16).

Perhaps the Old Testament passage is also significant for an understanding of why the harlot wears the mystical name 'Babylon' on her forehead. The usual explanation given is that public prostitutes in Rome were branded as such by wearing a label with their names on their brows, reference being made to Seneca and Juvenal.[31] That such an allusion could be made is certainly possible, but the case cannot be regarded as proved because of those other passages in Revelation which refer, outside the context of harlotry, to the wearing of a seal, a name, or a distinguishing mark (cf. 7.3; 13.16; 19.12). In the context of Jer. 3.3 the significance of the 'harlot's brow' is in the nation's refusal to be ashamed. The original Hebrew refers to the forehead, while the Septuagint broadens the reference to the face; Kittel suggested an emendation which would be a parallel to Isa. 48.4 'brow of brass' – a similar figure for a self-willed and brazen effrontery. So the harlot Babylon can be seen wearing boldly and shamelessly the sign of her depravity, in a way that might have reminded the author of the prostitutes in the streets of the city to which he was referring. The author may well have found much to criticize in the sexual morality of Roman life, but the fact remains that the chief target, which he attacks in this Book, is the idolatrous worship of the Emperor. And in the Old Testament he could find ready for use a vivid image of the idolatrous city or nation.[32]

The harlot is given 'a name of mystery: Babylon the great' (17.5). This too fits with the Old Testament background. As Kuhn says,

> The historic city and empire of Babylon were always depicted by the prophets as the ungodly power par excellence. Thus even after the fall of Babylon, Babel, as they saw it, represented for later Jewish readers of Scripture, and also for early Christians, the very epitome and type of an ungodly and domineering city.[33]

Later Judaism commonly applied the title of Babel, and its reputation as an ungodly power, to Rome, both city and empire.[34] A confirmation within the New Testament is provided by 1 Pet. 5.13 – 'She who is at Babylon, who is likewise chosen, sends you' (the churches in Asia Minor) 'greetings; and so does my son Mark.' Christian exegesis from an early date accepted this as a reference to the church in Rome, and this is supported by the traditional association of Peter with Rome rather than Mesopotamia.[35] On this basis Schlatter deduced 'not merely that Peter expects the destruction of Rome and sees it in the prophetic utterance against Babylon, but that the whole Church both in Rome and Asia Minor shared this view'.[36]

The second group of ideas in this passage to be investigated are those concerning the cup, wine, and drunkenness. In the Old Testament the cup 'was symbolic of the kind of life experience which God the host pours out for his world. For the saints there was the cup of the blessings of God. For the wicked there was the wine cup of the wrath of God.'[37] In the cup of suffering the predominant idea is that of God's punishment of human sinfulness. '... in the hand of the Lord there is a cup, with foaming wine, well mixed; and he will pour a draught from it, and all the wicked of the earth shall drain it down to the dregs' (Ps. 75.8). In Isa. 51.17–23 there is an appeal to Jerusalem to rouse herself from the despair into which she has sunk. Her condition is due to Yahweh's having given her 'the cup of his wrath' to drink. But after the punishment of the exile comes the assurance that now Yahweh has taken his cup away from Jerusalem, and will instead give it to her tormentors.

Very relevant to the imagery of Revelation is Jer. 51.7–8a: 'Babylon was a golden cup in the Lord's hand, making all the earth drunken; the nations drank of her wine, therefore the nations went

mad. Suddenly Babylon has fallen and been broken; wail for her!'
Here the oracle's reference is to the geographical Babylon which
has been Yahweh's instrument in the punishment of other nations;
now she herself has provoked Yahweh's avenging wrath and will be
laid low. The adjective 'golden' may well add the idea of Babylon's
luxury; it does not affect the basic meaning of the cup symbolism
which is expressed very concisely by identifying Babylon (the agent
of God's wrath) with the cup which symbolizes God's wrath. This
represents an extra stage of development beyond Isa. 51. In Ezek.
23.31–4 the cup which Jerusalem will drain is a 'cup of horror and
desolation ... the cup of your sister Samaria' that is God's punishment for her lewdness and harlotry.

In the Messianic suffering of Mark 14.36, Jesus is to drink the cup
of God's wrath against sin. 'In his identification with sinful men he is
the object of the holy wrath of God against sin, and in Gethsemane
as the hour of the Passion approaches the full horror of that wrath is
disclosed.'[38] According to Mark 10.39 Jesus says that James and
John will indeed drink the cup that he drinks, and share in the same
baptism.[39] The disciples ask for a share in Christ's glory, and are told
that they will indeed have a share in the divinely appointed tribulation through which one must pass. Largely because of the world's
hostility to the disciples as to their Lord, the disciples will indeed
have a share in drinking the cup of God's wrath, and in being
baptized in the woes that arise from human sin.

In Revelation there are three groups of references which apply
the cup or wine imagery in different ways. In the first case there are
three passages where the cup refers to punishment by God, perhaps
administered by a human agency. Anyone who worships the beast
'shall drink the wine of God's wrath, poured unmixed into the cup of
his anger' (14.10). The word for unmixed wine is used figuratively of
God's anger in full strength.[40] 'And God remembered great Babylon, to make her drain the cup of the fury of his wrath' (16.19). In
the command from heaven the people are exhorted to 'render to her
as she herself has rendered, and repay her double for her deeds; mix
a double draught for her in the cup she mixed' (18.6). In the second
category of references are those where the cup of wine imagery is
closely linked with the harlotry of Babylon: 'Fallen, fallen is Babylon the great, she who made all nations drink the wine of the wrath
of her fornication' (14.8; 18.3). It is the great harlot 'with the wine
of whose fornication the dwellers on earth have become drunk'

(17.2). She holds in her hand 'a golden cup full of abominations and the impurities of her fornication' (17.4). Thirdly, because of the similarity of language, we must note those references to the winepress. The vintage gathered from the earth is cast into the great winepress 'of the wrath of God' (14.19). The figure of the 'Word of God'... 'will tread the wine press of the fury of the wrath of God the Almighty' (19.15).

The wine harvest was an occasion for joyful festivities;[41] thus when the Old Testament uses the imagery of the winepress to depict the fearful horror of God's judgement the power of the metaphor is enhanced by the contrast (Isa. 63.1–6; Jer. 25.30; Lam. 1.15; Joel 4.13). The passage most echoed in Revelation is that from Isaiah about Yahweh's judgement over Edom: 'I have trodden the wine press alone, and from the peoples no one was with me; I trod them in my anger and trampled them in my wrath; their lifeblood is sprinkled upon my garments, and I have stained all my raiment.' The winepress is linked with God's wrath in the symbolism for judgement. The connection with Old Testament imagery appears to be equally close in the first group of references mentioned above. Here is the cup of God's wrath, his punishment for human sin, which will be administered to the guilty, to the idolaters as well as to Babylon herself. But in the second group of references the thought is somewhat different.

The great harlot holds in her hand a golden cup; we have already noted the relevance of Jer. 51.7, where Babylon herself is described as 'a golden cup in the Lord's hand'. In Revelation, Babylon is not now herself the cup, but she holds it as an identification symbol. In view of the use of the image of harlotry alongside that of the cup, it is possible to say that Babylon offers herself as a harlot to the nations, and her harlotry has an intoxicating effect (the expression of this idea being the contribution of the cup and wine imagery), just as Babylon of old was offered as the maddening and intoxicating draught from the Lord's cup. What the passage from Jeremiah makes explicit is the control which God exercises over Babylon – the punishment which she measures out to the nations is ordained by him. But we shall see that this idea is also expressed in Revelation, although less directly.

Rev. 14.8–10 is a significant passage for the understanding of the imagery as a whole (since it contains two references apportioned to two different groups). Firstly there is the problematic phrase 'the wine of the wrath of her fornication' in 14.8, repeated in 18.3, and in 14.10 'the wine of the wrath of God'.[42] Whereas *thumos* usually means anger, wrath, or rage, and, in particular, the outpouring of God's wrath, it could also mean passion or strong feeling.[43] Some interpreters have therefore taken *thumos* closely with 'wine' and translated 'the raging wine of her fornication'. Others have taken it closely with 'fornication' and render it, as the RSV, 'the wine of her impure passion'.

Let us consider what happens if we translate as 'wrath' consistently in both verses, seeing if we can still apply the strict Old Testament sense of God's wrath. We then have, in 14.8, a mixed metaphor in which the wine of harlotry, with which Babylon intoxicates the nations, becomes the wine of God's wrath for them. There is no direct connection in the Old Testament between the cup and the harlot images; Jer. 51.7, however, with its reference to the golden cup that is Babylon, offers the author of Revelation the starting-point for his exposition (Rev. 17.4). It is because Babylon is a harlot, decked in all her gold and finery, that she has this intoxicating effect upon the nations. So far the contents of the cup, if considered at all, are merely intended as a metaphorical expression, the cause of the intoxication which results from addiction to prostitution as much as to drink.

But Babylon, as well as being the harlot with all her allurements, is also the one who administers the cup of wrath, and this aspect can be understood as fully in accordance with the Old Testament model. By her undoubtedly evil influence Babylon has involved all the nations in her destiny: 'the wine of her fornication means the wrath process, whereby not only individuals but also whole nations are involved in the complex of sin and suffering which is the history of the Roman Empire'.[44] We have seen reason to regard the figure of Babylon in Jer. 51 as the agent of God's wrath, who is herself eventually brought low. A similar picture is represented here – we are concerned with the doom of Babylon as well as with the punishment of all who have sinned through her. As with the historical Babylon, the punishment meted out to the nations by her – which they experience through association with her – is ordained by God, is very much part of the cup of God's wrath. The second angel refers to the two stages in the process of God's judgement; the nations have been punished, now Babylon herself is to fall. Similarly the third angel draws a parallel situation in terms of the beast and its mark; those who come under the influence of the beast, and are guilty of idolatry, are likewise subject to the wrath and punishment of God, and we know too that the beast will eventually be destroyed. The unsavoury contents ('abominations and impurities' – 17.4) [45] of the luxurious and impressive cup held by the woman in her finery are the idolatrous practices with which Rome has perverted the world. In view of the exegesis of the imagery of the cup of wrath, it might have been expected that the cup would contain the divine wrath ready to be poured out. The explanation for this apparent inconsistency of symbolism is to be found in the condensed expression of these ideas in 14.8. The Book of Revelation leaves its readers in no doubt that nothing, good or bad, happens outside God's knowledge or without a part to play in the divine plan. Babylon, in Old and New Testaments, had her role – through her harlotry, her incitements to idolatry, the sinfulness of paganism is revealed. At the same time, and by this same agency of Babylon, the judgement of God is made clear and the nations drink from the cup of his wrath.

Finally, in this examination of the details of the picture of the harlot, we must turn to the other incidental features of her description. She is 'seated upon many waters' (17.1), a phrase which recalls Jer. 51.13 – 'O you who dwell by many waters, rich in treasures, your end has come, the thread of your life is cut' – which is a description of Babylon. A literal application to Rome is difficult, so that v. 15 explains the many waters as many peoples. It may well be that this quotation is applied because of the ideas, explicit in the context of Jeremiah, of apparent great wealth and security. Originally in the prophecy the reference may have been, as G. B. Caird suggests, [46] to the elaborate irrigation system on which Babylon's prosperity depended; in its present context it could refer to Rome's mercantile empire. We cannot exclude the possibility of an allusion to the waters of evil and chaos, especially as the woman, as well as being seated upon many waters, is also sitting on a scarlet beast – the seven-headed beast from the sea. Such ideas, not necessarily mutually exclusive, may have influenced the author to employ this Old Testament allusion.

The woman is seated upon a scarlet-coloured beast, and is herself 'arrayed in purple and scarlet'. For the prophets these colours were symbolic of ungodly and worldly luxury, represented by the extravagant attire of the daughters of Zion (Isa. 3.18ff.; Jer. 4.30).

The link with ungodly and sinful conduct is also shown by the use of scarlet in a cultic context where it is the opposite to white wool (cf. Isa. 1.18; also the unknown quotation in 1 Clement 8.3–4).[47] But such imagery would be considered especially appropriate because of its application to the contemporary setting of Roman civilization. Perhaps the author would have agreed with the comments of the Elder Pliny:

> moral corruption and luxury spring from no other source in greater abundance than from the genus shell-fish. It is true that of the whole of nature the sea is most detrimental to the stomach in a multitude of ways, with its multitude of dishes and of appetising kinds of fish to which the profits made by those who catch them spell danger. But what proportion do these form when we consider purple and scarlet robes and pearls![48]

Purple dye was valued so highly by the Romans that it became for them the symbol of power and luxury; robes dyed wholly or partly in this colour were the insignia of office. The standard equipment of a Roman legionary of the first century A.D. included a rust-red cloak; a cavalry standard of this period was a purple banner with a gold fringe, surmounted by a gilt statue of victory. On departure for a campaign a general assumed a red mantle on the Capitol, and on his return exchanged it for a toga upon entering the city. In the period of the Empire the purple *paludamentum* of the Emperor as commander-in-chief became a token of the imperial power. It was a purple mantle, embroidered with gold, that was worn when celebrating a triumph. Against this background the colours of Revelation – purple, scarlet and fire-red – acquire special significance over and above the original connotations of their various sources.

Is it possible on the basis of the details examined to isolate any one figure as the model for the Seer's picture of the harlot? Can we consider among the possibilities the Old Testament figure of Babylon, the personification of evil, to whom much of this imagery is applied; the Daughter of Zion who plays the harlot and revels in luxury; Jezebel, Ahab's queen, to whom the Seer refers specifically earlier in the book; a celebrated female figure from Roman history, such as an Empress, or Cleopatra, whose path crosses with the leaders of Rome at a decisive stage; or 'Roma' worshipped as the genius of the Roman Empire?

Babylon, in that she has given her name to the harlot, has a strong claim to be the model as well as the label for the figure. To take account of the contribution which Old Testament material, not originally addressed to the historical Babylon, made to the picture given in Revelation is not to reject this claim; there was a real possibility of the collecting together, whether by the author of Revelation or by someone before him, of similar ideas into a common tradition, with the necessary blurring of the precise original applications. The same process of amalgamation and reapplication can have taken place with the larger body of material relating to Israel's unfaithfulness to Yahweh (to which the important references in Jer. 3 and 4 belong). It seems better to regard this as a type of evil, namely idolatry, which is included within the epitome of evil, rather than attribute to the figure of the Daughter of Zion a more active and formative role, as the basic pattern for this imagery. By making Israel the epitome of evil, one is wrenching out of its total context one aspect of the Old Testament ideas about Israel. Either a view is adopted that is more one-sided than the Old Testament ever seems to be, or the writer is more violently anti-Jewish than any interpreter of Revelation would be prepared to assert; both would present considerable problems in relating ch. 17 to the rest of the Book and to ch. 12 in particular.

The explicit influence of Jezebel seems to be confined to the letter to the Church at Thyatira. An identification with a particular Roman Empress, such as Messalina,[49] will appear to confine the author to an attack upon contemporary immorality rather than upon the idolatry of Emperor-worship. Despite the notoriety of Cleopatra,[50] there is little evidence of a sustained tradition about her from the last days of the Republic which could connect with the author's other contemporary and historical references.

The idea of a patron goddess Roma was not a Roman creation, but rather, as something foreign to Roman religion, was developed under Greek influence in the Hellenistic period.[51] It derived from the Greek tradition of individual patron deities of the city-states; in the Hellenized East the 'Fortuna' of a city was worshipped in the local cult. As the sphere of Roman control and influence extended it was natural that districts accustomed to pay their respects to the 'Fortuna' of the local centre of government should transfer their allegiance and worship to the conquering power; they could hardly do other than acknowledge the existence of a power greater than their own and endeavour to propitiate it. Among the Italian allies and the dependent communities of Greece, as Franz Altheim expressed it, 'there men recognized in the existence of the ruling city a divine element and therefore gave a religious form to their devotion to it'.[52] In areas where Ruler-worship was traditional these cults would be transferred to the Roman generals and proconsuls. The goddess Roma probably achieved her important place in the cult offered to the new power of the Romans because of the practical consideration of her permanency in contrast to the Roman officers and magistrates who changed frequently.

Temples to Roma were soon erected in cities beyond the eastern boundaries of Greece – Smyrna had one as early as 195 B.C.[53] There the new rulers were worshipped, as the former kings had been, alongside the 'Fortuna' of the city they represented. Doubtless practical, political considerations permitted, and even fostered, this continuation of the Hellenistic ruler cult. The cult was celebrated in many centres with games and festivals called 'Romaia'; some of these festivals continued to be celebrated for a long time.

After the defeat of Antony and the confirmation of Octavian in power, leagues of cities in Asia and Bithynia requested permission to express their loyalty to the new rule of Octavian by erecting community temples to him. This offer was accepted, but with the enforced condition, which had not always been made by earlier proconsuls, that no temple should be erected to him except in union with the goddess Roma.[54] The temple of Roma and Augustus at Pergamum was depicted on coins for general circulation in Asia. The two divinities were closely linked in the title of the quinquennial games, the 'Romaia Sebasta'. It is probable that leagues of cities in other eastern provinces were organized just as speedily for cultic purposes. A sharp distinction seems to have been made between what was permitted to Roman and to foreign subjects. Roman citizens in Ephesus and Nicaea were allowed to erect shrines dedicated to Roma coupled with Divus Julius, but not with the reigning Emperor.[55] The worship of Roma and the Emperor was not restricted to the East; the combined cult was practised in the West at least at Lugdunum and Tarraco. But the cult of the city's goddess was not officially admitted to Rome itself until A.D. 118, when Hadrian dedicated a temple to Venus and Roma. There was no mention of Roma at the 'Parilia', the native feast celebrating the city's foundation; but by Hadrian's time the name 'Parilia' had been changed to 'Romaia'.

Alongside an emperor who reigned for so long as Augustus there was a tendency for Roma to be relegated to a subordinate position – the name does not figure so frequently in the titles of temples and priests. This may well be explained by the same hypothesis of practical considerations suggested for the rise of the cult. When one man is in power over a very long period his personality naturally assumes a greater importance than an idealized abstraction. But this is a restricted phase rather than ultimate decline. After Augustus 'the veneration of the Emperor was no longer understood as the expression of the effect of a unique and personal greatness, but was applied to the institution of the principate as such'.[56] So there follows a succession of personifications of abstract qualities, characterized as blessings from the Emperor ('Clementia Caesaris' etc.). Even in the later stages of the Empire the role of Roma remains important. In this name the greatness of the past can be incorporated; this expression could sum up the belief in the eternity of the city and the Empire, in its unique role as determined by fate, and could contain within itself those traditional ideas that survived from the old religion. In Symmachus' speech before Valentinian II, Roma begs for respect:

> Permit me to continue to hold to my ancestral belief, for I take my delight in it. Permit me to live after my own fashion, for I am a free woman. This religion has laid the circle of the earth at my feet, has beaten back Hannibal from my walls, the Gauls from the Capitol. Was I to be kept alive, only to be attacked in my old age? Whatever these desires that you present to me may be, it would be too late, it would be shameful to try innovations in my hoary age.

Roma appears to be depicted in the sculpture at the east end of the Ara Pacis Augustae – although this section is not in a good state of preservation.[57] She is seated on a pile of armour, and faces a goddess with two children and attendants, on the other side of the entrance, who is some earth or mother goddess, perhaps Italia. The Gemma Augustea from Vienna depicts Augustus as an ageless god seated beside the goddess Roma, who wears a helmet. On one of the silver cups found at Bosco Reale illustrating the glorification of Augustus, Roma is depicted in the processional group, her left foot supported on a helmet; the spear she was resting on has been lost. On the left panel of the archway of Titus in Rome the Emperor is shown in the triumphal chariot, with Victory at his side, escorted by allegorical figures of Roma and the Roman people. Roma is shown in full panoply at the head of the horses. In the sculptured friezes representing the exploits of Trajan on the Arch of Constantine, which may originally have decorated the Forum of Trajan, Roma welcomes the hero of the Dacian campaigns and Victory crowns him. Roma also figures on a relief which, it is suggested, belongs to the early period of Hadrian's principate; on the Arch of Trajan at Benevento; seated receiving a procession of captives and wagons laden with booty and trophies on the Arch of Septimius Severus; and on the keystone of the Arch of Constantine.

On the basis of inscriptions and of such illustrations in Roman art, it would seem reasonable to assume that there was an active cult of Roma throughout at least the first century of the imperial period. There may well have been fluctuations in the degree of its popularity, and such fluctuations would seem likely to bear some relation to the popular view of the reigning emperor, since the cults of Roma and the Emperor were closely associated, at least in the older-established temples of the East. We have seen that Asia Minor was among the first districts to establish a cult of Roma, doubtless agreeing enthusiastically to such an acceptable and logical adaptation of the traditional practices of Ruler-worship. It would seem highly significant in establishing a connection between the cult of Roma and the ideas of the Book of Revelation that among the cities to which John is writing the first three, Ephesus, Smyrna and Pergamum, are known to have had temples to the goddess Roma.

Is the author therefore, in using the figure of the harlot Babylon, with all its Old Testament imagery, as a symbol for Rome, making a definite reference to the goddess Roma, who was worshipped in the cities where his readers lived, and who was regarded as embodying all that Rome stood for and symbolizing its power? If this was his intention, one might ask why he did not make the contemporary reference more explicit in the description of the woman, rather than relying so heavily in his description on the Old Testament material. At least one might expect a helmet, which seems to be a characteristic feature of the martial Roma. But the colour symbolism – scarlet and purple – is appropriate, as we have seen, to a Roman military context, as well as signifying luxury. John describes what he is attacking in Old Testament terms; what he is attacking is Rome, and there are precedents in apocalyptic literature for the equation of Roma and Babylon which he employs: he describes Rome in terms of Babylon, using Old Testament descriptions of Babylon and of kindred evils such as Babylon represented. But this description in terms of the woman Babylon is especially appropriate because Rome was currently regarded as symbolized by a woman, her patron goddess. From the point of view of the loyal Roman citizen, what John has done is to create a ghastly parody of the noble figure who stands for all that is best in Rome, its high ideals and renowned virtues, on which, at least according to the propaganda, the glorious age of the Empire has been founded. The significance of John's criticism would not escape anyone with a nodding acquaintance with the Jewish Scriptures.

One's confidence that the author is, in this figure, parodying the contemporary cult of Roma is increased by the intelligible explanation which this interpretation gives to the problem of the relation between the woman and the beast. Both the woman and the beast are attacked as evil by the author; they are closely related, as is shown by the way that the heads of the beast are seen as forming a seat for the woman. This is not merely a topographical reference, as might be deduced from Rev. 17.9, since the heads are also identified as seven kings or emperors. Rev. 17.3 reveals the woman, who is also 'seated upon many waters' because of her description in terms of Jeremiah's Babylon, as 'sitting on the scarlet beast'. Closely related as these figures are, some clear distinction must be drawn between them, to account for their individual existence within this vision, and, in particular, to make sense of the destruction of the harlot by the ten horns of the beast and the beast itself. 'And the ten horns that you saw, they and the beast will hate the harlot; they will make her desolate and naked, and devour her flesh and burn her up with fire, for God has put it into their hearts to carry out his purpose by being of one mind and giving over their royal power to the beast, until the words of God shall be fulfilled' (17.16–17).

This imagery does not seem appropriate to the idea of civil war within the Empire, even if such a situation could be envisaged at the time of the writing of the book. If the beast stands for all that is worst, all that is Antichristlike in the power of Rome, with special reference to the cults of Emperor-worship and its allied extravagances, and if the woman is the patron goddess of the city of Rome, this interpretation offers both the degree of connection and the element of conflict as the result of the relationship which the imagery of this chapter seems to require. The assault on the woman, symbol of Rome, that is envisaged is that of 'Nero Redivivus' and the hordes from the East under their captains, marching against the city, in accordance with the popular fears of the time. The mythology represented a bad dream which many expected to become an historical reality – Rome being overwhelmed by powers from the East incited by one of her own emperors, who had merely carried to extremes the imperial policy inaugurated by Augustus.

As the author of Revelation expresses it, there is strong criticism of both Rome itself and of the imperial cult with which the name and reputation of Nero is associated. The harlot Babylon is a bitter parody of Rome's patron goddess. Perhaps, by the use of some Old Testament material relating to Israel's unfaithfulness to Yahweh, the suggestion might be conveyed that Rome too is not inherently evil, that she has had her chances, but has not taken them. As it is, Rome, defiantly luxuriating, licentious and idolatrous, has worked for the destruction of others and is now to meet her own. This destiny, the working out of the wrath of God, is envisaged in terms of the Nero mythology; the end will be violent destruction at the hands of the invading hordes from the East which Rome has brought upon herself.

7

The New Jerusalem

The significance of Jerusalem in the history and future expectation of the Israelite nation is given at least its due prominence by most Old Testament studies. There are, broadly speaking, three phases in the complex of ideas about Jerusalem: the historical reality of Jerusalem fulfilling the role of neutral capital for which David had chosen the city; then, after this heyday, the hopes that the city might achieve again its former glory – the this-worldly, national and political hopes of the prophets, and the other-worldly, universal and transcendent hopes of the apocalyptists. Such an analysis must of necessity be an over-simplified generalization; the two complexes of future hope do not fall apart into these easy divisions, for they are often confused and blended together. But even if these divisions are somewhat artificial, it is helpful to be able to sort out the various expressions by their dominant idea, so long as one does not expect to find a neat line of development linking them in a chronological or thematic chain.[1]

A significant theme of apocalyptic is the belief that 'the usurped creation will be restored; the corrupted universe will be cleansed; the created world will be re-created'.[2] Expression is given to the principle 'that the End should in some way correspond to the Beginning: what the Creator willed and planned at the time of his creation of the world will reach its fulfilment in the last days when he will redeem his universe'. For this reason the idea of the return of Paradise is important, and it is in this context that an associated theme of the heavenly Jerusalem, designed by God at the beginning of creation, makes its appearance. One concept of Paradise has been formulated as the New Jerusalem, under the influence of a combination of historical and mythological factors.

The perspectives of apocalyptic presentations vary tremendously. Broadly, where, in the earlier writings, God's kingdom is to be established on this present earth, it is the old Jerusalem which is purified as a preparation for the coming of the Messianic kingdom (1 Enoch 10.16–19; 25.1; Psalms of Solomon 17.25, 33), or as the setting for this temporary kingdom (2 Baruch 29; 39–40; 72–4; 4

Esdras 7.27–30; 12.32–4; 13.32–50). Even so there is a tendency for some writers to idealize the concept where the city is so purified as to be a new Jerusalem or an actual replacement of the old city (1 Enoch 6–36; 83–90; Testament of Dan. 5.12f.). In other writings the earth is transformed, and sometimes the heaven too; God's eternal kingdom is in heaven, although there may be a temporary Messianic kingdom on earth as a climax to the present age. Then the new Jerusalem is God's creation in heaven, a counterpart of the earthly Jerusalem (Tobit 13.9ff., 14.5; Jubilees 4.26; 2 Baruch 4.3; 32.2–4; 4 Esdras 7.26; 8.52–3; 10.44–59; 13.36).[3] Heroes of the Old Testament, such as Abraham and Moses, have been allowed to see this heavenly Jerusalem (2 Baruch 4.4–5), and the apocalyptic Seer claims to have been shown it in anticipation of the general revelation (4 Esdras 10.26f.; Rev. 21.2ff.).

When apocalyptic writers have attempted to weave together into a single fabric the various strands of tradition concerning God's kingdom and the last things – including the varied concepts of an eternal earthly kingdom, a millennial kingdom, and an eternal reign in heaven – the result has not been entirely successful, nor has it followed any consistent pattern. What can be termed a compromise picture is achieved by a combination of the temporary earthly kingdom with the revelation of eternity in heaven. What R. H. Charles regarded as incompetent editing at the end of the Book of Revelation may well be a confusion of ideas produced by the attempt to weld together a variety of traditions.

Strack-Billerbeck contains this comment at Rev. 3.12 on the description of the New Jerusalem as 'coming down out of heaven' (cf. 21.2, 10): 'The Jerusalem coming down from heaven is mentioned in the Pseudepigrapha seldom, in the older rabbinic literature not at all, and in the later small Midrashim only a few times.'[4] An examination of the passages cited suggests that an explicit reference to the descent of New Jerusalem from heaven to earth may not be attested prior to the Book of Revelation itself. This aspect could be an unexpressed assumption of those apocalyptic writers who combined traditional expectations about Jerusalem which were originally distinct; it is certainly 'taken as read' by many scholars, including R. H. Charles when he writes, 'If it was believed that the heavenly Paradise had come down to earth to be Adam's abode, there could be no objection to the hope that the Heavenly City should come down to be the abode of the Messiah.'[5]

If it is true that the explicit reference to the descent of New Jerusalem is a distinctive contribution of the Book of Revelation, it is reasonable to ask whether it bears a special significance. To follow R. H. Charles's suggestion would be to make this into a reference to Adam typology: 'If the heavenly Paradise could appear on earth for Adam, it was only natural that the heavenly Jerusalem should appear on earth for Christ – the Second and greater Adam.' H. B. Swete supplied a spiritual interpretation: 'It is perhaps unnecessary to think of a future visible fulfilment.... What is primarily intended is doubtless the heavenly origin of the Church and her divine mission.' Preferable to either of these constructions is the interpretation which allows the literal eschatological sense of the imagery to stand,[6] and, following up the indications provided by the text itself, relates the description of the heavenly city of New Jerusalem as fulfilment to the promises made to those who conquer in the seven earthly and historical cities of Asia Minor.

The heavenly Jerusalem of Rev. 21–2, as C. J. Hemer observed, 'is set in implicit contrast with the imperfections of the seven actual earthly cities. The parallels are not in this case', in comparison with the relationship between the Letters and Rev. 1, 'obtrusive or systematic; there are repeated echoes of the same images, promises developed in a larger context, particular opponents overcome and disabilities reversed.' Hemer draws special attention to three points where there are echoes in the imagery:[7] the promise 'to eat of the tree of life, which is in the paradise of God' in the Ephesian letter (2.7) which is resumed by the 'paradise' imagery of the New Jerusalem, and in particular by the 'tree of life' of 22.2, 14, 19; 'a grouping of rare words' – *themelios* ('foundation'), *tetragōnos* ('foursquare'), *endōmēsis* ('construction'), are found in Rev. 21.15–19 and also in a contemporary inscription of Smyrna describing a sacred enclosure;[8] and thirdly the 'visual impact of ... modern Alasehir ... a town strikingly "foursquare", and to its (Philadelphia's) church was made the promise of the coming of the new Jerusalem'.

Further parallels are supplied by Paul Minear, although he is reluctant to say more than that 'the inheritance of the victors as spelled out in this vision' (the seven letters) 'is wholly consistent with the promise given in the later chapters'. His cross-references include: Smyrna, 2.11, cf. 21.4 (and surely 21.8); Pergamum, 2.17, cf. 22.4 (although no parallel to 'manna' or 'stone'); Thyatira, 2.28, cf. 22.16; Sardis, 3.5, cf. 21.27 (and surely 20.15), 22.14; Philadelphia, 3.12, cf. 21.22, 22.4 as well as 21.2, 10; Laodicea, 3.21, cf. 22.3. Minear also notes 'in that final vision the climactic occurrence of the formula itself as a succinct summary of all the promises of the Book' – 'he who conquers shall have this heritage' (21.7). Much less convincing is what Minear says about the eight terms in 21.8, 'five of which echo the deceptive threats in the seven cities: the cowards (2.10, 13), the disloyal (2.10, 13), the fornicators (2.14, 20), the idolaters (2.14, 20), and finally the liars (deceivers and deceived) (2.2, 9, 20; 3.9)'.[9]

Throughout these parallels there is little indication of a close literary dependence; it is possible to envisage either the promises or the final vision being rewritten to take a much fuller account of the material in the other section. But the verbal correspondences are sufficient to suggest not so much a deliberately contrived literary connection as an actual relationship of ideas. It is for theological reasons that one would explain the apparent strict contradiction between 3.12 and 21.22 which would prove fatal to a theory of literary dependence. And the interpretation one would wish to defend, of the New Jerusalem as an eschatological fulfilment of promises made in a specific historical situation, demands just such a relationship of ideas as is visible in the text.

It is also instructive to examine the characterization of the three supposedly female figures to be found in the Book of Revelation:[10] the woman clothed with the sun in ch. 12, the harlot Babylon in ch. 17, and the New Jerusalem in ch. 21 who is 'the Bride, the wife of the Lamb'. We should not expect precise correspondences or parallels between three very different symbols. But in the same way as there can be a 'polemical parallelism', which is devised intentionally, between the first horseman of Rev. 6 and the victorious figure of Christ in Rev. 19, so there is abundant scope for contrasts between these three women. The woman who is Jerusalem could be said to represent a perfect, divinely ordained fulfilment, where her predecessors have demonstrated their inadequacies and falsehood.

The 'bride adorned for her husband' is the antithesis of the prostitute, and both are identified with cities. Babylon the mighty city comes to judgement, made desolate and devoured by those who might have been expected to defend her (17.16); Jerusalem comes down from heaven to be the dwelling place of God with men (21.3). Israel through many vicissitudes of her history had held firm to an expectation of the glories of Jerusalem. In Revelation, Israel, who gives birth to Christ and the Church, waits in the wilderness for the vision of the city that is pure gold (12.6; 21.18). The expectation of the New Jerusalem throws into sharp contrast the incompleteness of Israel and the false hopes of Rome. It also expresses the incompleteness of the Christian Church in its manifestations as local communities such as the seven churches of Asia. The earthly communities are by no means identical with the heavenly Jerusalem, nor is there direct continuity between them.

Akira Satake[11] makes an interesting comparison between Eph. 2.20, where the apostles and prophets are seen as the foundation of the world-wide earthly Church, which 'grows into a holy temple in the Lord', and Rev. 21.14, according to which the twelve apostles alone are the foundations of the heavenly Jerusalem. The absence of a foundation of prophets is possibly explained by their continuing operations within the present communities; they are not regarded as belonging to the closed circle of the Great who serve as foundations for the future glorious manifestation. But this is to assume some sort of connection between these two passages, which is by no means proved.

It is important to observe the way in which a close relationship is expressed between the New Jerusalem and Christ. Jerusalem is the Bride and the Lamb is her husband (21.2, 10). This represents a final affirmation of the truth which is declared in Rev. 5, where only the Lamb is worthy to open the sealed book, and the total demonstration of God's purpose is indissolubly linked with Christ's sacrifice on the Cross. If, as we have suggested, the participle *katabainousa* (= 'coming down') is John's distinctive articulation of the natural connection between earthly and heavenly expectations of Jerusalem, then this Christological motif could be an additional reason for his choice of words. Just as the full revelation is inaugurated by Christ's self-sacrifice, so the final manifestation of new Jerusalem is made possible by Christ's Incarnation. A characteristically Johannine expression for Christ's manifestation (*katabainō* = 'descend' used at John 3.13; 6.33, 38, 41, 42, 50, 51, 58) is now applied to the realization of the hopes of New Jerusalem (Rev. 3.12; 21.2, 10).

There is much more that could be said about the imagery of New Jerusalem; indeed there is material for a thesis by itself[12] in the development of these concepts from Old Testament beginnings, through the New Testament to St Augustine's *De Civitate Dei*. But enough has been said to show that this topic is not of primary relevance for the present study. What is from its origin a future expectation preserves this eschatological time-reference within John's Apocalypse. The Seer envisages an historical continuity from present events, through cosmic developments to the final judgement and manifestation of God's kingdom. To express the last stage of this process he is deeply indebted to traditional material, as we have seen, but he also contributes his own distinctive emphases. But there is little scope here for an interplay between traditional mythology and the historical background, simply because the image is, by definition, an expectation for the future. Historical elements appear only to emphasize the incompleteness of present realities in the earthly cities over against the perfection of God's heavenly city.

8
Conclusions

As was said in the Introduction, the main purpose of this study has been to investigate the possibilities of a relationship between the historical background of the Book of Revelation and its author's use of traditional mythological ideas. Let us go through the seven selected topics again and draw together the main lines of our conclusions.

In the investigation of the letters to the seven churches, where we drew extensively on the work of Sir William Ramsay and its subsequent vindication in C. J. Hemer's thesis, a visual summary was offered of the cumulative strength of the historical interpretation. The most significant features of the letters combine in this exegesis to present an intelligible picture of these cities and churches in Asia Minor at the end of the first century A.D. Although the majority of local allusions are to general characteristics relevant over a long period, there are a sufficient number of pointers to the reign of Domitian to make the traditional date a reasonable working hypothesis. We also saw evidence for the author's use of the Old Testament and other traditional themes, and his adaptation of them so that they might bear a specific application to the contemporary situation of the churches.

The three sequences of Plagues – seals, trumpets and bowls – show very clearly the author's debt to traditional material; his work indicates a further stage in the use of imagery which originated in Israel's historical or prophetic traditions. The seals are closely related to the apocalyptic tradition found in the 'Little Apocalypse' of the Synoptic Gospels, while the trumpets and the bowls represent developments in the Egyptian plagues tradition, emphasizing in the first place the call to repentance and secondly the systematic punishment. In the sequence of the seals there is a reapplication of the apocalyptic tradition to the new circumstances of the Church in the years following the Fall of Jerusalem; each of the first five seals relates to an issue of concern for the churches of Asia Minor in the reign of Domitian. These historical elements are represented as part of the revelation of God's plan, a revelation inaugurated by the work of Christ in his life and death. The programme of apocalyptic expectation, modelled on the Synoptic tradition, is followed through by the Seer as he moves from an exposition of contemporary concerns, through the expectation of the cosmic woes, to the climax of judgement and vindication.

The episode of the two witnesses represents a significant 'interlude' within this total scheme. In a 'flash-back' the author in ch. 11 refers to the historical events of the siege and fall of Jerusalem (the forty-two months approximating to the period of the Flavian war from A.D. 67–70) and depicts the earlier but related episode of the witness of Peter and Paul in Rome and their martyrdom – the 1260 days covering the period from the fire of Rome in 64 to the martyrdom in 67/8. The account combines historical references with traditional material, such as the imagery of Zech. 4, expectations concerning Elijah and Moses, the theme of the beast and the Antichrist legend associated with Jerusalem and Rome. Observations can also be made about the way in which the historical and traditional material interacts: the martyrdom of Peter and Paul represents the foundation on which the author's deliberate association of Moses and Elijah is based; continuity and essential identity is established between Nero as the beast in this historical context of Rev. 11 and 'Nero Redivivus' as the beast in chs. 13 and 17; the reinterpretation of the Antichrist tradition, and the historical activity of Peter and Paul, together justify the author's treatment of the symbolic 'cities' in 11.8.

Attention was drawn, in the introduction, to the variety of theories about the mythological origins of the material in Rev. 12. My own theory concerning the interpretation of this chapter recognizes the likelihood that the imagery is derived either from one specific tradition (if a relationship can be established) or from a popular syncretism of traditions. Literary analysis by computer has also focused attention on this chapter as the one place in Revelation where it is most likely that the author has incorporated traditions in their original form. This makes it more important than ever to recognize the historical application of this material within John's overall scheme. With this imagery he establishes a broad historical perspective for the ultimate earthly manifestation of Antichrist. One can see that this is provoked by the circumstances of the birth of a male child; in an unusual mythological guise John emphasizes the centrality of the Incarnation and represents the essential relationship between the ideals of Israel and the contemporary phenomenon of the Christian church.

The mythological form of a beast with seven heads underlies the characterization of the dragon in Rev. 12.3 and also the picture of the beast from the sea in chs. 13 and 17. The identification of this second beast is presented as a riddle; the solution we propose takes due account of the historical references as well as the traditional formulation. The beast, fashioned from the imagery of Daniel and ultimately from creation mythology and the tradition of Leviathan, is to be understood in its new context in terms of the contemporary legend of 'Nero Redivivus'; all this traditional material is applied in turn to the immediate circumstances of the worship of the Roman emperors. John is characterizing as Antichrist the aspect of imperial organization most inimical to Christianity, the Imperial Cult under Nero's model which is a bestial parody of the true worship of God through Jesus Christ. It is 'Nero Redivivus' and his Eastern host who, the author believes, will fulfil God's purpose in their destruction of Rome (17.16f.). A suggestion is also made to reconcile the indications in this material of a date in the reign of Titus with the traditional Domitianic date attested elsewhere; the use of the author's own historical shaping of traditional elements in these two contexts would correspond to 'Jewish' expectation and its approaching fulfilment.

In examining the beast we were considering one part of a total picture which also includes the image of the harlot Babylon. Old Testament material relating to Israel's unfaithfulness to Yahweh is an important element in the characterization of this woman, and perhaps carries with it some of the original prophetic significance. It is applied to a new historical context in a way which illuminates the concept of Rome then current in Asia Minor. The patron-goddess Roma, worshipped in association with the Roman Emperor, had been readily accepted in this district as a means of perpetuating the tradition and practices of Ruler-worship. The traditional character of Babylon as the epitome of an ungodly power, and the association of Babylon in this sense with Rome, as represented in later apocalyptic and other Jewish and Christian writings, complete the principal feature of John's careful blend of history and tradition.

The final topic that has been examined is the expectation of the New Jerusalem; this has the least immediate relevance to the theme of our study of all seven topics, and for that reason the treatment was brief. But even here the author's debt to traditional material, and his distinctive contribution to its development, can clearly be seen. The New Jerusalem remains a future expectation, and for that reason has only limited connection with the historical circumstances of the author's own time. But attention has been drawn to some points of correspondence and contrast between the heavenly Jerusalem and the earthly cities, and between the Bride, the Woman clothed with the Sun, and the Harlot, all of which serve to emphasize the limitations of present realities over against the eschatological hope, and the reassurance of heavenly perfection and the fulfilment of promises for those who are victorious in the current situation.

It can be said with fairness, on the basis of this appraisal of the seven topics, that what began as the possibility of a relationship between the historical background of the Book and the author's use of traditional material has been substantiated and abundantly justified. But before we explore further the significance of such conclusions, a general word of caution is needed. The introductory chapter indicated some of the practical problems inherent in both the *zeitgeschichtlich* and the *traditionsgeschichtlich* methods of interpretation – problems in working with incomplete data and in drawing out superficial relationships. The scope of research must be limited by the resources available. For these reasons I am conscious that in writing this concluding chapter I am effectively writing also an introduction to a much larger work, which will require the endeavours of a lifetime on the part of several scholars. In order to complete the appraisal of the relationship between history and tradition, ideally we should possess more historical data, and – more important still – we need a fresh clarification of the actual historical relationships between those antecedent traditions to which reference can be made.

This view of what is still required can be reinforced by a quotation from the impassioned book by Klaus Koch, *The Rediscovery of Apocalyptic*. Koch says:

> The efforts of Stuhlmacher and Strobel show clearly yet again how shaky is the ground which is generally presented as 'late Judaism' – and how urgently work needs to be done on the pre-Christian and non-Christian material. The Qumran discoveries especially have revived the question of whether, and how far, 'Judaism' really existed before A.D. 70; and, if it did, whether

that 'Judaism' was in any way a spiritual unity. How far can the positions held by religious historians, especially Bousset and Volz, still be adhered to? To what extent have the views of Moore or Strack-Billerbeck stood the test of time? [1]

What is true as far as Revelation is concerned, of the immediate background of apocalyptic and inter-testamental Judaism, is true also of the possible debt to thought forms and mythologies from further afield.

Meanwhile I rashly offer a few tentative general conclusions and comments on the basis of my work on Revelation. I want to consider the significance of the relationship between the historical background and the use of traditional mythology in the book, and also to say something about the broader contexts of the book, such as the connections between the Apocalypse and apocalyptic, the Apocalypse and the New Testament, and the Apocalypse and its function in the early Christian world.

The impression I have formed of the author of Revelation is of a creative literary artist expressing himself with material from a wide variety of sources. The combination of historical allusion and traditional imagery is therefore a deliberate and highly skilful achievement and not simply the unconscious product of the influences in a particular environment. This is not to exclude the real possibility of a genuine spiritual experience underlying this work, but rather to suggest that here we have that rare situation of a creative artist with the ability to translate his experience into words and communicate it effectively so as to do justice to the experience. It is reasonable to conclude that the application of traditional ideas to a particular historical context is partly due to the original spiritual experience localized in a man's mind, and that this basic association is developed into a substantial literary expression of the combination, by the skill of the author.

The author of Revelation seems to stand in the Old Testament tradition even in this special respect of combining history with traditional mythology. Ancient myths such as those of the creation were borrowed by Israel's early thinkers and applied as theological statements about Yahweh; such applications were characterized by restraint rather than by elaboration. The assertion that 'the God of Israel has no mythology' [2] is a misleading exaggeration; what should be said is that, for Israel's faith, historical experience and reflections upon it, rather than upon the natural world, form the primary sphere of revelation, and so the story of past events takes precedence over nature myths.[3] But the myth becomes historicized and is used metaphorically to describe Yahweh's achievements in history[4] or used eschatologically to describe God's victory over his enemies on the Great Day to come.[5] The distinction between the historicization of myth and the mythical presentation of history appears as a question of the degree of emphasis in the work of individual writers.

Klaus Koch admits that 'the picture language of the apocalypses is so noticeable and so curious that it stands out clearly from the normal framework of the literature of the time and suggests a particular linguistic training, perhaps even a particular mentality'. But he rightly emphasizes that mythical images and richness of symbolism are by no means confined to strictly apocalyptic writings. For this reason the idea that the apocalyptists were deliberately 'remythologizing the long-since demythologized religion'[6] belongs among the distortions and popular misapprehensions of apocalyptic. The intensive and esoteric use of imagery needs to be coupled with the understanding of history in any characterization of apocalyptic, and then the line of development, admittedly taken to the extreme, from Israel's historic and prophetic writings becomes apparent.

What the author of Revelation achieved was a supreme statement of this attitude of mind, incorporating a highly significant range of contemporary and traditional imagery with Israel's insight into the meaning of history and the apocalyptists' vision of what – or, more accurately, who – transcends history. Koch's statement of the essence of apocalyptic can be applied pre-eminently to the Book of Revelation:

apocalypse means not only the revealing of details ... but the disclosure of possible participation in the final and unique, all-encompassing coming of God among men. An apocalypse is therefore designed to be 'the revelation of the divine revelation' as this takes place in the individual acts of a coherent historical pattern.[7]

Nowhere is this better demonstrated, nowhere can the 'continuous scarlet thread running through the whole' be seen more clearly than in the plague sequences of Revelation and in particular the seven seals opened by the Lamb.

The relationships between the Apocalypse and apocalyptic, and between apocalyptic and prophecy, are controversial in current scholarship. Revelation refers to itself as *apokalupsis* 'of Jesus Christ' (1.1), but this term should not be construed automatically as referring to the literary genre, for which scholars have used the names 'apocalypse' and more loosely 'apocalyptic' only within the last 200 years.[8] James Kallas posed the question sharply ('The Apocalypse – an Apocalyptic Book?') and established as a criterion the attitude towards suffering. If this criterion has been criticized subsequently and doubt cast on its validity as regards both Revelation and apocalyptic, how much less satisfactory are other subjective criteria for separating Revelation from this literary genre![9] The real fallacy in such arguments lies in the adoption of popular misapprehensions as a characterization of apocalyptic, and this results in the drastic separation of apocalyptic from prophecy and the natural desire to retain Revelation on the side of prophecy.

But if we allow the predominantly British and American exegesis which maintains that apocalyptic represents a continuation or development of prophecy,[10] and accept for the most part Klaus Koch's characterization of the forms and ideas of apocalyptic, with his critique of popular misconceptions,[11] then we can cease to be purely defensive in our attitude to Revelation and can offer a positive appraisal doing justice to the author's use of imagery and his understanding of history within a single broad perspective of developing traditions. It is interesting to note the variety of reasons given for the argument, frequent in Continental scholarship, that there is a great gulf between prophecy and apocalyptic. For G. von Rad 'the decisive factor ... is the incompatibility between the apocalyptic literature's view of history and that of the prophets'. He could, however, comment on 'the ability of the writers of apocalyptic literature to reduce history to the primary forces at work within it'. But what he describes as a 'positively hybrid-seeming universal Gnosis', characterized by determinism, makes him 'ask whether such a conception is not indicative of a great loss of historical sensitivity, whether history has not been excluded from the philosophy which lies behind this gnostic idea of epochs that can be known and calculated, a philosophy which has dispensed with the phenomenon of the contingent'.[12] Rudolf Bultmann speaks of 'the dehistoricizing of history by apocalyptic', but for the different reason that 'its end is determined by God and is not the organic close, the consummation of a course of development'.[13] Koch comments: 'For Bultmann, therefore, it is the very contingent character of the end which makes him feel the lack of a historical mode of thought, whereas for von Rad the lack of contingency is decisive.' [14] It becomes apparent that an influential factor in these discussions is the exegete's own understanding of history[15] and this tends to prevent an appreciation of the rather different understanding of the apocalyptist.

Klaus Koch refers to 'the agonised attempts to save Jesus from Apocalyptic' and to 'the great chorus of New Testament scholars who view apocalyptic of every kind with mistrust and discomfort, even when it appears in Christian guise, within the canon, in the book of Revelation'.[16] Ethelbert Stauffer could write: 'the world of apocalyptic ideas is the one in which the New Testament writers were really at home. This proposition provides the required indication of the place of Christianity in the history of religion.' But his is an unusual attitude in Continental scholarship of the period. W. G. Kümmel, who describes the chequered career of the Book of Revelation and the opposition it has faced over the centuries, concludes:

> there still remains no doubt that the Apocalyptist is in danger of falsifying the message of God's goal with world history.... The theological task of exposition of the Apocalypse can be properly fulfilled only if the impropriety of these conceptions and symbols is expounded and maintained. Just as there is no reason to exclude the Apocalypse as a whole from the New Testament, so there is every reason to regard detailed theological criticism of this writing as indispensable.[17]

Questions of detail certainly can only be settled by detailed exposition, but what has been said in this present study about the broad lines of interpretation for the Book might justifiably alleviate some scholarly discomfort. The Apocalypse declares its message within the framework of the New Testament. The relationship that has been examined between the historical background and the use of traditional mythology can be set in the wider context of the role of mythology within the New Testament and early Christian Theology. The evaluation and interpretation of New Testament mythology which has been discussed extensively by scholars, especially since the work of Rudolf Bultmann, provides a critical perspective against which to examine John's 'historical mythology', the form in which he chose to present his teaching about Christ and his Church. If the Book of Revelation requires 'demythologizing' for the general reader, it is no different from the rest of the New Testament in this regard.

Where the New Testament speaks with many voices to the ears of modern scholarship, this does not necessarily mean that all the voices are raised in anger against one another. Different emphases and various points of view can provide ultimately a richer and more satisfying expression of complementary attitudes, representative of the Early Christian world in the same way as the diversity we accept in our own day. So, as we have observed, John and Paul can speak of the authorities in their world, using rather different language, not because their situations are so radically different, but because they are speaking of different aspects – the political and the religious – of the relationship between Church and State. For these general reasons, we should recognize the voice of apocalyptic within the New Testament, and try to understand it in its context, rather than giving preference to some aspects and justifying our selectivity by the application of different labels. In this way we may be surprised by the richness of our discoveries and their essential harmony with what we already know.

For the Book of Revelation, we have been encouraged by the evidence to attempt an historical exegesis, to explain the text against the background of the contemporary circumstances, while recognizing the influence of a range of already developed traditions. But can one say more about the conditions and potentialities of the Book's temporal, geographical and linguistic environment? Can what has been established on the basis of internal evidence be further clarified by other external evidence? For example, does what is known about the *Sitz im Leben* of apocalyptic literature in the Old Testament and inter-testamental periods suggest the possibility of a similar setting and function for the Christian Apocalypse? Herein lies the problem already mentioned of an absence of information and an abundance of theories. Klaus Koch's survey 'indicates how completely obscure the sociological basis of the apocalyptic writings still is', so that he can only suggest, as a working hypothesis, that

if we are to arrive at a historical perception of the background against which apocalyptic ideas grew up, as well as a serviceable and generally applicable concept of apocalyptic, we must start from the writings which were composed in Hebrew or Aramaic, or in which, at least, the Hebrew or Aramaic spirit is dominant.[18]

In our examination of the seven letters, the two witnesses, and the imagery of Rev. 12, we found reasons for resisting the view that the Christian Apocalypse is anti-Jewish in feeling. John uses Jewish terminology, forms and traditions in his writing; he speaks of the Jews not merely as a type of the Christian Church, but also as a people who in principle still have a role to play in God's ultimate purposes. This suggests a situation within Christianity after the Fall of Jerusalem where there is intense sympathy for the tradition of Israel and correspondingly intense anger against those who were born Jews but have 'sold their birthright' in collaboration with the blasphemies of the Imperial cult.

It is hard to see how one could go further in reconstruction without more evidence, and without the necessary clarification of the historical relationships between different traditions in Judaism and beyond. If the apocalyptic strand within Judaism is representative of a particular religious party, rather than of a mental attitude found in all parties, and if this is developed as a cohesive and self-contained tradition,[19] perhaps transmitted through a community such as that at Qumran, then one might be justified in seeing the Book of Revelation as the product of that movement, transformed through contact with the Christian Gospel.

Bibliography and Notes

Commentaries – A Select List

Allo, E. B. Paris 1921 (Études Bibliques)
Baldensperger, G. Paris 1928
Barclay, W. Edinburgh 1959 (Daily Study Bible)
Beasley-Murray, G. R. London 1974 (New Century)
Beckwith, I. T. New York 1919
Behm, J. Göttingen 1949 (NTD)
Benson, E. W. London 1900
Boismard, M.-E. Paris 1953 (Jerusalem Bible)
Bonsirven, P. J. Paris 1958 (Verbum Salutis)
Bousset, W. Göttingen 1896 (Meyer)
Burnet, A. W. London 1946 (Russell Lectures)
Caird, G. B. London 1966 (Black)
Carrington, P. London 1931
Cerfaux, L. and Gambier, J. Paris 1955 (Lectio Divina)
Charles, R. H. Edinburgh 1920 (ICC)
Farrer, A. M. Oxford 1964 (cf. *A Rebirth of Images* London 1949)
Ford, J. M. Garden City, N.Y. 1975 (Anchor)
Gelin, A. Paris 1938 (La Sainte Bible)
Glasson, T. F. Cambridge 1965 (Cambridge Bible Commentary)
Hadorn, W. Leipzig 1928 (Theologischer Handkommentar)
Harrington, W. J. London 1969
Hartenstein, K. Stuttgart 1954³
Hendriksen, W. London 1962
Holtzmann, H. J. Tübingen 1908³ (W. Bauer)
Hort, F. J. A. London 1861 (chs. 1–3)
Kepler, T. S. New York 1957
Kiddle, M. London 1940 (Moffatt)
Kraft, H. Tübingen 1974 (HNT)
Ladd, G. E. Grand Rapids, Michigan 1972
Läpple, A. München 1966
Lilje, H. Hamburg 1955⁴; Philadelphia 1957
Loenertz, R. J. London 1947

Lohmeyer, E.   Tübingen 1926, 1953 (HNT)

Lohse, E.   Göttingen 1960 (NTD)

Loisy, A.   Paris 1923

Milligan, W.   London 1886

Moffatt, J.   London 1910 (Expositor's Greek Testament)

Morant, P.   Paderborn 1969

Morris, L.   London 1969 (Tyndale)

Müller-Jurgens, W.   Nürnberg 1968

Niles, D. T.   London 1962 (*As Seeing The Invisible*)

Oman, J.   Cambridge 1923

Orr, R. W.   Glasgow/London 1972

Peake, A. S.   London 1919

Preston, R. H. and Hanson, A. T.   London 1949 (Torch)

Reisner, E.   Göttingen 1949 (*Das Buch mit den sieben Siegeln*)

Rist, M.   Nashville 1957 (IB)

Schlatter, A.   Stuttgart 1938 (Erläuterungen zum N.T.)

Scott, C. A. A.   Edinburgh 1902 (Century Bible)

Sickenberger, J.   Bonn 1939

Spitta, F.   Halle 1889

Swete, H. B.   London 1906

Torrey, C. C.   New Haven 1958

Turner, N.   London 1962 (Peake's Commentary)

Weiss, J.   Göttingen 1908² (*Die Schriften des N.T.*)

Wikenhauser, A.   Regensburg 1947

Zahn, T.   Leipzig 1924–6

1

The Interpretation of the Book of Revelation

W. Bousset, *Die Offenbarung Johannis* (Göttingen 1896), pp. 49–119.

R. H. Charles, *Studies in the Apocalypse, being lectures delivered before the University of London* (Edinburgh 1913), Chs. 1, 2: 'History of the Interpretation of the Apocalypse'.

A. Feuillet, 'Les diverses méthodes d'interprétation de l'Apocalypse et les commentaires récents', *L'Ami du Clergé* 71 (1961), 257–70. *L'Apocalypse. État de la Question* (Paris 1963).

R. Halver, *Der Mythos im letzten Buch er Bibel* (Hamburg 1964).

E. Lohmeyer, 'Die Offenbarung des Johannes 1920–1934', *Th R* 6 (1934), 269–314; 7 (1935), 2–62.

O. Piper, 'Johannesapokalypse', *RGG³* (1957–65), III. 825f.

N. Cohn, *The Pursuit of the Millennium: revolutionary millenarians and mystical anarchists of the Middle Ages* (London 1970).

F. Kermode, *The Sense of an Ending: Studies in the Theory of Fiction* (New York 1967).

E. S. Shaffer, *Kubla Khan and The Fall of Jerusalem* (Cambridge 1975).

NOTES TO PAGES 1–19

1   W. Calder, 'Philadelphia and Montanism', *BJRL* 7 (1922–3), 309–54.

2   Feuillet, article, p. 258.

3   R. H. Charles, *A Critical and Exegetical Commentary on the Revelation of St. John*, 2 vols (Edinburgh 1920), I. clxxxiv.

4   Charles, commentary, II. 144ff.

5   Origen, *princ.* 4.2.4.

6   P. R. Ackroyd and C. F. Evans, *Cambridge History of the Bible*, Vol. I (Cambridge 1970), p. 379.

7   Millar Burrows, *The Dead Sea Scrolls* (London 1956), p. 248.

8   cf. M. Black, 'The Christological Use of the Old Testament in the New Testament', *NTS* 18 (1971), 1–14.

9   G. Bonner in *Cambridge History of the Bible*, I. 554.

10   Migne, *P.L.*, 5. 281–344.

11   See chapter 3.

12   cf. Marjorie Reeves, *Joachim of Fiore and the Prophetic Future* (London 1976).

13   It is hardly surprising that this line of interpretation was turned against the Papacy itself, in the first place by certain Franciscans, notably Peter John Oliva in his *Postilla super Apocalypsim*, and subsequently by sectarian and reforming movements. This tradition was inherited by Luther and the Lutheran exegesis of the sixteenth and seventeenth centuries.

14   Charles, commentary, I. clxxxiv.

15   E. Lohmeyer, *Die Offenbarung des Johannes* (Tübingen 1926; 1953).

16   P. Minear, 'Ontology and Ecclesiology in the Apocalypse', *NTS* 12 (1966), 89–105; p. 93.

17   *ibid.*, pp. 94, 96.

18   M. Rissi, *Time and History – A study on the Revelation* (Richmond 1966): quotations from Foreword, pp. 112–13, 115, 134; cf. Mathias Rissi, *Zeit und Geschichte in der Offenbarung des Johannes* (Zürich 1952); *The Future of the World – an exegetical study of Rev. 19.11–22.15* (London 1972).

19   Charles, *Studies*, p. 8.

20 S. Neill, *The Interpretation of the New Testament 1861–1961* (London 1964), pp. 141–2.

21 *Dictionary of National Biography 1931–40* (Oxford 1949), pp. 727f.

22 'Sir William Ramsay and the New Testament', *Studia Evangelica*, 5 (1968), 277–80; cf. W. Ward Gasque, *Sir William Ramsay: Archaeologist and New Testament Scholar* (Michigan 1966).

23 W. M. Ramsay, *The Letters to the Seven Churches of Asia and Their Place in the Plan of the Apocalypse* (London 1904), p. viii.

24 E. B. Allo, *L'Apocalypse de St. Jean* (Paris 1921).

25 *Adnotationes in Novum Testamentum* (Paris 1644).

26 *RB* 56 (1949), 507–41.

27 G. Mussies, *The Morphology of Koine Greek as used in the Apocalypse of St. John* (Leiden 1971), p. 3.

28 *The Jerusalem Bible* (London 1966), N.T., p. 429.

29 Work carried out by the author in collaboration with G. Jagger.

30 A. Dieterich, *Abraxas. Studien zur Religionsgeschichte des spätern Altertums* (Leipzig 1891), pp. 117ff.; H. Gunkel, *Schöpfung und Chaos in Urzeit und Endzeit. Eine religionsgeschichtliche Untersuchung über Gen 1 und Ap Joh 12* (Göttingen 1895), pp. 171–398; A. Jeremias, *Babylonisches im Neuen Testament* (Leipzig 1906), pp. 34–45.

31 W. Bousset, *Die Offenbarung Johannis* (Göttingen 1896), pp. 354ff.; H. Lietzmann, *Der Weltheiland* (Bonn 1909).

32 W. G. Kümmel, *Introduction to the New Testament* (London 1966), p. 332.

2

The Letters to the Seven Churches

W. Bauer, *Orthodoxy and Heresy in Earliest Christianity* (Philadelphia 1971).

G. E. Bean, *Aegean Turkey* (London 1966).

G. E. Bean, *Turkey Beyond the Maeander* (London 1971).

M. J. Brunk, 'The Seven Churches of Revelation Two and Three', *Bib. Sac.* 126 (1969), 240–6.

F. Hahn, 'Die Sendschreiben der Johannesapokalypse. Ein Beitrag zur Bestimmung prophetischer Redeformen' *Tradition und Glaube* (ed. Jeremias, Kuhn, Stegemann) (Göttingen 1971), 357–94.

C. J. Hemer, *A Study of the Letters to the Seven Churches of Asia with Special Reference to Their Local Background*: PhD thesis, University of

Manchester 1969, scheduled for publication in the SNTS Monographs series.

D. Magie, *Roman Rule in Asia Minor to the end of the third century after Christ*, 2 vols (Princeton 1950).

W. M. Ramsay, *The Letters to the Seven Churches of Asia and Their Place in the Plan of the Apocalypse* (London 1904).

A. Satake, *Die Gemeindeordnung in der Johannesapokalypse* (Neukirchen-Vluyn 1966).

NOTES TO PAGES 20–42

1 Edgar J. Goodspeed, *New Solutions of New Testament Problems* (Chicago 1927).

2 Ramsay, *Letters*, pp. 35ff.

3 J. Stevenson, *A New Eusebius* (London 1957), p. 145.

4 F. Spitta, *Die Offenbarung von Johannes* (Halle 1889).

5 Charles, commentary, I, xciv, 43–6.

6 M. Goguel, *L'Église primitive* (Paris 1947), p. 66.

7 M. Dibelius, 'Rom und die Christen im ersten Jahrhundert', *Botschaft und Geschichte* 2 (1956), p. 224.

8 M. Kiddle, *The Revelation of St. John* (London 1940), p. 18.

9 A. Farrer, *The Revelation of St. John the Divine* (Oxford 1964), pp. 11, 83ff.

10 Ramsay, *Letters*, pp. 70f.

11 *ibid.*, pp. 245f. Ramsay uses 'denunciation' in the sense of 'prophecy'.

12 D. G. Hogarth, *Excavations at Ephesus. The Archaic Artemisia*, 2 vols (London 1908).

13 Tacitus, *Ann.*, 3.61.

14 cf. Xenophon, *An.*, 5.3.6ff.

15 *Cambridge Ancient History*, Vol. 11 (1954), p. 39.

16 Apollonius of Tyana, *Ep.* 27, 65, 66.

17 Hemer, thesis, p. 95.

18 cf. R. Roberts, 'The Tree of Life (Rev. 2.7)' *ET* 25 (1914) 332.

19 *ET* 69 (1957–8), 176–8.

20 Some of Rudwick and Green's material was anticipated by Ramsay in *Cities and Bishoprics of Phrygia* (Oxford 1895), I, 48f., where he deals with the problems of the local water supply, but he drew no inferences from this for his discussion of the seventh letter.

21 Rudwick and Green add that, because each of the city gates opened on to a busy trade route, 'the inhabitants must have been very familiar with the belated traveller who "stood at the door and knocked" for admission' (Rev. 3.20).

22 Warm water was used as an emetic.
23 Ramsay, *Letters*, p. 41.
24 e.g. P. Minear, *I Saw A New Earth – An introduction to the visions of the Apocalypse* (Washington 1968), with an examination of parallels between the Letters and the New Jerusalem. cf. C. H. Parez, 'The Seven Letters and the Rest of the Apocalypse' *JTS* 12 (1911), 384–6.
25 Ephesus – cf. J. Keil, *Ephesos, Ein Führer durch die Ruinenstatt und ihre Geschichte* (Vienna 1955); F. Miltner, *Ephesos, Stadt der Artemis und des Johannes* (Vienna 1958). Quotations: Gen. 2.9; 3.22, 24; Ezek. 31.8; Test. L. 18.11; cf. 1 Enoch 24. 3–6; 25. 4–6; 2 Enoch 8. 2–4; Ps. Sol. 14. 2, 3; 1 QH 8. 4–14; 6. 15–16. Allusions: Exod. 25.13ff.—Jer. 2.2; Hos. 1–3—Ps. 139.21f.
26 Smyrna – C. J. Cadoux, *Ancient Smyrna* (Oxford 1938); W. M. Calder, 'Smyrna as described by the orator Aelius Aristides', *Studies in the History and Art of the Eastern Provinces of the Roman Empire* (ed. W. M. Ramsay) (London 1906), 95–116. Quotations: Isa. 44.6; 48.12—Dan. 1.12, 14. Allusions: Num. 16.3; 20.4; 27.17; 31.16; Josh. 22.16; Ps. 73.2; cf. Str.-B. 3.830f.
27 Pergamum – E. V. Hansen, *The Attalids of Pergamon* (New York 1947); P. Wood, 'Local Knowledge in the Letters of the Apocalypse' *ET* 73 (1961–2), 263f. Quotations: Num. 31.16; 25.1, 2—Ps. 78.24f.; cf. 2 Baruch 29.8; Sib. 7.148–9—Isa. 62.2; 65.15; cf. Exod. 28.17–21; Test. L. 8.14. Allusions: Ps. 89.37 (Heb.)—Isa. 11.4; 49.2—Exod. 16. 13–15, 32–4; 2 Macc. 2. 4–8; 2 Baruch 6. 7–10; Yoma 52b.
28 Thyatira – E. Schürer, 'Die Prophetin Isabel in Thyatira' *Th LZ* 18 (1893), 153–4. Quotations: Dan. 10.6; Ezek. 1.4, 7, 21; 8.2—1 Kings 21.25; cf. 16.31ff.; 18.19; 2 Kings 9.22f.—Num. 25.1f.—Ezek. 33.27; Jer. 21.7—Jer. 11.20; 17.10; 20.12; Ps. 7.9; 26.2; cf. 1 Sam. 16.7; Prov. 17.3; 21.2—Ps. 62.12; Prov. 24.12—Ps. 2.8f.; cf. Jer. 18.1–11. Allusions: Ps. 41.3—2 Kings 10.7; or 2 Sam. 12.14—Ps. 2.7—Num. 24.17; Dan. 12.3; CD.7; ctr. Isa. 14.12; Sib. 5. 516, 527 (Lucifer).
29 Sardis – P. Wood, 'Local Knowledge', *ET* 73 (1961–2), 263f.; D. G. Mitten, 'A New Look at Ancient Sardis' *BA* 29 (1966), 38–68. Quotations: Exod. 32.32f.; Ps. 69.28; Dan. 12.1; Mal. 3.16; cf. Isa. 4.3; 1 Sam. 25.29. Allusions: Isa. 11.2; Zech. 4.2, 10; Tob. 12.15—Ezek. 34.4; Obad. 5; Eccles. 9.8; 1 Enoch 71.1.
30 Philadelphia – W. M. Calder, 'Philadelphia and Montanism', *BJRL* 7 (1922–3), 309–54. Quotations: Isa. 22.22; Job 12.14—Isa. 45.14; 49.23; 60.14; Ps. 86.9; cf. 72.9ff.—Isa. 43.4—Ezek. 48.35; cf. Isa. 60.14; cf. 1 Kings 7.21; 2 Chron. 3.15, 17; Exod. 28. 36–8; Num. 6.27; Deut. 28.10; Isa. 43.7; 63.19; Dan. 9.18f.—Isa. 62.2; 65.15; cf. 1 Enoch 90.29; Test. L. 8.14. Allusions: Isa. 60.11, 22—Isa. 24.17; Hos. 4.1; Joel 2.1; Ps. 24.1; 33.8; 1 Enoch 37.5; 54.9; 55.1; 60.5; 65.6, 12; 66.1—1 Kings 7.21; Jer. 1.18; Isa. 22.23; 56.5; Berakoth 28b (figurative of R. Johanan ben Zakkai).

31 Anti-Jewish sentiments (cf. Charles, commentary, I. 57)? In view of
    later use of Jewish traditions (cf. Rev. 11, 12) it seems more likely to be
    an attack on particular instances of Jewish collaboration in Roman
    persecution of Christianity. By means such as the curse of the Minim,
    Christians who had sought refuge in the synagogue could be detected
    and disowned; cf. F. F. Bruce, *New Testament History* (London 1969),
    p. 382; C. J. Hemer, thesis, pp. 16f., 388f. John's view of relations with
    the Jewish synagogue is on a deeper theological level than that of
    seeking refuge in time of persecution.

32 Laodicea – W. M. Ramsay, *Cities and Bishoprics of Phrygia* (Oxford
    1895), I, 32–82; M. J. S. Rudwick and E. M. B. Green, 'The Laodicean
    Lukewarmness', *ET* 69 (1957–8), 176–8; S. E. Johnson, 'Laodicea
    and its Neighbours', *BA* 13 (1950), 1–18. Quotations: Prov. 8.22 –
    Hos. 12.8; cf. Zech. 11.5 – Eccles. 9.8; cf. Dan. 7:9 – Prov. 3.12; Song
    of Sol. 5.2. Allusions: Isa. 65.16; (or Prov. 8.22) cf. L. H. Silberman
    'Farewell to *ho amēn* – a note on Rev. 3.14' *JBL* 82 (1963), 213–15 –
    Isa. 55.1; Ps. 66.10; Zech. 13.9; Isa. 1.25.

3
The Plague Sequences

R. Bauckham, 'Synoptic Parousia Parables and the Apocalypse', *NTS* 23
(1977), 162–76.

A. Feuillet, 'Le premier cavalier de l'Apocalypse', *ZNTW* 57 (1966),
229–59.

Z. C. Hodges, 'The First Horseman of the Apocalypse', *Bib. Sac.* 119
(1962), 324–34.

T. Holtz, *Die Christologie der Apokalypse des Johannes* (Berlin 1962).

H. P. Müller, 'Die Plagen der Apokalypse', *ZNTW* 51 (1960), 268–78.

M. Rissi, 'The Rider on the White Horse – a study of Rev. 6. 1–8', *Int.* 18
(1964), 407–18.

W. S. Taylor, 'The Seven Seals', *JTS* 31 (1930), 266–71.

L. A. Vos, *The Synoptic Traditions in the Apocalypse* (Kampen 1965).

Y. Yadin, *The Art of Warfare in Biblical Lands in the light of archaeological
discovery* (London 1963).

NOTES TO PAGES 43–81

1 Charles, commentary, I, 155ff.

2 D. S. Russell, *The Method & Message of Jewish Apocalyptic* (London
   1964), p. 95, cf. pp. 92ff., 272ff.

3 G. von Rad, *Old Testament Theology*, Vol. 2 (Edinburgh/London
   1965), p. 124. e.g. Isa. 13; Joel 3.3f.; 4.15; Amos 8.9; Mic. 1.2–4;
   Nahum 1.2–10; Hab. 3.3ff.; Zech. 14.

4   J. Gray, *Archaeology and the Old Testament World* (London 1962), p. 19. cf. S. Mowinckel, *He That Cometh* (Oxford 1959), p. 269, n. 1.

5   cf. Str.-B. 4.977ff.

6   S. Mowinckel, *He That Cometh*, p. 295. cf. 1 Enoch 99.4ff.; Jub. 23.22ff.; 4 Esdras 4.51–5.13; 6.18ff.; 8.63–9.6; 2 Baruch 25–29; 48.30–37; 70.1ff.; Bab. Sanhedrin 96b.37; 97a. 5, 16, 36, 39; 98a. 4, 12, 21, 36; 98b. 2; Str.-B. 4.981ff.

7   e.g. 1 Enoch 80.2–7; 99.4ff.; 100.1ff.; Jub. 23.13–25; Sib. 3.538f., 633ff., 796ff.; 5.512ff.; Ass. Mos. 8.1; 10.5; Apc. Abr. 29f.; 2 Baruch 25–27; 32.1; 48.32ff.; 70.2ff.; 4 Esdras 5.1–12, 50–5; 6.21ff.

8   4 Esdras 5.4–8, 50–5; 6.16, 21ff.; 9.3; 2 Baruch 27; 32.1; 70.8; 1 Enoch 8.2; 80.2ff.; 99.5; 100.11; Jub. 23.18, 25; Sib. 2.154f., 164f.; 3.538ff., 633, 796–806; Josephus, *Bell*. 6.5.3; Apc. Abr. 29f.; Ass. Mos. 10.5; 2 Macc. 5.2f.

9   1 Enoch 99.4, 8; 100.1–2; 110.2; 4 Esdras 5.1–5, 9; 6.24; 9.3; 2 Baruch 25.3; 27.4; 48.32ff.; 70.2ff.; Jub. 23.16ff.; Sib. 3.633ff.; IQM.

10   1 Enoch 56.7; 90.16–19, 94ff.; Sib. 3.663ff., 670ff.; Apc. Elias 7.1ff.; Test. A. 7; D.5; Jos. 19; Ass. Mos. 10; Bab. Sanhedrin 95b.; 4 Esdras 13. Son of Man – Dan. 7.13; 1 Enoch 38.2f.; 51.3; 55.4; 61.8; 69.27ff.; 4 Esdras 13.1–3; Sib. 5.414f.

11   T. Colani, *Jésus-Christ et les croyances messianiques de son temps* (Strasbourg 1864), p. 204; H. J. Holtzmann, *Die synoptischen Evangelien, ihr Ursprung und geschichtlicher Charakter* (Leipzig 1863); G. R. Beasley-Murray, *Jesus and the Future* (London 1954), p. 11; cf. *A Commentary on Mark 13* (London 1957).

12   cf. Luke 21.12, for the same point made in a different way.

13   Charles, commentary, I. 158ff. On Mark 13, cf. R. H. Charles, *A Critical History of the Doctrine of a Future Life* (London 1899, 1913²), pp. 381ff.

14   cf. C. H. Dodd, 'The Fall of Jerusalem and the Abomination of Desolation', *JRS* 37 (1947), 47–54 (*More New Testament Studies*, Manchester 1968, 69–83); P. Winter, 'The Treatment of his Sources by the Third Evangelist in Luke XXI-XXIV', *St Th* 8 (1955), 138ff.; L. Gaston, 'Sondergut und Markusstoff in Lk 21', *Th Z* 16 (1960), 161ff.; T. Schramm, *Der Markus-Stoff bei Lukas: eine literarkritische und redaktionsgeschichtliche Untersuchung* (Cambridge 1971).

15   Charles, commentary, I. 158f., 181f.

16   Mark 13.21ff.; cf. 13.5f.; Matt. 24.23ff.; cf. 24.4f., 11; Luke 21.8; cf. 21.17, 20f., 23f., 37b.

17   G. R. Beasley-Murray, *Jesus*, p. 216; R. H. Lightfoot, *History and Interpretation in the Gospels* (London 1935), pp. 94, 104; C. K. Barrett, *Jesus and the Gospel Tradition* (London 1967), p. 52.

18   K. Stendahl in M. Black and H. H. Rowley (eds), *Peake's Commentary on the Bible* (London 1962), p. 794.

19　Hans Conzelmann, *The Theology of St. Luke* (London 1960), pp. 131f.

20　See note 14; cf. Beasley-Murray, *Jesus*, pp. 100, 212–16.

21　P. Minear, *I Saw A New Earth*, pp. 74, 78. On Rev. 5, cf. H. P. Müller, 'Die himmlische Ratsversammlung', *ZNTW* 54 (1963), 254–67.

22　Charles, commentary, I.136ff.; G. Schrenk, *TWNT*, 1.617ff.

23　'The Early Christian Symbol of the Open Book', *Exp*. 6 (1905), 294–306.

24　G. B. Caird, *The Revelation of St. John the Divine* (London 1966), p. 72; cf. Charles, commentary, I.138.

25　G. B. Caird, commentary, p. 71f.

26　P. R. Ackroyd in M. Black and H. H. Rowley, *Peake's Commentary on the Bible* (London 1962), p. 647.

27　On the use of the passive voice, avoiding reference to the divine name, cf. Blass Debrunner, 130 (1), 313, 342 (1).

28　M. Rostovtzeff, *The Social and Economic History of the Roman Empire* (Oxford 1957²), I, 145–7, 201; II. 599–600n.

29　Suetonius, *Dom*., 7.2; 14.2; Philostratus, *VA*, 6.42; *VS*, 1.21.520; Eusebius, *Chron*.; cf. Statius, *Silv*., 4.3.11f.; 4.2.34ff.

30　'La Mévente des Vins sous le Haut-Empire Romain', *Rev. Arch*. 3.39 (1901), 350–74.

31　W. M. Ramsay, 'Studies in the Roman Province Galatia', *JRS* 14 (1924), 179–84; cf. D. M. Robinson, 'A new Latin economic edict from Pisidian Antioch', *Transactions and Proceedings, Amer. Philol. Assoc*., 55 (1924), 5–20; cf. Dio Chrysostom, *Or.*, 46.8ff. (Prusa in Bithynia).

32　cf. Bertram, Rengstorf, *TWNT*, 2.896ff.; F. Boll, *Aus der Offenbarung Johannis* (Leipzig 1941), p. 85.

33　cf. Cicero, *Ver.* 3.81, 84; 2 Kings 6.25; 7.1, 18; D. Magie, *Roman Rule in Asia Minor* (Princeton 1950), 2.1443f. n. 38.

34　cf. Herodotus, 7.187; Thucydides, 4.16; Athenaeus, 3.20; Diogenes Laertius, *Pythag*. 8.18; cf. F. Stolle, *Der römische Legionar und sein Gepäck* (Strassburg 1914).

35　W. M. Ramsay, *Cities of St. Paul* (London 1907), pp. 430–2.

36　Irenaeus, *haer*. 4.21.3; M. Rissi, *Zeit und Geschichte in der Offenbarung des Johannes* (Zurich 1952), p. 90; W. M. Ramsay, *Letters*, p. 61; H. B. Swete, *The Apocalypse of St. John* (London 1909), p. 86.

37　H. Gunkel, *Zum religionsgeschichtlichen Verständnis des Neuen Testaments* (Göttingen 1903), pp. 53ff.

38　F. Cumont, *The Mysteries of Mithra* (London 1903); M. J. Vermaseren, *Mithras the Secret God* (London 1963); *Corpus Inscriptionum et Monumentorum Religionis Mithriacae*, 2 vols (Hague 1956–60); J. R.

Hinnells, 'Christianity and the Mystery Cults', *Theology* 71 (1968), 20–5.

39 Statius, *Theb.*, 1.717.

40 W. Harrington, *The Apocalypse of St. John* (London 1969), p. 123.

41 Xenophon, *Eq.*, 12.11; Josephus, *Bell.*, 3.94f.; W. Michaelis, *TWNT*, 4.524–7; 6.993–8.

42 Suetonius, *Ves.* 8.4.

43 D. Magie, *Roman Rule*, 1.577f.

44 cf. Rev. 8.7; 9.4.

45 ctr. R. Bultmann, *TWNT*, 3.7–21.

46 D. Magie, *Roman Rule*, 1.663; 2.1533, n. 8.

47 Aristides, *Or.*, 33.6; 48.38f.; 51.25; *CIG*, 3165.

48 cf. Charles, commentary, I, 155.

49 G. B. Caird, commentary, p. 80; cf. Rev. 1.18; 20.13f.; Ps. 49.14; Hos. 13.14; 1 Cor. 15.55 var.

50 cf. Lev. 26.22–6; Jer. 15.2f.; Ezek. 5.17; Epic of Gilgamesh, 11.4, 20–4.

51 Charles, commentary, I, 172–4; G. B. Caird, commentary, p. 84.

52 M. Kiddle, commentary, p. 121.

53 Charles, commentary, I, 179.

54 cf. A. T. Hanson, *The Wrath of the Lamb* (London 1957), pp. 159–80; G. B. Caird, commentary, pp. 91ff.

55 Bowls as altar vessels – Exod. 27.3; Num. 4.14; 1 Kings 7.40; 2 Kings 12.13; 1 Chron. 28.17; Neh. 7.70; Zech. 9.15; 14.20; Jer. 52.18; 1 Esdras 2.13; 1 Macc. 1.22.

56 cf. Str.-B. 3.461f.; S. Giet, *L'Apocalypse et l'histoire* (Paris 1957), pp. 5, 33; F. Boll, *Aus der Offenbarung*, p. 71.

57 cf. J. A. Thompson, 'Joel's Locusts in the Light of Near Eastern Parallels', *JNES* 14 (1955), 52–5.

58 Martin Noth, *Exodus: A Commentary* (London 1962), pp. 67–71.

59 e.g. Deut. 4.34; 6.22; 7.19; Ps. 105.27; 135.9.

60 cf. W. Harrington, commentary, p. 141.

61 J. Jeremias, *TWNT*, 1.468; 'Har Magedōn (Apc. 16.16)', *ZNTW* 31 (1932), 73–7; J. H. Michael, 'Har-Magedōn', *JTS* 38 (1937), 168ff.; C. C. Torrey, 'Armageddon', *HTR* 31 (1938), 237–50; O. Eissfeldt, *Baal Zaphon* (Halle 1932).

62 cf. Charles, commentary, II, 27.

63 G. B. Caird, commentary, pp. 108–11.

64 G. B. Caird, commentary, p. 111.

65 H. B. Swete, commentary, p. 200.

4

The Two Witnesses

L. Cerfaux, 'Témoins du Christ d'après le livre des Actes', *Recueil Lucien Cerfaux* (Gembloux 1954), II, 157–74.

J. S. Considine, 'The Two Witnesses – Apoc. 11.3–13', *CBQ* 8 (1946), 377–92.

A. Feuillet, 'Essai d'Interpretation du Chapitre XI de l'Apocalypse', *NTS* 4 (1958), 183–200.

S. Giet, *L'Apocalypse et l'histoire* (Paris 1957).

D. Haugg, *Die Zwei Zeugen – eine exegetische Studie über Apokalypse 11. 1–13* (Münster 1936).

P. S. Minear, 'Ontology and Ecclesiology in the Apocalypse', *NTS* 12 (1966), 89–105.

J. Munck, *Petrus und Paulus in der Offenbarung Johannis* (Copenhagen 1950).

NOTES TO PAGES 82–105

1   P. S. Minear, *I Saw A New Earth*, p. 95.

2   For the idea that the symbolism of Rev. 7.9–10 is founded on the ceremony of Tabernacles, see F. J. Badcock, 'The Feast of Tabernacles', *JTS* 24 (1923), 169–74.

3   In the context of Revelation a plausible interpretation is the diverse nature of the contents. But Ezek. 3.3, 14; Jer. 15.16f. (MT) are concerned with the reaction of the prophet.

4   Dan. 8.26; 12.4, 9; Rev. 22.10. In origin this is a literary device (cf. Isa. 8.16) to account for the fact that, although Daniel lived at the time of the Exile, his 'writings' did not appear until the age of Antiochus Epiphanes; cf. W. M. Ramsay, 'The Early Christian Symbol of the Open Book', *Exp.* 6, 6 (1905), 294–306; ctr. Rev. 10.4: 'seal up', which represents a different idea – the suppression of the seven thunders; they are not sealed as a prophecy for the future, because they are not even recorded.

5   cf. G. Bornkamm, 'Die Komposition der apokalyptischen Visionen in der Offenbarung Johannis', *ZNTW* 36 (1937), 132–49.

6   J. Wellhausen, *Analyse der Offenbarung Johannis* (Berlin 1907), p. 15; W. Bousset, commentary, ad loc.; Charles, commentary, I. 270f.

7   Charles, commentary, I. 274ff.

8   cf. 1 Enoch 61.1–5 where angels with cords measure the righteous and faithful, so that they may never be destroyed, before the Lord of Spirits.

9   cf. 2 Kings 21.13; Isa. 34.11; Lam. 2.8; Amos 7.7ff.

10   see note 5.

11   S. Giet, *L'Apocalypse*, pp. 27, 36f.

12   Charles, commentary, I. 280; A. Farrer, commentary, p. 131.

13   Most recently A. A. Trites, *The New Testament Concept of Witness* (SNTS Monograph 31) (Cambridge 1977).

14   H. Strathmann, *TWNT*, 4.478, 489.

15   Origen, *mart*. 5, 22.

16   *Apostolic Fathers*, I. Clement of Rome, Vol. 2, pp. 26f.

17   Hs. 9, 28, 3/5/6; Hv. 3, 1, 9; 3, 2, 1; 3, 5, 2.

18   *TWNT*, 4. 506.

19   RSV (Ps. 89.37) corrects the text here, but preserves in the margin: 'the witness in the skies is sure' (faithful).

20   *TWNT*, 4. 496.

21   Charles, commentary, I. 62; *TWNT*, 4. 495.

22   cf. *TWNT*, 4. 484f.; T. W. Manson, 'Martyrs and Martyrdom', *BJRL* 39 (1956–7), 463–84.

23   Munck, *Petrus und Paulus*, p. 18.

24   *Apostolic Fathers*, I. Clement of Rome, Vol. 2, p. 26.

25   P. R. Ackroyd in M. Black and H. H. Rowley, *Peake's Commentary on the Bible* (London 1962), p. 648.

26   G. B. Caird, commentary, p. 134.

27   Th. Zahn, *Die Offenbarung des Johannes* (Leipzig 1924–6), p. 428; Bousset, commentary, p. 319; Charles, commentary, I. 282; cf. Str.-B. 3. 811f.

28   Deut. 17.6; 19.15; Num. 35.30; Matt. 18.16; 2 Cor. 13.1; Heb. 10.28; cf. John 8.17f.

29   G. B. Caird, commentary, p. 135.

30   2 Kings 1.10ff., but agreeing with 4 Esdras 13 in making fire proceed out of the mouth. Idea parallel to Jer. 5.14 or of mythological origin? If thunder is God's voice, it is natural to think of lightning proceeding out of the mouth; cf. Num. 16.35.

31   J. Jeremias, *TWNT*, 4. 863; 2. 928f.; Mal. 3.23 is RSV Mal. 4.5.

32   W. Bousset, *The Antichrist Legend* (London 1896), pp. 134–9.

33   Apc. Elias 163f.; 'Basically Jewish but ... thoroughly worked over by Christians at the beginning of the fourth century' (Jeremias, *TWNT*, 2.930).

34   Munck, *Petrus und Paulus*, p. 85; cf. R. Bauckham, 'The Martyrdom of Enoch and Elijah: Jewish or Christian?', *JBL* 95 (1976), 447–58.

35   Munck, *Petrus und Paulus*, pp. 113–18.

36   *TWNT*, 2.941; cf. W. Wink, *John the Baptist in the Gospel Tradition* (Cambridge 1968), pp. 13ff.; 'Elijah did suffer (1 Kings 19.2–10); but there is no basis for the much-advanced conjecture that pre-Christian apocalyptists expected Elijah to suffer at his return.'

37   *TWNT*, 4. 863.

38   *TWNT*, 4. 860f.

39   1 Enoch 90.31; 89.52; 4 Esdras 6.26; – Justin *dial*. 8.4; 49.1; Str.-B. 4. 748–89; Sopherim 19.9; Mark 9.11; Matt. 17.10; John 1.21, 25; Mark 6.15 //; 8.28 //.

40   Test. R.6; S.7; L.2, 8, 18; Judg. 21; D.5; N.8; G.8; Josh. 19; Str.-B. 3. 696, 812; 4. 460ff.; 789ff.

41   Qohelet rabba 1.28 on 1.9; Qumran usage – cf. R. E. Brown, *The Gospel According to John* (New York 1966), I. 49f.; J. Macdonald, *The Theology of the Samaritans* (London 1964).

42   The dominant Rabbinic tradition is concerned with the death of Moses based on Deut. 34.6.

43   It is only a possibility that these correspond, in the reverse order, to the Qumran expectation of 'the coming of a prophet and the messiahs of Aaron and Israel' (1 QS. 9. 11).

44   Munck, *Petrus und Paulus*, p. 27.

45   cf. A. Satake, *Die Gemeindeordnung in der Johannesapokalypse* (Neukirchen-Vluyn 1966); D. Hill, 'Prophecy and Prophets in the Revelation of St. John', *NTS* 18 (1972), 401–18; M. Green, *Evangelism in the Early Church* (London 1970).

46   A. Farrer, commentary, p. 136.

47   G. B. Caird, commentary, p. 138.

48   Ps. Hecataeus (in Josephus, *Ap*. 1.197) gives a figure *c*. 120,000; *The Beginnings of Christianity* (F. J. Foakes-Jackson, Kirsopp Lake) I.I (1920), p. 1, reckons, apart from festivals, a total not exceeding 50,000; Bousset/Gressmann, *Die Religion des Judentums* (Tübingen 1926), p. 65, thinks the figure exceeds 120,000; J. Jeremias, *Jerusalem in the Time of Jesus* (London 1969), pp. 83f. estimates between 25,000 and 30,000 at the time of Jesus.

49   P. S. Minear, article, pp. 94f.

50   Sib. 5.154, 226, 413; Josephus, *Ap*. 1.197, 209; Appian, *Syr*. 50; Pliny *H.N.* 5.14, 70 are the only references to Jerusalem.

51   Charles, commentary, I. 287.

52   Tacitus *Ann*., 14.27 dates the Lycus Valley earthquake in A.D. 60. According to Eusebius it seems to follow the fire of Rome. According

to Orosius, *Hist.*, 7.7.12 it is one of a series of judgements on the pagan world, consequent upon the fire and the Neronian persecution.

5

The Woman Clothed with the Sun

L. Cerfaux, 'La Vision de la Femme et du Dragon', *ETL* 61 (1955), 7–33.

A. Feuillet, 'La Messie et sa Mère d'après le chapitre XII de l'Apocalypse', *RB* 66 (1959), 55–86.

W. Foerster, 'Die Bilder in Offenbarung 12f. und 17f.', *Th St Kr* 104 (1932), 279–310.

W. H. C. Frend, *Martyrdom and Persecution in the Early Church* (Oxford 1965), Chapter 7, pp. 70–135.

B. J. Le Frois, *The Woman Clothed with the Sun* (Rome 1954).

J. McHugh, *The Mother of Jesus in the New Testament* (London 1975).

J. Michl, 'Die Deutung der apokalyptischen Frau in der Gegenwart', *BZ* 3 (1959), 301–10.

P. Prigent, *Apocalypse 12. Histoire de l'exégèse* (Tübingen 1959).

T. H. Robinson, 'Hebrew Myths', in S. H. Hooke (ed.), *Myth and Ritual* (London 1933), pp. 179ff.

A. Vögtle, 'Mythos und Botschaft in Apokalypse 12', *Tradition und Glaube* (ed. Jeremias, Kuhn, Stegemann) (Göttingen 1971), 395–415.

NOTES TO PAGES 106–121

1 Charles, commentary, I. 299ff.

2 London 1961.

3 2 Kings 19.21; Amos 5.2; Isa. 37.22; Jer. 18.13; 31.4, 21; Lam. 1.15; 2.13; cf. Ps. 9.14; 48.11; 97.8; Song of Sol. 3.11; Isa. 1.8; 3.16f.; 4.4; 16.1; 23.12; 47.1; 52.2; 62.11; 66.8; Jer. 4.31; 6.2, 23; 14.17; 46.11; Lam. 1.6; 2.1, 4, 10, 13; Joel 1.8; Mic. 1.13. G. Delling, *TWNT*, 5. 829ff.

4 Hos. 3; Jer. 2.1; Ezek. 16.23.

5 Hos. 13.13; Isa. 26.16ff.; 66.7ff.; Jer. 4.31; Mic. 4.10; cf. D. S. Russell, *The Method & Message of Jewish Apocalyptic* (London 1964), pp. 272f.

6 cf. S. Mowinckel, *He That Cometh* (Oxford 1956), pp. 114ff.

7 J. V. Chamberlain, 'Another Qumran Thanksgiving Psalm – further elucidation of a Messianic Thanksgiving Psalm from Qumran', *JNES* 14 (1955), 32–41, 181f.; L. H. Silberman, 'Language and Structure in the Hodayot (1QH3)', *JBL* 75 (1956), 96–106; J. Baumgarten and M. Mansoor, 'Studies in the New Hodayot (Thanksgiving Hymns) – II', *JBL* 74 (1955), 188–95; O. Betz, 'Die Geburt der Gemeinde durch

den Lehrer', *NTS* 3 (1956–7), 314–26; 'Das Volk Seiner Kraft – zur Auslegung der Qumran Hodajah III 1–18', *NTS* 5 (1958–9), 67–75; R. E. Brown, 'The Messianism of Qumran', *CBQ* 19 (1957), 53–82; W. H. Brownlee, 'Messianic Motifs of Qumran and the New Testament', *NTS* 3 (1956–7), 12–30.

8   cf. Farrer, commentary, p. 141.

9   cf. Dan. 12.3; Deut. 11.21; Str.-B. 3.1138ff. A. Feuillet, 'Le Cantique des Cantiques et l'Apocalypse', *Rech. de Sc. rel.*, 49 (1961), 321–53.

10 cf. Jewish practice of allegory, applied to High Priestly vestments, Josephus, *Ant.* 3.180; *Bell.* 5.212f.; Philo, *Fug.* 110; *Vit. Mos.* 2.117–35; *Spec. Leg.* 1.85–95; *Migr. Abr.* 102f.; on the basis of Exod. 28.1–43; 39.1–31; Ezek. 28.13.

11 Charles, commentary, I. 299f.; Farrer, commentâry, pp. 141f., 144.

12 cf. John 3.14; 8.28; 12.32ff.

13 cf. E. Schweizer, *Church Order in the New Testament* (London 1961), p. 132, n. 485; cf. Caird, commentary, p. 149.

14 cf. 4 Esdras 9.38–10.57.

15 Charles, commentary, I. 305ff.

16 W. Foerster, *TWNT*, 5.566ff.; 2.281ff.

17 W. Foerster and G. von Rad, *TWNT*, 2.71ff.; W. Foerster and K. Schäferdiek, *TWNT*, 7.151ff.

18 H. Braun, *TWNT*, 6.228ff.; A. Oepke, *TWNT*, 1.384f.

19 Farrer, commentary, pp. 145f.

20 Luke 10.18.

21 On Michael, cf. Str.-B. 1.142; Charles, commentary, I.323f.; 1QM. 17.5ff.; 11 Q. Melch. There appears to be a local tradition in Asia Minor that Michael struck a rock at Colossae with his sword during the first century A.D.

22 cf. Rev. 1.20, E. Schweizer, *TWNT*, 6. 332–451; 'Die sieben Geister in der Apokalypse', *Neotestamentica 1951–63* (Zurich 1963), 190–202.

23 cf. E. C. Hoskyns, 'Genesis I–III and St. John's Gospel', *JTS* 21 (1920), 210–18.

24 Homer *Il.* 24.310.

25 G. A. Cooke, *The Book of Ezekiel* (ICC) (Edinburgh 1936), pp. 181ff.

26 Charles, commentary, I. 331; On Pella cf. Eusebius, *h.e.*, 3.5; Epiphanius, *mens.*, 15.43.261.

27 M. Stein, 'Yabneh and her Scholars', *Zion* n.s. 3 (1938), 118ff.; cf. W. M. Christie, 'The Jamnia Period in Jewish History', *JTS* 26 (1925), 347–64.

28 J. Neusner, *A Life of Rabban Yohanan ben Zakkai ca. 1–80 C. E.* (Leiden 1962), p. 122.

29 Ketuboth 4.6; Eduyoth 2.4; Jer. Barakoth 4.1.

30 Th. Mommsen, *The Provinces of the Roman Empire* (London 1886), 2.216ff.

31 K. W. Clark, 'Worship in the Jerusalem Temple after A.D. 70', *NTS* 6 (1960), 269–80; cf. Dio Cassius, *h.r.*, 69.12ff.

32 M. P. Charlesworth, *Cambridge Ancient History*, Vol. 11 (1954), p. 42.

33 M. P. Charlesworth, 'Some Observations on Ruler Cult, especially in Rome', *HTR* 28 (1935), p. 34.

34 See note 13.

6

The Beast and the Harlot

M. P. Charlesworth, 'Deus Noster Caesar', *Classical Review* 39 (1925), 113–15; 'Some Observations on Ruler Cult, especially in Rome', *HTR* 28 (1935), 5–44.

M. Grant, *Nero* (London 1970).

J. Spencer Kennard, 'The Jewish Provincial Assembly', *ZNTW* 53 (1962), 25–51.

D. Magie, *Roman Rule in Asia Minor to the end of the third century after Christ*, 2 vols (Princeton 1950).

P. S. Minear, 'The Wounded Beast', *JBL* 72 (1953), 93–101.

B. Newman, 'The Fallacy of the Domitian Hypothesis: Critique of the Irenaeus source as a witness for the contemporary-historical approach to the interpretation of the Apocalypse', *NTS* 10 (1963), 133–9.

A. D. Nock, *Essays on Religion and the Ancient World*, 2 vols (Oxford 1972).

D. M. Pippidi, 'Le "Numen Augusti" – Observations sur une forme occidentale du culte impérial', *Revue des Études Latines*, 11 (1931), 1–29.

H. W. Pieket, 'An Aspect of the Emperor Cult – Imperial Mysteries', *HTR*, 57 (1965), 331–47.

J. A. T. Robinson, *Redating the New Testament* (London 1976), pp. 221–53.

R. Schütz, *Die Offenbarung des Johannes und Kaiser Domitian* (Göttingen 1933).

K. Scott, *The Imperial Cult under the Flavians* (Stuttgart 1936).

L. R. Taylor, *The Divinity of the Roman Emperor* (Middletown, Conn. 1931).

P. Touilleux, *L'Apocalypse et les cultes de Domitien et de Cybèle* (Paris 1935).

H. Wallace, 'Leviathan and the Beast in Revelation', *BA* 11 (1948), 61–8.

NOTES TO PAGES 122–153

1   A. Farrer, commentary, p. 155.

2   ctr. B. Murmelstein, 'Das zweite Tier in der Offenbarung Johannis', *Th St Kr* 101 (1929), 447–57.

3   W. Foerster, *TWNT*, 3.133ff.; cf. 'Die Bilder in Offenbarung 12f. und 17f.', *Th St Kr* 104 (1932), 279–310.

4   Sib. 8.157; Pliny *Pan.* 48.3; Philostratus *VA*. 4.38. cf. R. Schütz, *Die Offenbarung des Johannes und Kaiser Domitian* (Göttingen 1933), pp. 8f.

5   E. W. Heaton, *The Book of Daniel* (London 1956); A. Bentzen, *Daniel* (Tübingen 1952²); H. Gunkel, *Schöpfung und Chaos in Urzeit und Endzeit* (Göttingen 1895), pp. 29–82; *Zum religionsgeschichtlichen Verständnis des Neuen Testaments* (Göttingen 1903), pp. 38–64.

6   D. Winton Thomas, *Documents from Old Testament Times* (London 1958), pp. 129ff.

7   Tacitus, *Ann.*, 15.44.

8   Suetonius, *Lives*; Josephus, *Bell.* 4.9.2.; Sib. 5.35.

9   H. B. Swete, commentary, p. 164.

10   cf. Charles, commentary, I. 161.

11   Apart from primary sources (Suetonius, Tacitus, Dio Cassius); M. P. Charlesworth (ed.), *Documents illustrating the reigns of Claudius and Nero* (Cambridge 1939); E. M. Smallwood, *Documents illustrating the Principates of Gaius, Claudius and Nero* (Cambridge 1967); consult among recent works on Nero: J. H. Bishop, *Nero: the Man and the Legend* (London 1964); G. Charles-Picard, *Augustus and Nero – the Secret of Empire* (London 1966); B. H. Warmington, *Nero: Reality and Legend* (London 1969); M. Grant, *Nero* (London 1970).

12   Sib. 4.119f., 137f.

13   Tacitus, *Hist.* 1.2; 2.8, 9; Dio Cassius, *h.r.*, 66.15; Suetonius, *Nero*, 57, 40; Dio Chrysostom, *Or.*, 21.10.

14   Sib. 5.361f.; 8.88, 157; 5.29, 215ff.; 3.63ff.; 2.167f.; Ascens. Is. 4.2f. cf. Augustine, *De Civitate Dei*, 20.19.

15   Minear, article, p. 97.

16   Rom. 13.1ff.; cf. 1 Pet. 2.13; 1 Tim. 2.2. cf. W. L. Knox, 'Church and State in the New Testament', *JRS* 39 (1949), 23–30.

17   M. Rostovtzeff, *The Social and Economic History of the Roman Empire* (Oxford 1957²), I.86.

18 Suetonius, *Ves.*, 23.

19 Minear, article, pp. 98f.

20 Suetonius, *Tit.*, 1.

21 On Titus and Domitian, consult the primary sources (Suetonius and Dio Cassius); M. McCrum and A. G. Woodhead, *Select Documents of the Flavian Emperors including the year of Revolution. A.D. 68–96* (Cambridge 1961); *Cambridge Ancient History* Vol. 11 (1954).

22 Bauer (Arndt and Gingrich), p. 171.1; W. Grundmann, *TWNT*, 2.21ff. cf. Mark 8.31; 9.11; 13.7, 10; Luke 24.7, 26; John 20.9; Acts 3.21; 1 Cor. 15.25, 53; 2 Cor. 5.10; Rev. 1.1; 4.1; 22.6; cf. Dan. 2.28, 29, 45.

23 Suetonius, *Dom.* 12, 13, 37, 38; Tacitus, *Ag.* 2f., 44f.; Dio Cassius, *Epitome* 67.14; Eusebius, *h.e.*, 3.17–20; Juvenal, 4.38; Pliny, *Pan.* 53; Tertullian, *Apol.* 5; *De Pall.* 4; Sib. 5.218ff.; B. 4.4–5.

24 cf. Mark 13.20 and chapter three, above.

25 For further significance of the number eight, cf. Farrer, commentary, p. 158.

26 cf. Sulpicius Severus, *Chronicle*, 2.30.6. Titus reflects that to destroy the Jerusalem temple 'would be an invaluable way of doing away with both the Christian and the Jewish religions for, although mutually inimical, these two faiths had sprung from the same root ... and, once the root was dug up, the stem would soon perish'.

27 E. Stauffer, *Christ and the Caesars* (London 1955), p. 188.

28 F. Hauck, S. Schulz, *TWNT*, 6. 579–95.

29 cf. B. W. Bacon, 'The Apostolic Decree against *porneia*', *Exp.*, 8.7 (1914), 40–61; C. K. Barrett, 'Things Sacrificed to Idols', *NTS* 11 (1965), 138–53.

30 K. G. Kuhn, *TWNT*, 1.515, n. 11.

31 Seneca (Rhet), *Con.* 1.2.7.; Juvenal, 6.122f.

32 Mandaean parallels (cf. Lohmeyer, commentary, p. 142) are unnecessary.

33 *TWNT*, 1.515.

34 cf. 2 Baruch 11.1f.; 67.7; 4 Esdras 3.1f., 28; Sib. 5.1.43, 157ff.; Str.-B.3. 816; Num. R.7 on 5.2ff.; Midrash Ps. 121.

35 See the commentaries of E. G. Selwyn (1947), J. N. D. Kelly (1969), E. Best (1969). cf. C. H. Hunzinger, 'Babylon als Deckname für Rom und die Datierung des 1 Petrusbriefes', *Gottes Wort und Gottesland* (ed. H. Reventlow) (Göttingen 1965), 65–77.

36 A. Schlatter, *Die Geschichte der ersten Christenheit* (Gütersloh 1926), p. 303.

37 J. L. Kelso, *Interpreter's Dictionary of the Bible* (Nashville 1962), 1. 748f. cf. L. Goppelt, *TWNT*, 6.148–58. Cf. Ps. 16.5; 23.4; 116.13, for

symbol of joy; Ps. 11.6; 75.8; Isa. 51.17–23; Jer. 25.15–28; 49.12; 51.7; Lam. 4.21f.; Ezek. 23.31–4; Hab. 2.16; Zech. 12.2 for punishment and suffering. J. G. Davies, 'The Cup of Wrath and the Cup of Blessing', *Theology* 51 (1948), 178–80.

38   C. E. B. Cranfield, *The Gospel According to St Mark* (Cambridge 1959), p. 433; cf. V. Taylor, *The Gospel According to St Mark* (London 1952), p. 554; C. E. B. Cranfield, 'The Cup Metaphor in Mark 14.36 and Parallels', *ET* 59 (1948), 137; M. Black, 'The Cup Metaphor in Mark 14.36', *ET* 59 (1948), 195.

39   W. L. Knox, *The Sources of the Synoptic Gospels* (London 1953/7), 1.71; A. Oepke, *TWNT*, 1.530.

40   cf. Jer. 25.15f.; Ps. 75.8; Ps. Sol. 8.14; Aeschylus *Pr.* 678.

41   G. Bornkamm, *TWNT*, 4. 254–7.

42   cf. Charles, commentary, II. 14.

43   cf. Plato *Cra.* 419E; F. Büchsel, *TWNT*, 3.167–72; G. Stählin et al., *TWNT*, 5. 382–447.

44   A. T. Hanson, *The Wrath of the Lamb* (London 1957), p. 161.

45   W. Foerster, *TWNT*, 1.598ff.; F. Hauck, *TWNT*, 3.427ff.

46   G. B. Caird, commentary, p. 213.

47   O. Michel, *TWNT*, 3.812ff.; F. Lang, *TWNT*, 6. 928–52.

48   Pliny *H.N.* 9.53; cf. E. Wunderlich, *Die Bedeutung der roten Farbe im Kultus der Griechen und Römer* (Giessen 1925).

49   e.g. Messalina (W. Barclay, *The Revelation of John* (Edinburgh 1959), 2.187f.).

50   E. Stauffer, *Christ and the Caesars* (London 1955), p. 188; cf. W. Bousset, commentary ad. loc.; *The Antichrist Legend* (London 1896), p. 62; Sib. 3.75–7; 5.18; 8.200; W. W. Tarn, *Cambridge Ancient History*, 10 (1952), Ch. 2.

51   cf. L. R. Taylor, *The Divinity of the Roman Emperor* (1931), pp. 35ff. F. Pfister, 'Romaia', Pauly-Wissowa, 2nd series, I A, 1.1061ff.

52   F. Altheim, *A History of Roman Religion* (1938), Bk. 4.

53   Tacitus, *Ann.*, 4.56.1; for evidence on the cults of Roma, and Roma and Augustus, see D. Magie, *Roman Rule in Asia Minor* (Princeton 1950), Vol. 2, Appendix 3.

54   Suetonius, *Aug.*, 52.

55   Dio Cassius, *h.r.*, 51.20.6–8; Tacitus, *Ann.*, 4.37.

56   F. Altheim, *A History of Roman Religion*, p. 350.

57   A. W. van Buren, 'The Ara Pacis Augustae', *JRS* 3 (1913), 134–41; cf. E. Strong, *JRS* 27 (1937), 114; M. A. Momigliano, 'The Peace of the Ara Pacis', *Journal of Warburg and Courtauld Institutes* 5 (1942), 228–31.

7

The New Jerusalem

A. Causse, 'Le Mythe de la nouvelle Jérusalem du Deutéro-Esaïe à la IIIe Sibylle', *RHPR* 18 (1938), 377–414. 'De la Jérusalem terrestre à la Jérusalem céleste', *RHPR* 27 (1947), 12–36.

M. Noth, 'Jerusalem and the Israelite Tradition', *The Laws in the Pentateuch and Other Essays* (Edinburgh/London 1966), 132–44.

K. L. Schmidt, 'Jerusalem als Urbild und Abbild', *Er Jb*, 18 (1950), 207–48.

A. Wikenhauser, 'Die Herkunft der Idee des tausendjährigen Reiches in der Johannesapokalypse', *Römische Quartalschrift* 45 (1937), 1–24.

NOTES TO PAGES 154–159

1 cf. Noth article; G. Fohrer and E. Lohse, *TWNT*, 7. 292–338; G. von Rad, 'The City on the Hill', *The Problem of the Hexateuch and Other Essays* (Edinburgh/London 1966), 232–42; A. Causse articles; R. E. Clements, *God and Temple* (Oxford 1965); N. W. Porteous, 'Jerusalem/Zion: the Growth of a Symbol', *Living the Mystery* (Oxford 1967), 93–111; K. L. Schmidt, article.

2 D. S. Russell, *The Method & Message of Jewish Apocalyptic* (London 1964), pp. 280ff.

3 cf. Heb. 12.22; 11.10, 16; 13.14; C. K. Barrett, 'The Eschatology of the Epistle to the Hebrews', *The Background of the New Testament and its Eschatology* (Davies and Daube) (Cambridge 1956), 363–93; Gal. 4.25f.; Hv. 3; Hs. 9. '

4 Str.-B. 3.796.

5 cf. 1 Enoch 90.29; 2 Baruch 4.3ff.; 4 Esdras. 7.26; 10.54; 13.36; T. Holtz, *Die Christologie der Apokalypse des Johannes* (Berlin 1962), p. 192, n. 5; Charles, commentary, II. 158.

6 Charles, commentary, II. 161; H. B. Swete, commentary, p. 277; A. Feuillet, *L'Apocalypse. État de la Question* (Paris 1963), pp. 45f. G. B. Caird, commentary, pp. 55, 271.

7 Hemer, thesis, pp. 41, 98f.

8 *SIG³* 996.30 (1st century A.D.).

9 P. Minear, *I Saw A New Earth*, p. 61.

10 cf. J. E. Bruns, 'The Contrasted Women of Apoc. 12 and 17', *CBQ* 26 (1964), 459–63.

11 A. Satake, *Die Gemeindeordnung in der Johannesapokalypse* (Neukirchen-Vluyn 1966), p. 25.

12 cf. W. W. Reader, *Die Stadt Gottes in der Johannesapokalypse* (Dissertation zur Erlangung des Doktorgrades – Theologischen Fakultät) (Göttingen 1971).

8
Conclusions

Klaus Koch, *The Rediscovery of Apocalyptic* (London 1972).

NOTES TO PAGES 160–169

1   Koch, *Rediscovery*, p. 86. P. Stuhlmacher, *Gerechtigkeit Gottes bei Paulus* (FRLANT 87) (Göttingen 1965); A. Strobel, *Kerygma und Apokalyptik* (Göttingen 1967).

2   G. Ernest Wright, *The Old Testament Against its Environment* (London 1950), p. 26.

3   cf. H. Frankfort, *Before Philosophy (The Intellectual Adventure of Ancient Man)* (Chicago 1946); Th. C. Vriezen, *The Religion of Ancient Israel* (London 1967); H. Wheeler Robinson, *Inspiration and Revelation in the Old Testament* (Oxford 1962).

4   e.g. Isa. 51.9–10.

5   e.g. Isa. 27.1.

6   Koch, *Rediscovery*, p. 27.

7   ibid., p. 33.

8   cf. J. M. Schmidt, *Die jüdische Apokalyptik. Die Geschichte ihrer Erforschung von den Anfängen bis zu den Textfunden von Qumran* (Neukirchen-Vluyn 1969).

9   James Kallas, 'The Apocalypse – An Apocalyptic Book?' *JBL* 86 (1967), 69–81; B. W. Jones, 'More about the Apocalypse as Apocalyptic', *JBL* 87 (1968), 325–7; G. E. Ladd, 'The Revelation and Jewish Apocalyptic', *EvQ* 29 (1957), 94–100; D. Hill, 'Prophecy and Prophets in the Revelation of St. John', *NTS* 18 (1972), 401–18.

10 H. H. Rowley, *The Relevance of Apocalyptic* (London 1944); S. B. Frost, *Old Testament Apocalyptic* (London 1952) (ctr. 'Apocalyptic and History', *The Bible in Modern Scholarship*, ed. J. P. Hyatt; Nashville 1965, 98–113); D. S. Russell, *The Method & Message of Jewish Apocalyptic* (London 1964); C. K. Barrett, *The New Testament Background: Selected Documents* (London 1956), p. 227; O. Plöger, *Theocracy and Eschatology* (Oxford 1968).

11 Koch, *Rediscovery*, pp. 23–33.

12 G. von Rad, *Old Testament Theology*, Vol. 2, pp. 303ff. quoting variously from English edition 1965 and 4th German edition 1965.

13 R. Bultmann, *Geschichte und Eschatologie* (Tübingen 1964), pp. 34f.

14 Koch, *Rediscovery*, p. 140, n. 39.

15 cf. the use made of the apocalyptic concept of history in the work of Wolfhart Pannenberg.

16 Koch, *Rediscovery*, ch. 6 and p. 63.

17 E. Stauffer, *New Testament Theology* (London 1955), p. 21; W. G. Kümmel, *Introduction to the New Testament* (London 1966), p. 333.

18 Koch, *Rediscovery*, pp. 22f.

19 cf. G. Bornkamm, *TWNT*, 6. 668ff.; J. Massyngberde Ford, *Revelation* (Anchor Bible) (Garden City, N.Y. 1975).

Index of Authors

193

Index of Subjects

In view of the importance of numbers throughout the Book of Revelation it has seemed advisable to list certain subjects below under the number(s) with which they are prominently associated.

Allegorical interpretation 3–5, 184
Antichrist 7, 61, 80, 83, 85, 94–5, 99–105, 123, 125–6, 129, 130–2, 134, 136–7, 152, 161
Antipas 32, 89–90
Artemis of Ephesus 29, 36, 108

Babylon/the woman/the harlot 52, 84, 90, 102, 125, 130, 132, 139–53 *passim*, 157, 162–3
Balaam, the teaching of 32, 139
beast 52, 99–100, 111, 122–38 *passim*, 152, 162; from the sea 79, 83, 104, 111–12, 117, 122–4, 130, 146, 162; mark of 79, 145–6; number of 5
beast from the earth (ram) 52, 122, 130–1
Beliar 129
blasphemy 79, 126, 131–2
book: *see* Scroll; of life 56

Chiliastic interpretation 2–3
Cleopatra 147–8
comparative religion 16–18, 106, 161
computer analysis 16, 109, 161
conqueror, promise to 23, 71, 156
Contemporary-Historical interpretation 11–13, 27, 122, 159, 163
crown 30–1
cup/wine/drunkenness 142–6

daughter of Zion 106–7, 110, 115, 141, 146–8
Day of the Lord 43–5, 68
Devil 111–12
Domitian, Emperor 35, 39, 41, 60, 126–7, 134–8, 160, 162
dragon 107, 111–12, 114, 117, 122–4, 129–33, 162

eagle 115, 120

Elijah 93–9, 161, 182
Emperor-worship 13, 32, 34–5, 39, 41, 108, 113, 119–20, 126, 130–3, 135, 137, 141, 149–53, 162
Ephesus 24–5, 29, 89, 149, 151, 156, 175
Eschatological interpretation 8–11

fifth seal 58, 66–7, 77
forty-two months 85, 87, 104, 116
four angels 74
four horsemen 57, 59, 61, 65, 72–3; first 61–3; second 63–4; third 59–61; fourth 64–5
four plagues 65
four winds 70, 74

Gog and Magog 44, 61, 100, 102
Greek used by John 14–16

Hades 65
harlot: *see* Babylon
historical applications 7–8, 172

Jabneh, flight to 117–20
Jerusalem 52–3, 85–7, 100–4, 117–18, 120, 125–6, 129, 142–3, 154–5, 161, 182
Jews 30, 37, 38, 86–7, 92, 110–11, 118–21, 134, 138, 148, 162, 169, 176, 184
Jezebel 34, 139, 147–8

kings from the east 74, 78–9, 153

Laodicea 25–6, 40–1, 67, 157, 174–6
Leviathan: *see* beast
literary analysis 13–16
little scroll 55, 84–6, 104
locusts 72, 78, 82
lukewarmness 25–6, 40

manna 42–3

195

Index of Biblical References

197